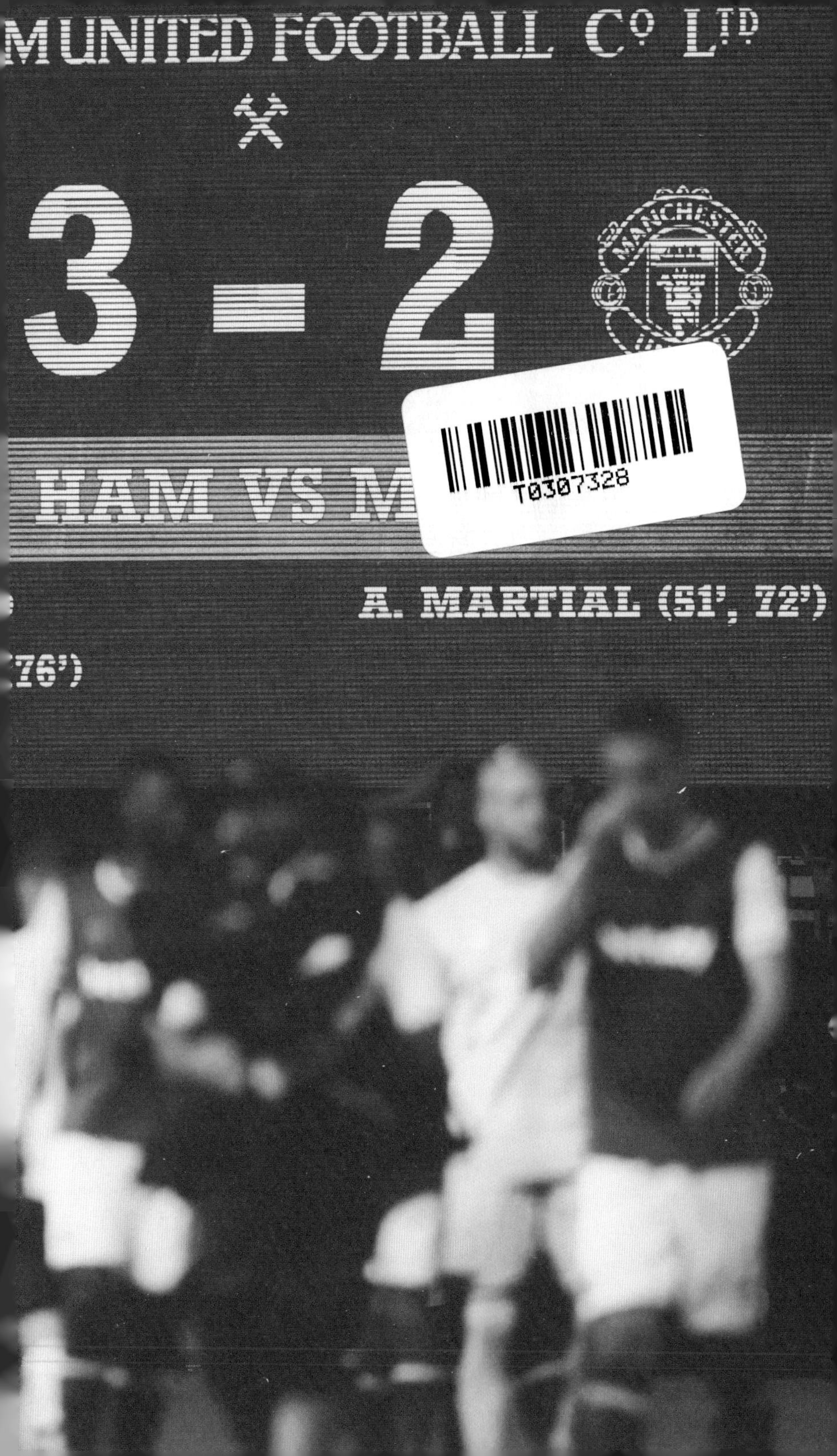
MUNITED FOOTBALL Cº LTD
3 - 2
MANCHESTER
HAM VS M
A. MARTIAL (51', 72')
76')

THE BOLEYN'S FAREWELL

DANNY LEWIS

THE BOLEYN'S FAREWELL

WEST HAM UNITED'S UPTON PARK SWANSONG

pitch

First published by Pitch Publishing, 2021

Pitch Publishing
A2 Yeoman Gate
Yeoman Way
Worthing
Sussex
BN13 3QZ
www.pitchpublishing.co.uk
info@pitchpublishing.co.uk

A CIP catalogue record is available for this book
from the British Library.

ISBN 978 1 78531 774 3

Typesetting and origination by Pitch Publishing

Printed and bound in India by Replika Press Pvt. Ltd.

Contents

Foreword by Tony Cottee

WHAT DOES the Boleyn Ground mean to me? Memories.

As much as I enjoy the new experience of going to the London Stadium as the passionate West Ham fan that I am, it's not quite the same day out as it used to be. Like many other supporters, I yearn for the good old days.

From the moment that I first went to a game at the Boleyn in 1972, I was hooked, but the memories of my fore-bears had already been planted deep inside me by my dad. Tales of my great uncle being a founding member of the Supporters' Club, the 1923 White Horse FA Cup Final, 1964, 1965 and the West Ham World Cup winners of '66 were repeatedly recounted by all members of my elderly family in my early years.

But such wonderful stories always seemed to end back at the Boleyn, with more talk about the great nights under the floodlights there and the special atmosphere that only Hammers fans can generate. I can remember my dad giving me permission to stay up late and watch the legendary Gordon Banks save Geoff Hurst's penalty in 1971: if only!

By the late 1970s, I was a teenage season ticket holder going to every game and I loved every minute of it, watching my heroes Pop Robson and David Cross bang the goals in. I loved the whole day and my journey to and from the Boleyn. Two buses from Collier Row to the top of Green Street, then walk down the road to the stadium. Lower West Side, opposite the six-yard box to start with and normally ending up opposite the 18-yard box after all the surging on the terraces during the game! After the match, another walk back up Green Street, with a regular stop at the chip shop for my saveloy and chips and then home to watch *Match of the Day*. The Boleyn fan experience was the best.

The Villa quarter-final in 1980, the Coventry semi-final in 1981 and the West Ham fans clapping off the Dinamo Tbilisi team after we had lost 4-1 at the Boleyn are quite simply some of the best memories of my time as a fan. The halcyon days!

On 1 January 1983, I made my debut and scored the first of my 146 goals for the club. I scored over 300 goals in my career, but I can honestly say that the feeling after my first one, at the South Bank end of the Boleyn, was the best I ever felt in my career.

Not all of my memories are good ones, which goes without saying as a Hammer. The saddest is the death of my grandad from a heart attack in January 1980 before the kick-off of the FA Cup third round replay against West Bromwich Albion. All I can say though is what a way to go – under the nameplate in front of the West Stand! If I could nominate my way to leave this life, I would love to emulate my grandad.

Apart from my playing days, one of my best days as a fan was the last game at the Boleyn, which I've described in this book. The ground was given a proper send-off that night and I will always cherish what happened there back in May 2016.

I've not been back to where the ground used to stand since that night, and I don't have any plans to either. The reason is quite simple: memories.

All my love for the club, the fans and all my personal achievements happened at the Boleyn and although the old lady is no longer with us, my memories will never die!

Enjoy the book.

Introduction

IT'S FRIDAY, 11 September 2020, the day before West Ham United kick off their 2020/21 Premier League campaign. The Hammers just about managed to stay up last season, and pessimism is in no short order. After making his loan move permanent, Tomáš Souček is the only signing so far, while Grady Diangana being sold has created uproar among the entire fanbase.

However, in my mind, all of that can wait until tomorrow, as my head is stuck firmly in the past. Today is the day I return to Upton Park for the first time since the final game at the Boleyn Ground. I had never really had a reason to come back before now, but it was also something I would have gone out of my way to avoid at all costs – I never wanted to see anything filling the space the club's spiritual home once stood on. There is something about writing this book that compels me to go back, though. Despite the stadium no longer being there, while writing about that historic night in 2016, it feels important to be close to the area where it had taken place at least once.

Still, there is a very real sense of nervousness as I leave the house, fumbling around with my keys and checking I have everything I need a million times. It feels like I'm making a pilgrimage of sorts, only in this one, the very thing that made this site feel holy has been razed to the ground and is still being built on.

To fit in with the book's theme, I would have loved to have taken the same route as I did for the Boleyn's swansong. However, that would involve me going back to my old university halls in Bournemouth. Instead, I do the next best thing and take the route from when I was growing up, back when I was a fresh-faced kid who couldn't wait to wolf down a bacon sandwich after football training and get to my favourite place in the whole world.

As I get off the train to switch at West Ham station, I have vivid memories of sprinting through it with my dad, purely so we could catch the next train and get to the ground as quickly as possible. As I step on to the platform for the last leg of the journey, I recall the excitement of standing alongside others in claret and blue and how the mere sight of other fans got me up for each and every game. There had always been an unspoken bond between all of us, which is something I had loved.

However, as much as all of this is going on in my mind, this is just a normal day for everyone else. That fact is made abundantly clear to me when I get off the train at Upton Park station to be hit by a wall of silence, with everyone else just going about their daily business. There is nobody shouting 'Irons' at the top of their voice, no hustle and bustle, just a couple of people on the opposite platform wondering why I'm taking a picture of the Upton Park sign.

If I'm honest, I don't really know what to expect as I journey out on to Green Street. Coronavirus has meant that I'm now used to places feeling slightly different than they had before lockdown. It has, however, been more than four years since I last walked on these pavements and the difference was always going to be drastic.

First impressions tell me this is just a normal place now. The market is still going, shops still tick along and there is a little bit of activity from local residents. Normal isn't what I had known this place for, though. There is now no Gary Firmager on his step selling copies of *Over Land and Sea*. No burger vans. Nobody shouting out to buy two bags of sweets for a pound. Nobody competing to shout 'Irons' the loudest and longest. No one selling a matchday programme. No score predictions. No excitement in the air. Nothing out of the ordinary at all.

A place that had once lived under the shadow of the Boleyn Ground is now only towered over by a crane and some flats. Where this site had once been filled with the noise of chants, cheers, boos and everything else that comes when football fans convene, all I can hear now is constant drilling and machines at work.

The site where the Boleyn Ground once stood is now occupied by flats, but it is still a work-in-progress. There is a mixture of works and scaffolding that is impossible to ignore when walking past, with diggers on the go and labourers carrying parts. As I head to the back of the development, there are people entering one of the completed parts of the building with shopping bags. That used to be the ticket office where I got my replacement ticket for the Leicester City game in that final season, having forgotten my season card. I had hoped to see the section where the Bobby Moore Upper entrance had once been, as that's where I had sat for our beloved stadium's final few seasons, but that is currently cordoned off.

I knew all of this was coming, but it still doesn't prevent the immense change from being a shock to the system. This means I can feel my heart racing as I walk down the same roads I had done every other weekend for 11 years. There's something in the fact that the work still isn't finished despite all the time that has passed, which makes it feel almost like the Boleyn is hanging on to everything it had represented and stood for – even though in reality that is ludicrous.

One thing that gets me is the famous 'LONG LIVE THE BOLEYN' graffiti. Two people – one of whom clearly goes by Gabz – had decided to add their own mark to the wall. There is also a collection of bin bags and litter directly beneath the wall that had been spread across social media so many times. This means there are flies buzzing about with more enthusiasm and vigour than Cheikhou Kouyaté on the Upton Park pitch. Seeing it desecrated only goes to show that what has been left behind following the move is far from untouchable. That sense is only accentuated when seeing Ken's Cafe and Nathan's Pie and Eels both closed for good.

However, there are still signs that West Ham lives on in Upton Park. Most obviously, the World Cup winners statue still stands proudly in its spot, looking down a very different Green Street to the one Bobby Moore, Sir Geoff Hurst and Martin Peters knew during their playing days. There's also a mural of Billy Bonds and Sir Trevor Brooking right next to Erkan Fish Bar – which still has its West Ham-style logo.

The club also lives on in those people who remain there. As I mention the Boleyn's final game in Newham Bookshop, the response is jubilance in reminiscing about the day. When I speak of my book in The Queens, I'm met with a massive grin as the barmaid enthusiastically goes, 'Oh, all right', clearly turning her mind back to that historic night. When I walk up the road and mention it in B.J.'s Pie and Mash, I'm met by a cry of 'this place used to be packed on a matchday' from a customer.

West Ham, and more specifically the Boleyn Ground, was always at the heart of this community, its main centrepiece and its pride and joy. It was impossible for it not to be. When I journeyed to Upton Park, a part of me had feared that its impact would have been largely forgotten by now. That couldn't be further from the truth. So, while the ground is no longer physically there, the memories that were made in it, as well as its legacy for the local area, will continue to endure. This can also be said for the Boleyn's final game, which will forever be remembered as one of our beloved stadium's greatest.

1
The Backdrop

INCLUDING THE club's time as Thames Ironworks, the Hammers had already played at three stadia before moving in at the Boleyn Ground: Hermit Road, Browning Road and Memorial Grounds. The move to Upton Park came about when, in 1904, Thames Ironworks and Shipbuilding Company owner Arnold Hills was having financial issues. Hills was unwilling to re-negotiate a deal for the club to remain at Memorial Grounds, meaning the Hammers needed to find a new place to call home. Upton Park was settled upon, where the club would play its football from the 1904/05 season right up until 2016.

The stadium, which was originally named The Castle, was built next to and in the grounds of Green Street House. The pitch was laid on an area that had previously been used to grow cabbages and potatoes. The stadium originally consisted of a small West Stand, a covered terrace backing on to Priory Road and changing rooms placed in the north-west corner between the West Stand and North Bank.

West Ham's first game at Upton Park came on Thursday, 1 September 1904, when they beat long-standing rivals

Millwall 3-0 in front of 10,000 fans. Syd King was putting out a new-look side, with Billy Bridgeman scoring a brace and Jack Flynn notching the other.

Developments were made to the ground throughout the following decades, although a lot of that work was ruined during the Second World War. In August 1944, a German V-1 flying bomb landed on the south-west corner of the pitch. The initial blow caused severe damage to the ground, while the ensuing fire destroyed the club's offices, which housed historical records and documents. After playing ten wartime games away from home while repairs were carried out, West Ham returned to the Boleyn Ground in December that year.

One specific part of the stadium that had been famed was the 'Chicken Run', due to how close fans were to the pitch. This helped to create the intimidating atmosphere that the Boleyn became so synonymous with – it also allowed fans to make life especially hard for opposition wingers and full-backs. This was a part of the ground that became the stuff of legend in terms of fandom and I would often hear about how brilliant it was when growing up. However, that was replaced by the East Stand in January 1969.

There were further developments made in the early 1990s, following the Taylor Report, which was brought into effect after the Hillsborough disaster. This led to the Bobby Moore Stand being built on the stadium's south side in 1993. Just two years later, the North Bank was replaced by what was first named the Centenary Stand and was then re-named after Sir Trevor Brooking in 2009. The last stand to be replaced was on the west side of the ground, which was opened by Queen Elizabeth II in 2001, and contained a hotel, executive boxes and various other facilities.

While there had been various changes to the Boleyn Ground, Freddie Bonfantini, who was born in Italy and grew up in Scotland, feels it still gave a taste of the area's past, 'You've got this area of London that is traditionally very distinctively white working-class and the people that live there have gone through a lot, with the Blitz and the poverty and the slums. I think that generated a type of personality that is unique and many of the people that used to live in that area left and went to Essex. The only tie they had left to east London was that football club. I think it was so amazing to see people coming back every Saturday and making that part of London a bit more like it used to be.

'For me, it was all about that Saturday routine where the football was sort of irrelevant; you just meet with some like-minded people and you get a sample of what London used to be like back in the day. It's not that commercialised corporate London that you see on the news now with social media. It was everything: the way the stadium was built, the way it was so shit with the scaffolding towers outside, the Belly Busters parked on the side of the road. All that crap was a way of going back in time, personally. I just really liked that because, for once, you could go back to something that was a little different.'

In March 2013, it was confirmed that the Hammers would be moving from the Boleyn Ground to London Stadium in 2016, leaving the past behind and stepping into what was seen as the future. The arena had been used during the 2012 Olympics in London, and the Hammers moving in would ensure that it would not become a white elephant – a fate that is often feared when infrastructure is built for major events.

This announcement came not long after West Ham had earned promotion from the Championship, beating Blackpool 2-1 in the play-off final. 'I always say the best day of my life for West Ham was the play-off final because of what it meant. That final night at Upton Park wouldn't have happened if we hadn't won that day at Wembley,' Rob Pritchard, the club's media officer, says. 'Having been part of the wider team that got relegated at Wigan the year before, I remember how shattering that felt. Sitting there live blogging that game and the devastation of getting relegated, to bounce back immediately and the feeling of sitting in the dressing room at Wembley having a beer with Matt Taylor. Just sitting on this medical table to cheers glasses with him and saying, "Thank goodness for that." Then having that night going out and going back to Upton Park and having a few beers with some of the lads. I remember we went out with a lot of staff, the medical team, marketing and media, we all ended up in a bar in Shoreditch and Sam Baldock came with us, which was bizarre but lovely. That was an unbelievable day and night that I'll never forget.'

The Hammers took on a 99-year lease, with the stadium being altered to accommodate football – as well as other events including athletics, various sports and concerts. Tottenham Hotspur and Leyton Orient were among the other clubs chasing the arena, but it was eventually awarded solely to West Ham for use throughout the football season. While this was seen as a progressive step for West Ham as a football club that was aiming to move forward, this did mean the Hammers would have to leave Upton Park. The 2015/16 campaign would put an end to their 112-year stay at the Boleyn Ground.

The summer of 2015 saw some monumental changes at West Ham, which would go on to shape the club's final season and game at the Boleyn. The first and most significant was that Sam Allardyce was relieved of his duties as manager. The club captain Kevin Nolan followed him out of the door. Consequentially, two of the biggest roles at the club were vacated, eventually being filled by Slaven Bilić and Mark Noble respectively. Stewart Downing, Modibo Maïga, Dan Potts and Nenê were among the players who followed Nolan out during that summer.

Dimitri Payet was undoubtedly the biggest signing made ahead of the final campaign at the Boleyn, joining from Olympique de Marseille. Other summer acquisitions included Angelo Ogbonna, Michail Antonio, Pedro Obiang, Darren Randolph and the initial loan of Manuel Lanzini, who came in from Juventus, Nottingham Forest, Sampdoria, Birmingham City and Al-Jazira respectively.

The last season at Upton Park could easily have had a Europa League campaign running through it, but any hopes of that faded fairly quickly. The men in claret and blue started the European campaign off by beating Andorran side Lusitanos 4-0 on aggregate, then getting past Maltese outfit Birkirkara on penalties. However, they were knocked out in the third qualifying round by Astra Giurgiu. West Ham had taken a 2-0 lead in the first leg, following goals from Enner Valencia and Mauro Zárate, but two late goals for the Romanian side meant they went into the away leg with a draw. A weakened team was beaten 2-1 by a brace from Constantin Budescu.

The Premier League campaign got off to a brilliant start for the Hammers with a 2-0 win over Arsenal at the Emirates. However, a slow start was endured at home with defeats at the hands of Leicester City and Bournemouth. Despite this, the home form for the rest of the campaign would go on to be near-impeccable – helping the side to force their way into the Europa League places, while at one stage it looked as though they could even reach the Champions League.

There were some superb results achieved throughout that campaign, including a 3-0 victory at Anfield, a 2-1 win at

Manchester City, and a 0-0 draw at Manchester United, as well as wins against Chelsea, Liverpool and Tottenham Hotspur and draws with Manchester City and Arsenal at Upton Park. There were also a number of club Premier League records broken that season, with a highest points total being posted, while recording the most goals scored and the least games lost.

Excitement was also to be had in the cups – specifically the FA Cup, as Bilić's side had earlier been knocked out in the third round of the League Cup, having been beaten 2-1 by Leicester after extra time. The FA Cup campaign started with a 1-0 win against then-Championship outfit Wolverhampton Wanderers, which led to a tie against Liverpool. After a well-earned 0-0 draw at Anfield, the Hammers won 2-1 in extra time in the replay when Ogbonna scored in the 120th minute. A routine 5-1 victory against second-tier Blackburn Rovers set up a tie against Manchester United, which was eventually lost when the Hammers were defeated 2-1 in another replay, after a 1-1 draw at Old Trafford. The tie meant that the Premier League match between West Ham and the Red Devils was delayed, resulting in it becoming the final game at Upton Park, rather than the fixture against Swansea City.

While the campaign was mostly known for uplifting fans with quality performances and results, there was also some controversy towards the end. Pretty much every West Ham supporter wanted to secure their ticket for the final game. They lined the streets before the match, with plenty of them likely maintaining some sort of hope that they would still be able to get within the Boleyn's walls one last time. Touts had a field day, but they were not the only ones giving the non-regulars a chance of getting in.

That is because the club introduced a ballot for the final three home matches – against Arsenal, Swansea and the big one against Manchester United. The ballot was made exclusive to Academy Members, with supporters being encouraged to sign up to have a chance of being one of over 35,000 fans there for the historic night.

This was seen as a massive opportunity for many, as they were suddenly given a lifeline – whether they had been to games throughout the season or not. However, on the flipside, there were plenty of members who would go on to miss out because of the scheme. Joe England is one of those who felt let down by the board when the ballot was introduced. The man behind the fanzine and book *5Managers* had been a season ticket holder in various parts of the ground for just under 20 years combined, before taking a job that required him to work at weekends.

Joe managed to negotiate with his bosses to allow him to get down to Upton Park for the final season, though. 'I wanted to go to every game, visit every part of the ground that I had stood and sat in, which I did – the only game I missed was Wolves in the cup. I was getting tickets through my club membership, no problem. I knew the club members tickets were available at nine o'clock and got my ticket in the part of the ground I wanted.'

The lifelong Hammer had understandable frustrations about the scheme. 'I was fuming about it because I thought somebody who'd never been before could go to that Man United game. Well, of course, I got a ticket for Arsenal, for Swansea, did I get a ticket for Man United, the one I wanted? No. So I've been to almost every home game, but I didn't get the Man United ticket. I was so disappointed, so let down, I felt such a sense of betrayal, as every single club member would when the news came out about the ballot for the last few games. It wasn't just me; it was thousands of us.'

For some who missed out, this felt like an injustice on a par with the Bond Scheme, which was introduced in November 1991. Following the Hillsborough disaster in April 1989, the Lord Justice Taylor Report led to the introduction of all-seater stadiums in England's top tier. In order to fund the Boleyn Ground's redevelopment, West Ham attempted to sell bonds – costing £500, £750 or £950 – which would give fans the right to buy a match day or season ticket in a designated seat for 150 years.

Because the club had a largely working-class fanbase, this was far from a success and was met with outrage, with just 808 bonds being sold before the scheme was eventually closed down in 1997. This led to various protests, which included one supporter running on to the pitch and planting the corner flag in the centre spot, before proceeding to sit next to it, with a number of other disgruntled Hammers fans joining him on the pitch.

While the ballot may not have been costly from a financial standpoint, fans felt they were being robbed of a once-in-a-lifetime experience and their place in history. It had taken their chances of getting a ticket and turned it into complete pot luck. This is something that Joe had a strong sense of. 'I still love West Ham, of course I do, but from that moment onwards, my emotional connection to West Ham, which I've had all my life, became a detachment. Even during the Bond Scheme, I still wanted to ride it through. I still believed it would all be all right in the end. I wouldn't stay around for demonstrations, I went home. But I feel like I got shafted that last season.'

This meant that the Swansea match was Joe's last game at Upton Park. It's a good job it wasn't the final game at the Boleyn Ground for everyone, though, as there won't be a West Ham fan out there who would want to read a book on what happened that day. Instead, it is remembered as the last Saturday game at the Boleyn, and one West Ham went into with hopes of Champions League football intact. While this was an important game for the club's European aspirations, Georgina Hunt, the fashion director at *Season Zine*, feels there was a carefree attitude from Hammers fans outside the ground. 'It was almost like no one really cared about the football. It was about being at Upton Park, and everyone was super pissed. I just remember everyone was drinking on the streets and everyone was in a party mode, celebrating the last weekend game.'

While that was the case before kick-off, supporters were heavily invested in what occurred on the pitch once the starting whistle had blown. The men in claret and blue actually had chances when the score was still 0-0: a Dimitri Payet free kick whistled just over the crossbar, grazing the net as it travelled; Łukasz Fabiański saved a Winston Reid header and Mark Noble fired off an effort that was closer to the Sir Trevor Brooking Upper than the goal.

Francesco Guidolin's side made the Hammers pay for their missed chances when they took the lead in the 25th minute. Kyle Naughton crept in at the back post to get on the end of Ki Sung-yeung's clipped ball over Aaron Cresswell's head, before squaring it to Wayne Routledge with a first-time pass, giving the winger the simplest of finishes.

It was 2-0 just six minutes later, when Stephen Kingsley was given the freedom of Upton Park to run down the left wing. The full-back utilised the acres of space afforded to him and sent a low cross to André Ayew, who made no mistake from the edge of the six-yard box.

After 51 minutes, it was 3-0. Modou Barrow got the better of Michail Antonio before fizzing the ball in towards the penalty spot. It wasn't the easiest of chances for Ki, but he controlled his volley well, sending it into the bottom corner and giving Darren Randolph no chance of making the save.

The Hammers did get a goal back in the 68th minute to get a glimmer of hope, but even that came in calamitous fashion. After Payet's initial corner delivery was unconvincingly headed clear, the Frenchman put another cross into the box. Antonio's header was saved by Fabiański, who then managed to block Diafra Sakho's follow-up effort. In trying to clear the ball away under pressure, Kingsley ended up smashing the ball into his own net.

This gave many of the claret and blue army belief that our team could potentially come away with something. However, with more chances being squandered, any remaining remnants of hope disappeared in the 93rd minute. The away side caught West Ham on the break, with Bafétimbi Gomis sprinting forward with the ball, playing a one-two with Ayew and then stroking his shot into the back of the net.

When the full-time whistle was blown, plenty of Hammers were already out of their seats and walking out of the Boleyn with a feeling of disgust. However, there were those who knew they would never be coming back inside their spiritual home, so they tried to savour the place as much as possible, even if the performance and result were something to erase from the memory.

After his lack of luck in the ballot, Joe was one of those. 'I think I was the last person to leave the ground. The stewards let me stay because I asked them to have some time just to take some photos, to have a little wander around. They let me do that. They even told the guy at the gate, who was locking it while I was still in the ground. That was a nice thing, but that comes from the genuine stewards. They let me sit there and watch the groundsmen. They had their job, but I think they understood this was my last game.'

The match's nature hasn't helped Joe accept the fact he wasn't able to get in for the Boleyn's swansong. 'To be at that undignified final game, where we were so poor, it almost felt like I got the joke. I didn't get tickets for Man United and we've lost this one 4-1, we were awful. It was an awful game. To me it's quite an emotional one, the Swansea one, because that was it for me.'

Joe was not alone in this, as Joseph Fordham says, 'My uncle booked a holiday to leave the day after the Swansea game. My uncle thought, well, we all thought, the Swansea game would have been the last one, so he left Upton Park for the last time after that 4-1 smashing. He walked away a little bit disheartened and missed out on a classic three days later, while he was on a walking trip up in the Peak District. Went for 50 years, then missed the last game.'

While this match was it for Joe, Joseph's uncle and many other fans, there were so many who had to maintain focus on the Boleyn Ground's final fixture, despite the shocking result. In his programme notes for the United game, Mark Noble wrote, 'I won't dwell too long on Saturday's game, because it was just a blip and it serves no purpose going over it and digging ourselves out. We didn't take our chances and Swansea did – simple as that.' Looking back, Tony Cottee says, 'It was sort of like the calm before the storm and I think all the players knew that there was an emotional night coming up.'

Aaron Cresswell adds, 'I remember the build-up, because let's be honest, it was all about that game three or four weeks before but we were actually doing well in the league. Then we played Swansea and we were fully confident going into the game, fully expecting three points – whether that was a good thing or bad thing. Then before we knew it, we were beaten 4-1. After that it was like, "We've got Man United coming up, this is arguably one of the biggest games in the club's history." So that was an eye-opener and maybe something we kind of needed going into the Man United game.'

That final night was all about West Ham United and celebrating Upton Park, but the opponents in these occasions can also play a part. There may be slight bias involved, but it feels as though the final games at other stadiums simply can't compare to the one at the Boleyn and part of this would be down to the team faced on the day. An example of this was Highbury's swansong, which was a comfortable 4-2 win for Arsenal against Wigan Athletic, while elsewhere the Hammers helped them secure Champions League football by beating Tottenham Hotspur. They, understandably, had their eyes elsewhere, while we as fans were in our bubble locked away from the world, with no thoughts that strayed away from West Ham in any way entering the majority of our minds.

While it is believed that this sort of emotion and intensity would have come against any opponent, it certainly helps if there is a gripping match taking place on the pitch. When it was announced that the ground's swansong would actually be against Manchester United, there was an even greater sense of excitement around the occasion. In hindsight, facing the Red Devils helped to give everyone involved with the club a far greater experience – not just because of the debacle that would unfold against the Swans.

Hatred is arguably something that could have taken away from the event, so as eye-catching as it would have been to have a Spurs or Millwall, it's probably for the best that it didn't happen. However, facing a club that the Hammers have history with can only be a good thing – especially in the build-up – and that is there in abundance between West Ham and Manchester United. This was the 124th meeting between the two clubs, with the first being a 2-1 FA Cup third-round win in 1911. There had already been quite a few matches to stay in the memory before the Boleyn's farewell game, especially since the start of the 1990s.

In 1991/92, English football was witnessing the final season of the First Division as everyone prepared to enter the era of the Premiership, which is now known as the Premier League. The Hammers were already relegated when they met Alex Ferguson's United side, with the Scotsman still chasing his first league title in Manchester. Ferguson had the trophy pretty much in his grip as his team were narrowly ahead of Leeds United.

This may have been a group whose fate was written in stone, but West Ham weren't meek in the slightest. The likes of Stuart Slater and Kevin Keen let off ambitious efforts, while Alvin Martin missed a header. United had chances of their own, as Ryan Giggs was denied by the offside flag and Luděk Mikloško stopped a spectacular effort from Mark Hughes.

It was after the corner resulting from that very save that West Ham scored the game's only goal, as Keen emerged with the ball and got the men in claret and blue tearing up the pitch for a counter-attack. The ball eventually found itself with Slater on the left. He crossed in as far as Gary Pallister, but the United defender's clearance was a weak one and went straight to Kenny Brown, who side-footed it past Peter Schmeichel with a first-time effort. Having lost that game, United then suffered defeat in the following match against Liverpool and missed out on the league to Leeds by four points.

The more famous example of West Ham preventing United from winning the title came in the 1994/95 season's final match. United had to win and hope for a Blackburn Rovers loss on the final day to overtake them and win the league. Despite a goal from Alan Shearer, Blackburn were defeated 2-1 by Liverpool.

However, United weren't having their own way either, as Michael Hughes put the Hammers ahead with a volley just after the half-hour mark. Brian McClair equalised with a 52nd-minute header, but Mikloško wasn't about to be beaten twice and was in outstanding form. Shot after shot was fired in at West Ham's goal, but the behemoth from Czechoslovakia was equal to every one of them. As the final whistle blew, there was understandable despair among the visiting ranks.

Over at Anfield, Tony Gale was a centre-back for the title-winning Blackburn side. When asked about whether there was gratitude from Rovers towards West Ham, he says, 'There certainly was from me, definitely towards Ludo Mikloško because he had an absolute blinder that day. He probably was the reason they were able to hold Manchester United. I obviously was at Anfield with the lads and they were most pleased with the way West Ham went about it, but I don't think West Ham did it for Blackburn. They did it for themselves because the fans always wanted a good performance against Manchester United. I don't think anybody could have thought about the way that it would pan out over those 90 minutes. So, I was forever grateful to what was a bunch of friends that I'd left the season previous.'

Martin Godleman, who has worked for West Ham since 1991 and was stadium announcer for Upton Park's final game, recalls a unique encounter after the draw in 1995. 'Jules, who's my wife now, was my girlfriend then, was with me on the day and she was a Manchester United fan. She said she'd really love to meet Alex Ferguson. At the end of the game, I just did my interviews and then wandered around.

'We walked into this section where they used to sometimes warm up at the back of Upton Park, and there was this mountain of Carling cans – they were the sponsors at the time, they probably weren't real cans of lager – and at the top was clearly a fake trophy, because the real one was in Blackburn. Then, over in the corner was Alex Ferguson looking miserable. I had asked Jules not to go up to him and that it wouldn't work, but she's completely fearless and went to get his autograph and he gave her it. He must have worked out she was a Man United fan.'

These past interventions may have played into United's psyche on Upton Park's big day, especially among the fans, as Martin suggests, 'They probably thought they owe it to us to screw up our special day because we've screwed theirs up twice, both near the end of the season. Then here we are with the last one at Upton Park. So, I know there will be Manchester United fans with long memories who will remember '92 and '95.' Even the manager remembers what the Hammers had done to his title hopes on various occasions, as Gale points out, 'When Sir Alex came to some of our functions, because he was a big friend of John Lyall, he would always joke about the way that West Ham had done them up on a few occasions. A really good man he is as well.'

Not all of West Ham's joyous moments have come at such a severe cost to the Red Devils. The win that meant the most for many Hammers will undoubtedly be the victory that completed the Greatest Escape of 2006/07. West Ham had looked doomed, but six wins in the eight games preceding the match at Old Trafford meant they still had a chance of survival if things went their way on the final day. Over at Bramall Lane, Paul Scharner's strike and a David Unsworth penalty were enough for Wigan Athletic to beat Sheffield United despite Jon Stead's header.

Meanwhile, Carlos Tevez, who had been the hero of the club's late resurrection, was on target again. The Argentine magician played a one-two with Bobby Zamora and the ball flicked up following Wes Brown's challenge. Many would have panicked in this situation, but not Carlos. He waited for the ball to hit the floor and slotted it past the onrushing goalkeeper Edwin van der Sar. United came back with threatening efforts from the likes of Cristiano Ronaldo and Paul Scholes, but Robert Green and his defence stood strong. The group kept hold of the clean sheet and a place in the Premier League, sparking mad celebrations among Alan Curbishley and his team, which included a young Mark Noble.

It wasn't only those at Old Trafford going wild that day, though, as 11-year-old me was jubilantly jumping up and down on a table in the pub when Tevez scored, then did it again following the final whistle. Daniel Hurley also recalls that moment in his book, *The Greatest Escape*, 'I was sat indoors nigh on open-mouthed at what I'd witnessed. I'd given it up two months ago, and always had a hunch that in the end it would be the hope that killed me, and despite the surge in form we would meet the same result at the end anyway. But I was wrong and rarely in my life had I ever been happier to be so.'

Going far further back, West Ham faced Manchester United on the 1976/77 campaign's final day, needing a victory to stay in the top tier. That aim was achieved as goals from Frank Lampard Snr, Geoff Pike and a brace from Bryan Robson led the Hammers to a 4-2 victory.

There have been so many other great matches and moments against Manchester United, such as Paolo Di Canio embarrassing Fabien Barthez in the FA Cup in 2001, as well as Jonathan Spector and Carlton Cole both scoring braces in the snow during a 4-0 win in the League Cup in 2010.

Looking at the 2015/16 campaign, the league game played at Old Trafford was a 0-0 draw but it's in the FA Cup where the drama had occurred. The tie – which caused the league game at Upton Park to be postponed – started at United's home ground. Despite what ensued, this will be remembered for Dimitri Payet's incredible strike in the 68th minute. It was the sort of distance nobody had any business beating David De Gea from, but the Frenchman did it. He had stepped up to take the free kick and sent it careering off the post, giving the Spaniard absolutely no chance.

The Hammers had already felt hard-done-by when Payet wasn't given a penalty, despite seemingly being fouled by Marcos Rojo. Those frustrations with the referee were only accentuated when United scored a controversial equaliser in the 83rd minute. Ander Herrera had got to the byline and played the ball towards the back post where Anthony Martial was on hand to finish. Amid all of this, Bastian Schweinsteiger had jumped into Darren Randolph, but was not adjudged to have fouled the Republic of Ireland international. Rob Pritchard states, 'Darren says it still leaves him awake at night, when Schweinsteiger sort of blocks him off. If we'd held on and won that we'd have got to Wembley, which I think would have been fitting because we were box office. We were just so good to watch.'

This meant that there was a replay, taking the tie back to the Boleyn Ground, just shy of a month before the stadium would see its final game. United were the team on the front foot this time and Marcus Rashford opened the scoring in the 54th minute by sticking the ball right in the top corner. Again, West Ham had a big call for a penalty turned down, which often leaves fans feeling it would be typical if the opposition were to go and score.

That is exactly what happened as, 13 minutes after Rashford's opener, Jesse Lingard played a ball to Martial at the back post. The Frenchman's strike took a deflection off James Tomkins and went in off Marouane Fellaini's thigh. Tomkins scored a brave header from close range with 11 minutes left, but it was to be a night of frustration for the men in claret and blue. Andy Carroll missed a header by a matter of inches before Cheikhou Kouyaté saw a goal ruled out for offside.

West Ham were out of the FA Cup, which Manchester United went on to win, and suddenly there was the motivation of not letting the Red Devils ruin yet another massive night in this historic season. Another thing that played beautifully into Upton Park's final fixture is that the away side were also desperate for a result to stay in the top four and qualify for the Champions League. All of the historical context behind the fixture, both clubs needing a result and what had happened just a month before set the scene perfectly for one of the biggest and best matches this wonderful ground would ever host.

The stadium witnessed so many heroes, from the likes of Billy Bonds, Bobby Moore, Sir Geoff Hurst, Martin Peters and Sir Trevor Brooking, to modern greats such as Paolo Di Canio, Carlos Tevez, Scott Parker and Dean Ashton. It was now time for West Ham's current crop to etch their own names into Upton Park's history on arguably its most important and historic night.

2

Preparation

AN EVENT as big as this was always going to require plenty of preparation. Whether it was players, club staff, media or tradesmen, they all needed to ensure that they were ready for the big night. Plans began months in advance, as Rob Pritchard recalls, 'I was heavily involved in getting in contact with every former player to get them back to the ground. That was quite a task because going back five decades, some players have completely fallen out of contact with the club. Others had moved on and their contact details were out of date. Players are living all over the world, not only the international players, even two members of our 1964 FA Cup-winning team live on other sides of the world. We've got players in Australia, Asia, Africa, all over Europe. So, that was a major task, to get in contact with them all and try and get as many of them back as possible.'

There were also plans that had to be made for the entertainment and ceremony, with Cockney Rejects singer Jeff Geggus being contacted back in February. As much as West Ham were trying to get hold of various people, there was also a plethora of media companies scrambling to get as much access as they possibly could for the final game. Suri Krishnamma, who was director of the *Iron Men* documentary, states, 'We had to go through quite a long process of getting approval from West Ham. One of the difficulties with the film was that West Ham themselves, in particular the co-owners David Sullivan and David Gold, and vice-chairman Karren Brady had to approve us as filmmakers. That's because in order to get the intimate access we got to the players, the manager, the ground and all the inner workings of the operation, we had to have them on side to some extent. There were several rivals who were also knocking at their door trying to get permission and, ultimately, we managed to get exclusive access, which no one else achieved.'

All of the club's media also had to be organised for the game. Clips on the big screens would play a key role in the ceremony, whether it was fans being interviewed or compilations that had been put together. Perhaps the most important of the lot was to come at the end, which featured Bobby Moore. His daughter, Roberta, had a big say in ensuring the club got the tone of the video right. 'They asked me to help with some input. I did and we changed it because I didn't personally feel the first attempt worked very well and they agreed. It got re-worked, and I thought it was very good at the end. So, they kind of included me because they wanted to get it right. Neil Felton is a big West Ham fan, and he's a creative, and we both had input into the final video. He did a lot and he spoke to me, I mean he always gets it right, so it was really worth it. West Ham just wanted to do the very best job they could, and it was important to handle it properly.

'I just felt that the first one that was made didn't capture my dad's mannerisms and he looked a bit mechanical. It just didn't have the right tone. So, in the end what they came up with just looked lighter and it had more of a spring in his step. When dad used to come out of the tunnel holding a ball, he used to pump it up with his fist. So, Neil and I came up with the idea that you immediately recognise that's what dad did and it gave it a bit more personality, it just felt warmer.'

Martin Godleman says, 'They had this evening absolutely immaculately prepared,' but there was still so much to be done in the weeks and days leading up to the game. Rob recalls, 'In the build-up, there was so much planning as the eyes of the world were on us. I remember Sky Sports News did a Farewell Boleyn day. I don't think the other clubs were overly happy about it, but I remember the whole day was dedicated to us. There was a press day where a lot of broadcasters came down. It was a really surreal few weeks because obviously it was a big build-up towards it. Prince Albert of Monaco also came to the ground that week and had a kickaround on the pitch, which was surreal, and we did an interview with him. So we had a royal visit.

'Then there was the programme, wanting it to be right. Also, because the game was rearranged, it was really busy because we played Swansea at home on a Saturday. I had to do a programme for that, and then the Man U game, and then we had Stoke away on the final Sunday. So, it was actually quite a busy end of the season, when normally you've only got one game a week at that time. I think everybody just wanted everything to go right, to go without a hitch, because we knew that everybody was going to be watching us.'

Once they had been produced, it was down to matchday programme manager Geoff Martin to ensure they were safe and ready to be sold. 'Rob Pritchard would get the programme together, then he'd send that off to a company and then they put it all together so that it's like you see on a matchday. I'd do some research behind the scenes about how many visitors are going to be allowed. I also used to speak to police, asking the same question and where they can be offloaded and picked up so I could maximise selling points for sellers around the ground. The vital question with that last match, the maximum for away visitors was 2,500 a match so nothing really changed position-wise. That's until they made the decision to print 50,000. I went, "What?" That last programme is quite a nice robust programme, so there were fewer per box. It was then planning for the volume of it and where you're going to stash it.'

Of all the people preparing for the night, it was most important that the players did it correctly. No matter how meticulously everybody else had planned everything that went around the game, there was no avoiding the fact that the match was the centrepiece. No matter how great the clips or programme were, they wouldn't be appreciated as much if the team had just got battered.

Speaking about the feeling in the lead-up, Darren Randolph says, 'It wasn't nerves, it was more the pressure. We knew it was the last game and obviously we didn't want the last game to be an embarrassment to look back on or a disappointing one for everyone. We didn't want to sign out and say goodbye on a negative note. So, I think that pressure was spread around the group in a good way.

'You get these feelings some days in football – we've all had games in football where you think, "We're not going to lose this game," and you lose it. But that day we just thought, for whatever reason, whatever happens we won't lose this game. We may not win but we're not going to lose.'

It's clear that the game's magnitude was not lost on the players, as Aaron Cresswell adds, 'I remember thinking it was one of the biggest. It wasn't a game in terms of you're going to win a trophy, you're going to get promoted. It was more the pressure of, "This is the last-ever professional game at this ground," and you don't want to be involved in it not being a good night.'

Looking away from the 90 minutes, plans for the ceremony had begun when the game was expected to take place on the Saturday, and Jeff Geggus recalls the challenges of the day change, 'Logistically, when they ask you to do it they think it's just a case of setting up a few amplifiers and away you go. It doesn't work like that; there was a lot of work that went in. It was the better thing, but putting it in midweek posed a lot of problems because there were all sorts of laws with Newham Council about how long the show can go on afterwards. You've got to be finished by a certain time and that, but when we knew it was Man United that was fantastic, the icing on the cake.'

There was a rehearsal in the stadium the night before the game, where Cockney Rejects did sound checks, and people ran through various parts of the final ceremony. Martin recalls watching the video that would end the night, 'There were probably 2,000 people the night before rehearsing. We tried it two or three times and everybody in the stadium was getting goosebumps because that was the clear moment: this is the last night at Upton Park and this place which has been your church for your life.'

Those rehearsals had gone on for longer than may have been anticipated, as Martin says, 'I was going home and I didn't realise they wanted me to meet Ben Shephard. I was pulling into Canning Town and Jane, my boss, texted me saying, "Where are you?" and I replied, "Didn't we finish?" and her text came back to me just as we were going underground saying, "Get back here now." I went back and we eventually got away at about 1.30 in the morning and West Ham put me in a cab with Hammerhead. So, he and

I were chatting about the game coming up. Thankfully he doesn't have to bring his kit home, can you imagine? But he had done all his bit and he had to be there right until the end.'

Those in the stadium weren't the only ones working at silly o'clock. Mark Gevaux, who is otherwise known as the Rib Man, was also busy preparing his ribs to be sold before the game. 'We cook it all through the night, that's probably why we look so tired when we're working, because we've been up all night cooking it. We cooked about 250 kilos of ribs for that game. We like to cook them slowly anyway. We cook them all through the night and then by the time they're ready to go, we take them straight to the place. We actually take them off the bones at the site so they're fresh and hot and absolutely delicious.'

When it came to anything to do with the final game, there was a clear desire from everyone at West Ham for it to be as close to perfect as possible. Whether it was a fan trying to take in every second, Martin ensuring he announced everything correctly, Mark getting his ribs right or Roberta having her say on the video, it was the preparation that played a key part in ensuring that the whole experience was the absolute best it could be.

3

Before The Game

Starting the day

Waking up with the knowledge it's a matchday is usually enough to excite most fans, no matter who the opposition is. Knowing that I would be among my fellow supporters, watching the players I adored and taking in the whole experience of being at Upton Park was always more than enough to enthuse me. It would get me out of bed a bit quicker than normal and put a spring in my step. For so many of our fans, waking up on such a momentous matchday meant the initial feelings that come around it flooded into the mind with far greater strength than usual.

In fact, some will have had so much anticipation for the game that they didn't get much sleep at all, as was the case with David Blackmore. 'I knew that it was going to be a big day, and I was just hoping and praying that we were going to get the result that we wanted and that we were going to, hopefully, send off the Boleyn in the best possible way.' Dan Lawless had a similar feeling to David. 'I knew it would be a momentous occasion. Mostly, I woke up feeling nerves because of how big the day was and thinking, "What if we get battered?" It could have been such a bad ending. I wanted it to be as perfect as possible – I didn't envision the story going the way it did, but I just remember waking up and feeling excitement and nerves about just not wanting it to end flat.'

There will have been plenty of fans who had something they did before a game that gave them comfort. It could be some sort of superstition, like taking the same route to the game or eating the same food before getting into the ground. My lucky charm was a pair of claret and blue boxers. I had worn them for the first home game after West Ham had been beaten by Leicester and Bournemouth. Having witnessed a 2-0 win against Newcastle United, I kept wearing them after that and they seemed to get results every week, so I always made sure I had them washed and ready whenever I was heading to Upton Park throughout the 2015/16 season.

I'm fully aware that Payet's genius, Noble's brilliant season and Bilić's tactical ability were the main reasons the team were picking up results, not my boxers. However, if there was ever going to be a season where a Hammers fan developed a silly lucky charm for home games, it was going to be that one. The only time the Hammers have lost fewer times at home in the Premier League era is 1997/98, when they were beaten just twice. The Swansea game had me wondering whether I should continue with this lucky charm, seeing as it hadn't exactly been a great game to watch. In the end, I decided to carry on with it, as a weekend of annoyance wasn't enough to counteract a season filled with joy.

While the 4-1 defeat to Swansea had planted some doubt in my mind, it actually acted as a comfort for Freddie Bonfantini on the morning of the Boleyn's swansong. 'There was a mixture of positivity and negativity. We're playing

Man United, it's West Ham. The good thing is we lost 4-1 to Swansea at home before that. I felt like we've done that, we've lost 4-1, there's no way we can lose that badly again. I remember thinking, "Wow, they're gonna turn up. It's not going to be a shit show, it can't be, it's the last game."'

Freddie wasn't the only fan who was confident that the hosts could get the win, although this was more down to an innate gut feeling rather than any sort of evidence that could be relied on. Joseph Fordham was one of those who believed. 'I did feel that we were going to win. I don't know if you've ever had that before, where you go to a game where you're not concerned about what's going to happen in a game at all, you just feel that energy. I had it a couple of times that season in particular – Spurs at home was another game where I openly claimed before the game there's no problem here, we've won this game. I just had a feeling that the Man United game was going to be another case of that.'

James Jones also had high expectations, as he recalls, 'The general feeling I and a lot of my mates had was that there was no way we were losing that football match on that day. The sheer size of the occasion and what it meant to everyone and what it meant to me personally as a West Ham fan, I knew it was going to be special.'

It wasn't all about the result, though. It always felt clear that this was never going to be a boring 0-0 draw, but the main point of importance was that the Hammers put in a good performance, showing the passion the historic night deserved. Pride played such an integral part in the whole event around the Boleyn's farewell: the pride around the spiritual home, being at its last-ever game, the club's history, the season that had preceded this match and the pride in being West Ham. It was vital that the team's performance reflected that.

With this being a night game, there will have been plenty of fans who got the day off work so they could completely immerse themselves in the event throughout the day's entirety. For many of us who had a completely free day, anticipation for what was to come filled every second of that morning and early afternoon. What magic will Payet show us tonight? What will the score be? What will happen in the ceremony? Will Noble get to take a penalty? How many people will turn up outside the ground? Will the atmosphere be celebratory or sad? I had all of these questions and so many more running through my head, as well as the constant feeling that this was surely going to be an incredible experience.

Even for those who did have work, it was difficult to focus on anything other than West Ham, as James Datson, the commentator for the blind and visually impaired, remembers, 'I wanted to take the time off, but it originally would have been on the weekend but it got moved. So, I had to work during the day in a secondary school in east London, and it was full of some West Ham supporters, and a lot of other London clubs and also Man United fans. So even during the day I couldn't really focus. I had to make sure I had all of my equipment and my preparation, because I was leaving from work to get to the stadium as soon as possible. I remember waking up in the morning and being quite nervous about the evening. I felt a lot of emotions around my time as a youngster at the club in terms of standing on the North Bank, and then just thinking, "Is this really the last time?"'

While countless people were at home or on their way to work thinking of Upton Park, Russ Budden, who is the stadium DJ, was doing what every other West Ham fan longed to be doing and got to spend time there. He looks back on that time gratefully. 'I was actually on jury service for two weeks around that time. Luckily, the case I was being a juror for was deferred to the afternoon. So, I drove up to the ground at about eight o'clock in the morning and I didn't have to be at court until the afternoon. I had my security pass and stuff, so I spent about two, three hours just walking around the stadium. There was no one there. I sat where I used to sit when I was a season ticket holder, where I first sat in the East Stand, where I used to sit in the Centenary Upper with my grandad, who passed a good few years ago but took me to West Ham.

'I had the most amazing time. I literally had two or three hours where there was no one there – I saw a few people setting up the mosaics. I walked around in the changing rooms, had a wee in the changing rooms, little things that no one would ever do and it was just incredible. I went to Ken's and had a quick bacon sandwich, all that stuff that I would never do again. It was a special time and I was fortunate enough to walk around and take pictures where nobody was really there. It was lovely walking around and it was really emotional.'

Being at the ground so early also gave Russ a chance to make a gesture on behalf of his loved ones who couldn't be there. 'As you came out of the changing rooms down on the corridors there was a big wall and people would sign it on the tours. I made sure that I'd signed it, but also signed it on behalf of my grandad, and also my wife's dad, who passed as well. So that was our little bit.'

Posting on social media has become a key part of the matchday experience for many supporters, especially since the rise of fan accounts. James Jones put a post of his own on Facebook before leaving for the ground, which read, 'Today my Boleyn Ground journey goes full circle. On 11 April 1992, my dad took me to my first West Ham game. I was so young and cried every time the crowd cheered. We won 4-0.

Today, after over 24 years, 588 home games and unlimited priceless memories, I say goodbye to the Boleyn Ground. And I know I will be in tears.

'It all began in tears for me, and now it'll end in tears too. For over 24 years the Boleyn Ground has become an important part of my life. It has been my escape every other Saturday afternoon, and where I have been able to share so many unforgettable memories, firstly with my dad and then with my brother.

'It is the ground in which I fell in love with football, and of course West Ham United. It's where I've laughed and cried, cheered and groaned, drunk way too many warm Carlsbergs at half-time and, most importantly, had the opportunity to see some of the greatest players in the world up close, like Paolo Di Canio, Carlos Tevez, Mark Noble and Jonathan Spector.

'It will always be my home, the greatest place on earth. Farewell Boleyn.'

There will have been thousands of posts with a similar sentiment behind them that morning and throughout the day; there were even more who relived their best Upton Park moments over and over again in their minds. Martin Godleman, the stadium announcer, is one of those. 'There are all of these wonderful games I've seen, I saw the great Eintracht Frankfurt semi-final and saw all the greats – except Martin Peters, I never saw him in a West Ham shirt. But, Geoff Hurst, Bobby Moore, Billy Bonds, Alan Devonshire, Phil Parkes, Tony Cottee, Ray Stewart, Julian Dicks. I started to think about them, I didn't mean to, but they started getting in my head. The first time I ever did a commentary was in the 1991/92 season against Luton Town and I was thinking what happens if a goal comes and of course the game was 0-0. There were hardly ever any 0-0s at

Upton Park and I was thinking, "Thank God I didn't have to describe a goal because I would have got the name wrong." It was a bit like your life flashing before you before the game.'

Russ may have initially been alone in the stadium, but all the other fans couldn't wait until they got to join him in the Boleyn Ground to say their own final goodbyes. Whether they were leaving in the morning, racing away from work as soon as their shift finished or sprinting out of the school gates, countless Hammers descended on Upton Park as soon as they could to take in the Boleyn's big day.

Travelling to the game

West Ham fans will have flocked from everywhere. Some only had to walk around the corner, others will have got the train or bus, some will have driven in, while there are even foreign fans who flew over especially for the big occasion. This may be a club in the heart of east London, but the diversity of fans who attended the game goes to show just how far its reach stretches.

Jeff Geggus, who performed as part of the Cockney Rejects that night, is one of those who didn't have far to go. 'I went to my mum's house in Custom House, it's still there, and I liked to do the ritual walk that I did as a kid, walking up to the ground that evening. I felt excitement, obviously, because of performing and hoping that everything goes right on the night. There was also a sadness because I was thinking of all the years I've taken this ritual walk to the ground since I was seven years old and thought, "I ain't ever going to do it again."'

I was one of those who went by train, travelling in from Bournemouth. I had got on the train early, so I could meet my dad after he finished work and spend time soaking up the atmosphere around the ground. Like many, we had wanted to get there as soon as possible to take in as much as we could. I remember feeling a sense of nervousness – something I didn't normally have before games. Of course, the excitement I usually felt before matches was also multiplied, but it was starting the journey that made it even clearer to me just how much this day meant. I'll never forget seeing the first fellow fan of the day sitting across from me in the carriage, as he gave me the sort of smile that said, 'Well, here we go.'

The fact that this was West Ham's final game at Upton Park was something that hadn't left my mind pretty much from the moment I woke up. There was something very final about it from the off in my case, but Dan Lawless had a different experience in the day's early stages. 'Going to Upton Park, it was that whole build-up where it doesn't quite dawn on you before you get there, and it didn't quite sink in that this is the last time you get to do it. As much as you realise that's true, you don't really process it that this train journey, going to eat here before the game and then travelling back to Upton Park, that's the last time you're going to get to do it, so it felt weird.'

Matt Datson also travelled in by train, coming from Western-super-Mare. He gets assistance due to the fact he's totally blind, but it comes across that Matt put a lot of planning into how he would get to the stadium. He recalls, 'I had to work in the morning, couldn't get the day off. I work very close to the railway station anyway. I worked until one o'clock, I then got the train at 1.10, had to change at Bristol Temple Meads, got a train at two o'clock, into Paddington just before four. I met Tony, who is my mate and guide and has been for several years, I met him at five o'clock at Upton Park and it was absolutely rammed. It must have taken a good 15 minutes to get out of the station.'

When speaking to Matt, it comes across that even years later he remembers specific details about his journey that I wouldn't have even taken notice of at the time – I was fine as long as I was at the ground before kick-off. He is also able to reel off his routine from the usual Saturday matchday times. Being a match-going fan, the journey to and from the ground can be an integral part of the overall experience, and Matt's day displays that.

Routine, and whether to stick to it, was a vital decision for many fans. This was the last time they would ever get to witness a game at Upton Park, so should they stick to what they know or change things to get to the stadium as quickly as possible? Perhaps caught up with his book, Joseph Fordham chose to stick to what he usually did. 'The journey was just like any other; there was nothing different about that in terms of how I got there or how our pre-match routine was route-wise and stopping off for a beer, that kind of thing. But there were just too many moving parts and I was worried that if I didn't meet up with those people that was it, it would be a headache getting them after that.'

David Blackmore had a completely different thought process. 'I changed my shift at work, so that I could finish at three and could get down there early. I got the tube there. It's probably the first time that I've actually done things differently to what I have done for any other West Ham game at Upton Park because normally, for me, I would go to Plaistow and would go to the Black Lion or the Vic Tav before walking up to the stadium. This time I wanted to kind of soak in the atmosphere, so I walked down Green Street and picked up some fish and chips on the way there. I wasn't sure how late the night was going to get, so I thought I had better line my stomach before I did it. And then I went down to the Boleyn.'

Then there were those who didn't need to worry about routine or times, making their way around in style. I challenge you to find someone who made a better entrance than Freddie Bonfantini and his mate, as he was picked up in a claret Jaguar to go to the Black Lion in Plaistow. Though he did make up for that afterwards, taking a walk through 'Dogshit Alley' to get to the stadium.

As mentioned above, the experience of getting to Upton Park was about more than just routes and logistics. There were also plenty of thoughts and emotions that approaching the ground stirred up in people. Georgina Hunt knew she wasn't going to be getting into the stadium, so travelling was a particularly emotional part of her overall experience. 'It was a mixed feeling. I never felt excited, I remember just feeling quite sad but almost like I was being part of a movement,' she says. 'None of us really knew what was going to happen when we moved to the new stadium, but I knew that this would be big. I remember just feeling sad but unified with all the fans because it was almost a feeling like we're all in this together that I wouldn't have at a normal game. We're all coming down to say our goodbyes to this magical place.'

There was also a lot going through Roberta Moore's head on the way to the Boleyn Ground, as she remembers, 'From my perspective, I knew it was going to be quite emotional, because as a child, I spent an awful lot of time over at Upton Park, I just had so many memories of it. Not just watching the games, but Dad used to go to training on Christmas Day, and it wasn't at the training ground, it was at Upton Park. It was always a bit special when they did the training at the stadium, rather than at the training ground. After matches I'd go into the players' bar and there was a gym and I used to run around the gym. I knew that it would stir that up and it would be a very reflective evening for me.

'I was also really excited and I remember as we pulled into Green Street, it was absolutely packed everywhere, absolutely packed. We got dropped off and we had to walk through all the crowds which was exciting; there was a real energy in the air. In a way, it kind of felt a bit sad but at the same time it was such a big occasion; it felt very momentous.'

For many, the emotions will have only grown in magnitude the closer they got to the stadium. As well as wondering what would happen in the evening, it was impossible to keep the mind away from all of the other memories that had come from days and nights spent watching West Ham at the club's spiritual home. Even without having seen the stadium, there was nothing else in the world many of us could think about.

Pre-match fill

Food and drink plays an integral part in any matchday experience, especially at home games. From the first time I set foot in the pie and mash shop, it became a part of my matchday routine. Getting my double pie, single mash and liquor before or after the game became just as much a part of my day as buying a programme or taking a certain route to the stadium. Aside from the fact the food tasted great, I loved that all of these West Ham fans were in one place discussing what they thought would happen or analysing what they had watched. It was a place where a real sense of community could clearly be felt. I could have a joke with the server and fellow customers before tucking into some lovely food.

A sign of the times to come, I didn't get to go there for the final game at Upton Park. The shop had already changed ownership, with the stadium move likely playing a part in the decision to sell up. Without the people I had come to know over the years it simply wasn't the same, while the food wasn't as good either. However, there were still so many options for people who wanted to grab something pre-game. Walking down Green Street, it was impossible to miss the offerings. Enticing smells came from fish and chip shops, kebab shops and burger vans, while stall sellers could be heard shouting to draw people in. Little kids could often be seen with flour around their face from burger buns, while there was always a bloke getting as much into his mouth in one go as possible.

Some establishments became synonymous not just with Upton Park, but with West Ham itself. In terms of food, there was Ken's Café and Nathan's Pies and Eels, while there was also the Boleyn Tavern to go and have a drink. The Boleyn was usually lively, but Dan Lawless recalls how the atmosphere in there was on another level before the final match. 'It was unbelievable. I've been in the Boleyn a few times before the game and there was nothing like that. It was an absolute party atmosphere. It was heaving, it was so hard to get served, it took ages, so people were buying multiple beers at a time.

'I was sort of squeezed up, talking to family, then I went into the back room where the pool table is and that was something else. Music, people were just throwing their beers everywhere, dancing all over the place. I nearly got hit with some beers. I wasn't throwing my beers anywhere because of how long it took to get them in the first place. I couldn't believe the people. It was unlike anything I've ever experienced in a pub because it was just an absolute party atmosphere.'

West Ham fans were desperate to enjoy themselves and came into this with the sort of energy that doesn't accompany a normal game. Many of them got to Upton Park much earlier than they usually would. That was only good news for those selling food and drink, as supporters went to their favoured sellers to get their fill. One very popular option was the Rib Man.

Mark Gevaux started serving his rib rolls at West Ham in 2012 and has become one of the best-known food sellers associated with the club. He says, 'I've got nothing but compliments, especially when we played rubbish, people would say, "The Rib Man was the best part of the day," and that kind of stuff and it's becoming such a tradition now where dads take their kids. The kids are actually the next generation and like with pie and mash there's now the Rib Man. That makes me very proud. To be considered as a West Ham matchday tradition amongst a lot of people, that really is awesome.

'For me, that was part of being the Rib Man of West Ham; people look forward to that matchday tradition. That was the hardest thing for me to break, because everyone had their thing, whether it was Ken's Cafe or Nathan's, to break that was the most difficult thing. But once they're on your side, people are loyal – especially West Ham fans – and to become part of the matchday tradition made me really proud.'

Even for someone who had been selling at games for so long, the Boleyn Ground's swansong was always going to be a special one. It's clear to see that it didn't disappoint when Mark looks back, 'The atmosphere was amazing; it was like serving in the middle of a stand at Upton Park. Everyone was around you. It was crazy but absolutely one of the best experiences I think I've ever had. To know it was that final time it was just so heartfelt – everyone was there, it was amazing. Everyone was singing and it was an unbelievable experience, one that you never forget.

'We sold out really, really early – it took everyone by surprise how busy it was. I always used to try to sell out 15 minutes before the game started, so I could go in and watch it. On that day it was like two hours before. It was absolutely incredible; we got there early to set up and from the moment we started setting up we had a queue and it just didn't stop. I've never known anything like it.'

As much as some former players probably will have loved to have been with the fans pre-game, they likely would have been mobbed. So, a lot of them gathered in the Ironworks Bar beforehand. Rob Pritchard, who was the club's media officer and helped with the evening's organisation, recalls the feeling of seeing them all there. 'I remember I went in there before the game – probably an hour and a half before kick-off. Any West Ham fan probably would have melted, it was ridiculous. Everywhere you looked, there were legends and to see them all back together in one place, sharing stories and just being part of it. They went from players who played one game to players who played 500 games. They were all in there swapping stories and enjoying each other's company. It was quite an emotional moment to see it all.'

There were, of course, those who simply grabbed a couple of cans to drink in the streets as they took in the atmosphere outside the ground and the World Cup winners statue. Though most people will have made sure they had food or drink from the place they had become loyal to over the years on their last chance to do so on a matchday.

Atmosphere outside the ground

'I went to The Queens, but before we went there, I went for a walk through the gates and around the shop and through the carpark just once more because I thought, "It's going to be so busy later,"' says Daniel Hurley. 'I've always wanted to have one last little walk around it. So, I went down from Upton Park station, through the market and everything, then through the main gates and back around, because I thought this would be the last time I ever go there.'

Daniel was right. Upton Park was absolutely teeming with energy. Even early on in the day, there were so many people who were all desperate to say goodbye to the Boleyn Ground in the best possible way. As Tony Cottee arrived at the stadium in the car, he immediately got a taste of how many people were there. 'You could sense that it was something special and different to any other game that I'd ever been to, because of the volume of fans at four o'clock in the afternoon. If you turn up three and a half hours before kick-off, normally there wouldn't be anyone in sight. So, when we got there, firstly, it was very difficult to get in the car park – I think I got one of the last parking spaces, right in the far corner. There wasn't that much room for cars anyway, but I managed to get in and as soon as I got out the car I just got deluged with fans.

'It was great. I'm a fan myself so I don't mind it all, but it was just so different. It was like there were fans everywhere wanting to talk to you, doing autographs, doing selfies, and the walk from the car to the main entrance was the longest it ever took me to do it. You always get stopped a few times, but this was just constant and trying to get through the front door was hard.' Tony Gale adds, 'Everybody wanted an autograph on that last home game of the season; it was as if we were all going to die and go away or something. I know it was the last game at the ground but everybody wanted a souvenir or something from that game. I must have signed hundreds of programmes on the evening, as did most of the other lads who were there as well.'

It wasn't just the big names who felt the magnitude of the occasion from those around them, though, as it was impossible not to. I clearly remember walking to the ground from Canning Town station and seeing more people the closer I got. There were people drinking, singing and dancing on the street, with plenty of those congregating around the World Cup winners statue. Having come out of the Boleyn Tavern, Dan Lawless was one of those who were in the thick of it. 'The big thing for me was getting to go there with my mum, who's a massive West Ham fan and we got to do it as kids, so that was really special. I was with her for most of the day. I went to go and get some beers and I bumped into Nicky [Hawkins] and Ryan [Archer]. They were standing there drinking by the Bobby Moore statue, just watching the sea of West Ham fans. We haven't really lived through a big cup win, so we haven't had that big trophy parade – that's probably the closest we'll ever come to it. Being around that statue as people were climbing on top, drinking on top of it, I was there with those guys and it was really special. It was just such a good moment that I didn't want it to end.'

Brian Holmes was a steward on the day, and had trouble making his way into the ground despite getting there early. He recalls, 'It reminded me of when we won the FA Cup in 1980 when the bus came down the high road. It was so jam-packed and it was a good atmosphere, but not for the little one – she must have been about eight. She had been to a few games but had never seen it that bad; she just liked the pie and mash, had to skip that.'

The feeling of the atmosphere being similar to a cup final was mentioned by plenty of people. The sheer number of people that had gathered on Green Street and the roads surrounding it, as well as the palpable excitement, created such a fantastic spectacle. Looking back on this, Joseph Fordham says, 'There was definitely a feeling of a lot of people being there that probably hadn't been there in a long, long time. It's kind of like when we play Millwall at home and you just see different people in the ground, a different kind of fan that was there just for whatever kind of reason, but it built really quickly.

'I wasn't expecting the streets to be packed like that, like it was a concert. It was unbelievable. I perhaps naïvely thought it would just be like any other game where the people that go into the game would be the ones that are around there, I didn't expect thousands more to be hanging off the statue, filling the streets singing and all that kind of thing. So that was a surprise, definitely. But it was definitely something quite special to witness because you're not going to see that again.'

If anybody had the best view of all this, it was surely James Datson. 'I was lucky enough to stand high up in the stadium. We had the boxes and directors' area and things like that. They have balconies, and I could squeeze through and see it was just mobbed, it was a sea of people. A sea of claret and blue for miles, you could see all the way towards Upton Park station. It was just full of people.'

Seeing so many fans in one place was breathtaking enough, but there was so much more for the senses to take in. On top of the singing and cheering, Gary Firmager could be heard on top of his stepladder selling *Over Land and Sea* for the last time, as well as Dean Tonkin bringing people in to buy his bags of sweets among his fellow stall owners. The smell of burgers filled the air, making me think of the countless times I had got flour all over my face or sauce on my top. Then there were the people nudging into others to remind everyone of just how many people had gathered outside the ground for this momentous occasion.

The people selling on the streets and in their shop undoubtedly added to the experience, but they also forced some fans to think about what would be left behind. 'When

I was there, I remember really thinking about the market owners, or the small business owners around the stadium – the merchandise stands and the burger vans and all those guys. I was really thinking about them in a concerned way,' Georgina Hunt says. There had been a lot of talk around what would happen to the area once West Ham moved over to Stratford. Businesses such as Ken's Café, Nathan's Pies and Eels, the Boleyn Tavern and many of the other stalls and sellers around the stadium had become synonymous with West Ham and the matchday experience. The businesses weren't going to be moved, so how would they be able to cope without the added income of thousands of Hammers fans descending on Upton Park every other weekend? There were also questions about whether the stalls and tradesmen that ran them would be able to go to the new stadium. Hope and scepticism seemed to intertwine during this conversation – the latter was eventually proven correct.

When thinking of the sheer number of people who were at the stadium, it's easy to forget that what makes the time outside that day so special is personal experience. Among the hordes of people, individuals were making memories they would hold on to for a lifetime. Some of these will have been private, while others were made more public due to involvements with the media. James Jones had moments that fit into both of these categories, the first of which was incredibly personal. 'I had a picture with my brother outside the front of the ground. It's something that I wanted to do straight away and absolutely had to do. The reason behind that is there's a picture of me, my brother and my dad outside the ground when it was the old West Stand. It was on the day of my brother's first game years ago – we beat Coventry 5-0. So, I was like, it's the last chance to get one of just me and my brother, similar to the one that we had all those years ago.'

That emotion-filled moment was soon to be followed by something that became infamous among James's friends and colleagues. 'We were pretty drunk and a guy comes up to me and goes, "Hi, guys, once you've had your photos done, do you mind doing something for Sky Sports?" I've got a bit of a reputation of sort of turning up for the opening of an envelope for anything media-related, so I just said yes without even asking what they wanted me to do. It turned out they were doing a montage and wanted someone to replicate Di Canio's famous volley against Wimbledon. After having a few beers, I just thought, "Yeah, why not? Let's go for it." My brother went first, and then I went and pulled a hamstring and just didn't think much of it after that; we just said thanks and walked off. It was at half-time, my phone started going mental and it turns out that they'd put it in the montage on Sky Sports. When I say my phone was going off, family, friends, people were tweeting me, people that I've never even met going, "Was that you just pulling a hamstring on television?" I don't regret it, I think it's funny but I'll watch stuff on YouTube of that last day and it will just surprise me every now and again that I'll pop up doing that, body in slow motion and it still gets me to this day. Took me a couple of weeks to get over that hammy, though.'

Nigel Kahn also appeared on television that day, but for a very different reason, as he spoke on ITV News alongside Dean Tonkin, discussing the impact of the move. Nigel had set up a Facebook group called West Ham Fans Against Olympic Stadium and had been fighting against the move for years. He remembers, 'I'd leafleted around the ground, I had a flag made, I petitioned. Then I went and met with the club and hung my flag outside the main gates saying no to the Olympic Stadium. I taught myself how to build and set up my own website. So, it was a bittersweet day.'

While a lot of fans had bought into the idea of moving to Stratford, Nigel is far from the only one who was against it. However, not many will have voiced that opinion on the day, feeling that they would rather just celebrate the Boleyn Ground and enjoy the whole day and night instead. That was certainly clear when looking around ahead of the game. West Ham fans were filling the roads to a point where none of the traffic could move at all. John Newman had the perfect view from Newham Bookshop and says, 'The buses and the cars just weren't moving. They were stuck there, and we were just wondering how long it would take people to realise they weren't going anywhere and get off the bus. Some people were sitting on there for over an hour, thinking it would move and it just built up and built up and built up. It was unforgettable.' Looking back on that scene, Rob Pritchard observes, 'There are a lot of clubs who have moved ground recently but there's only West Ham who's brought a whole part of London to a standstill. The sheer number of people that wanted to be part of it just shows how big this club is, it's huge.'

James had loved the atmosphere, but he reveals that there were perhaps signs that trouble might follow the Manchester United team bus's arrival. 'The West Ham bus obviously arrived first, but we didn't realise it was the West Ham bus and a lot of fans thought it was the United one. Some people started lobbing stuff at it until we realised it was West Ham and everyone stopped and started clapping.'

Still, the players seemingly loved the drive in, as Aaron Cresswell says, 'I remember coming down Barking Road and there was what felt like 300,000 fans. There obviously wasn't that many, but that's what it felt like and we were literally crawling through these thousands of people. It was just incredible from the minute we left the hotel all the way to the stadium, it was special.'

The Hammers had also arrived far earlier than the Red Devils, who had been instructed to get to the ground before they usually would due to the number of people who would be coming. That advice had been given with fewer fans expected to be on the streets than had actually turned up. However, United completely ignored what they had been told and approached at the usual time they would for a 7.45pm kick-off. Vivian Archer, who is the manager of Newham Bookshop, condemns the away side's decision. 'The bus stopped just by the shop and people were shouting at them. Nothing could move, it was such a ridiculous decision to allow the bus to arrive that late and take that route.'

There had been a strong police presence, with horses and vans in attendance, but that wasn't enough to get the United bus through the crowds without incident, as James recalls, 'I think by that point, a lot of fans were a little bit frustrated because the police had turned up and got a little bit heavy-handed for no real reason. I know it was reported that West Ham fans were misbehaving, and there were some fans that were misbehaving, but there were police horses about, and it just felt as if the police wanted something to go wrong to give them a reason to be a bit heavy-handed. By that time, you literally couldn't move and you had the poor old Man United bus stuck in the middle of thousands of West Ham fans and only one thing was actually going to happen by that point. It wasn't going to end well.'

The fans had been drinking in the streets for hours and used their bottles and cans as ammunition to throw at the bus. It didn't move properly for what will have felt like an age, leaving the vehicle as one big sitting target for anyone who fancied chucking something. Many people did oblige, whether that was playfully or with intent to do some damage.

For anyone aiming for the latter, they were successful as the coach's window ended up smashing.

Not all Hammers fans were comfortable with what was going on at this point, as Georgina Hunt remembers there being 'some dark, weird moments' and feeling worried. Personally, I can recall walking on the pavement at Green Street and not noticing a smashed window when I came up to a parked police van, but I spotted a hole in the black tint when I reached the other side and felt a sense of confusion. I had held a very idealistic view of the day beforehand and felt that nothing negative could possibly happen – I was hopeful of a victory on the pitch and hadn't comprehended anything going wrong off it. However, there was a media frenzy that began following the incident that threatened to take away from what this whole day was really about.

One of the first things to surface online was a video from Jesse Lingard. The visiting midfielder was known for being a big character and someone who posted online, so it was natural that he would want to document such a big situation. The 23-year-old's footage showed the Red Devils players sitting in the aisle to stay away from the windows in case the glass on the inside was also smashed. Watching the video, it seems as though he found it funny more than anything, repeatedly shouting 'oh shit' and 'mummy', before recording himself near the area that had been affected while covering his face and sticking his tongue out.

As would be expected, the events led to journalists springing into action, as James Datson, who was in the press lounge, says, 'There was talk in the press room like, "We'll be surprised if this kicks off on time." You can imagine inside the press area when you're hearing things like that, the journalists are quite keen to get whatever they can, so you can hear the taps on their laptops. It was well before kick-off, so a lot of things to report.'

Russ Budden recalls, 'I'm in the control room next to all the police control, looking at all the CCTV watching the Man U coach come in because they could obviously track it and see it getting pelted. They were all huddled around the CCTV. I don't know what they were saying, but you could see there was a lot of pointing and gesticulating at the screen, so they knew something was happening. Hindsight is a great thing but there was always going to be a delay; there was always going to be a little bit of naughtiness because you've got double the people outside that were in the ground and a lot of people didn't have tickets, but they went just to be there.'

Despite the media frenzy, much of which pointed towards potential bans and police action, there wasn't actually that much that happened in terms of fans being reprimanded. In response to a Freedom of Information Act request, the Metropolitan Police said, 'Police attended the bus and facilitated its movement through the ground where it was parked. A crime report was taken for the smashed window, but no offender was identified. No further incidents were recorded in regards to the bus.'

The match did end up starting late, with the whistle being blown at 8.30pm, 45 minutes after the initial start time. There was suddenly something else for news outlets to report on, as David Sullivan made a statement regarding Manchester United's role in the delay. 'United should have got here at 4pm. They know it's our last game,' it read. 'They had the same problem at Tottenham a few weeks ago. If you check the coach there won't be any damage to it. I think the police and officials have been kind. I'd make them kick-off at 7.45pm if I was in charge. What people forget is they've got trains and buses to get home and we've got a wonderful, wonderful show after the game for them. I'm gravely disappointed, more for our supporters.'

Having seen the ruckus, my dad had said something along the lines of 'Let's get out of here', gesturing to go towards the stadium and get into our seats. While the atmosphere calmed down quite a lot once the United coach passed, I had always wanted to get into the stadium as early as possible. That's because sitting and looking at the pitch and the stands is what I loved more than anything, so it made sense for me to be there rather than in the streets. Being normal fans, we were able to slip through the crowds, but not everybody could say the same, as the troubles were quickly forgotten by those who were there.

James Jones recalls, 'There was a bit of commotion behind me. I turned around and Russell Brand is behind me trying to push through everyone because he had VIP tickets and he's got his security guards pushing him out of the way. I've got some great close-up pictures of him literally right next to me; there are people mobbing him but he's trying to get through. It was just good fun and everyone was in really good spirits. When I look back at it now, I don't think of the bus incident or the police being heavy-handed or anything bad happening, not anything that was really reported afterwards. All I really remember was just thousands of West Ham fans being there to have a good time and to say farewell to a place where we've all got so many great memories.'

Roberta Moore also remembers the reception she received from the Hammers faithful on her way into the stadium, 'The fans were always so wonderful. They come up to you and say, "You're Roberta Moore. Are you Bobby's daughter? Your dad was just amazing. What a wonderful man. You must be so proud. I'll never forget." However he touched them, people would come up and tell me. There are lots of old faces who come up and say the same.'

There were so many people who simply wanted to celebrate the Boleyn Ground and be at Upton Park, whether or not they would be able to get into the ground. This made it one of the biggest pre-match spectacles I, or anyone else in attendance, had ever seen at a football game.

The programme

Like many others, I had made sure to buy a programme before going into the stadium. This brought about one of my biggest memories of the entire day, as looking back I can vividly see the seller resting a box full of programmes on his knee and supporting it with one hand, while rapidly handing them to people and taking the money with his other. The poor bloke was absolutely mobbed and there was a crowd that had swarmed around him in the hope of getting their physical piece of history.

Geoff Martin was the matchday programme manager and looks back on the experience from the sellers' point of view. 'People turned up buying fives and tens. It's fabulous, but people were desperate for these programmes. It was manic and I was going around making sure the sellers were okay, but even I ended up having to sell. It sold itself and I was really pleased. Nobody lost control, and the fans, give them their due, were quite orderly. When I initially heard about the volume of programmes I thought, "What am I going to do with these, where am I going to put them?" The average number of sales was about 8,500 that last season. We weren't talking about that here, it was over five times as much, but people had their normal sales pitches.

'Our sellers are all seasoned people. They've been there before I even got involved with it all. So, I inherited a staff that knew exactly what they were doing and went out and did it. Most fans are creatures of habit and they will come into the ground and they would buy off the same sellers they had always bought off.'

Rob Pritchard, who was West Ham's media officer, speaks about what went into the making of the programmes that term, 'That season we themed every programme as a hark back to the 112 years that we've been at Upton Park or the Boleyn Ground. We went through and our designer very cleverly recreated all the different designs throughout the history of the club. Obviously, they were very different from the basic print-only designs from the very early days through to the designs going through the 60s, 70s, 80s, 90s and up to the modern day. They were all historic in their own way because it was the final season at Upton Park and they were all collectible in their own way, but they were really well received by the fans. I thought they were a really fitting way to bid farewell to our 112 years at the Boleyn.'

Focusing on the programme for the Boleyn Ground's final game, he continues, 'It was a bigger issue, more pages, and it was probably a case of how much we could cram into it. We had the wraparound cover with the montage inside which tried to capture as many historical moments in the club's time as we could. I suppose it was a case of giving the place a fitting send-off and culminating a lot of the features that we'd done that season. We did a 50 greatest matches run-down that culminated in that one, we did all the stats of all the games that have been at the ground. We had a lot of help from contributors like Steve Marsh and Stuart Allen, who are programme and memorabilia collectors and historians, John Helliar, whose dad published the programme many decades ago and also edited it, so it was a case of bringing in as many different aspects of what was a one-off occasion. I'm never going to edit a programme that's going to be as widely read and widely circulated as that one. We sold, I think, over 60,000 copies of that programme which is far in excess of any other game. It was just nice to be a small part of such a historic occasion.'

The cover for the final game was different to all of those that had come before it that term or any other. It had a fairly minimalistic design with a claret background, the West Ham badge and 'Farewell Boleyn 1904–2016' in gold on the front and the lyrics to 'I'm Forever Blowing Bubbles' on the back. As Rob puts it, 'It was to make it more collectible and a coffee table sort of style, something that you could display or show to your family or friends or grandkids or whatever, and it will be something that looks a bit timeless.' This was certainly achieved with its simple yet striking look.

When Rob looks back on that specific programme, the feeling of pride attached for him is unmissable, 'I don't think you're ever 100 per cent happy, because I think with anyone who creates anything, whenever you look back on it you always think, "Oh, I could have done that better," but I was happy with it. Not only by the fact that it was well received and the fact it sold so many copies – I understand that was because of the occasion more than because of the content – but to think that tens of thousands of people were taking something home that I created and that it will have pride of place in their West Ham collection of memorabilia is great. We recently put a video up as a young boy who was a mascot a few years ago was talking about his supporter's story, and one of the things he mentioned was that his grandad had bought him a programme from the final game and that he'd kept it and it's his most prized possession.

'I've got a really deep affinity with West Ham United. I've been here a long, long time. We've had some really emotional moments, I've edited some programmes for what I would say have been really important games in the history of the club: the play-off semi-final in 2012 against Cardiff, I remember doing the programme for that. Nobes's testimonial, doing the programme for that, obviously Domžale and Juventus when we moved into the new ground, editing the programme for the first game at a new stadium was our moment. I also did the programme for Argentina v Croatia when that was played at Upton Park – I've got a cover of that signed by Messi because we had him on the cover. It's really nice to have something that's a lovely piece of memorabilia to keep. The final game programme, it was such an important night, there were 100,000 people in Upton Park that night. Sixty-four thousand who couldn't get into the ground just wanted to be there. To be part of an event that means so much to so many people, it's a privilege.'

One for the creatives

It can't be overstated just how important this match was for West Ham and the club's supporters. Whenever there is a monumental moment in history – whether it is within or outside sport – there will often be people who want to document it. While this book was written years after the historic night it focuses on, there are many who went about capturing events on the day.

As a first-year Multimedia Journalism student at Bournemouth University, I had initially wanted to do something of my own. I had managed to borrow one of the faculty's video cameras for free and put it in my rucksack in the hope of making a mini documentary about the game. It didn't come out at any point throughout the day or night, though, as when I came across my first fellow Hammer on the train, I had realised that I couldn't do it. I just wanted to take the entire event in for myself without worrying about trying to capture it in a way that attempted to look professional. I suppose writing this book makes up for that decision.

Luckily, there were those who followed through, largely documenting the events through the mediums of photography and videography. Some of these projects were undertaken solely on the day and night, while others had been going on throughout the final season at Upton Park or a series of matches. Joseph Fordham, Georgina Hunt, Freddie Bonfantini and Dan Lawless were all among those who were creating something.

The documentary *Iron Men* has also played a key role in documenting the Boleyn Ground's final weeks for future generations to look back on. This focused on more than West Ham's last night there, looking at the replay against Manchester United in the FA Cup, as well as the defeat against Swansea. It also examined the people affected by Upton Park's swansong as much as the action itself, using this as a way to look at the concept of home, what it means to people and how a community can be emotionally impacted when moving home is forced upon them.

Suri Krishnamma directed the documentary, despite usually being a fiction filmmaker. He's also a West Ham fan and says, 'I think there's a lot of directors out there that could have done that, but I think they chose me because I had a personal, emotional investment in the club and the move and the characters that would be involved in that. It wasn't a decision I had to even think about. As soon as I heard about the idea, I thought this is an opportunity to do something interesting.

'I knew this opportunity would never happen again, because this event will never happen again. Once we move; that stadium has gone. To document something that's been in my blood as a supporter for so many decades, and in my family's blood and in my friends' blood was a real honour. It's a real privilege and I couldn't quite believe I was being given this opportunity to do it.'

Joseph and Freddie had both been working on their own books. The former, who is the man behind *No Place Like Home*, was taking stills of various people involved with West Ham in or outside the stadium, while also adding quotes about their memories of the ground. The latter's book, *Long Live the Boleyn*, was solely photo-based, as he documented the final season at the Boleyn Ground, mainly from the Bobby Moore Lower.

Meanwhile, Georgina wasn't able to get into the stadium for the final game, having attended the three before, but she says, 'I was thinking about what I wanted to do as a creative and to remember those last moments at the ground, so I brought my camera and took some shots of the crowd. I wanted to go down there just to experience it for myself but also record it and try to document it as much as I could visually as well.'

Then there is Dan, who vlogged his own personal experience of the match and its build-up for West Ham Fan TV. He is an example of somebody who did something out of the ordinary for them, as he explains, 'Vlogging is not something I usually do, but I did feel it was important for that day. There's probably so much more footage I could have got, but I was sort of doing it as and when. It was kind of hard, but I felt at the time like I was documenting some really precious memories, but in between those clips I focused on just being present in that moment, just having a good drink and really enjoying that moment. It was the in between times when I really got to soak it in, so thankfully I wasn't vlogging non-stop.'

For these creatives, aside from Suri, it was important to strike a balance between getting the shots and enjoying their day. That is because above all else, they were primarily at the game as West Ham fans. That was certainly the case for Freddie, as he says, 'I had the attitude that if I can get some good shots I will, but mainly, this is all about me experiencing and enjoying this moment. I had already got enough shots to do the book by then. I was like, "Sure, I want more but I don't want this to take over what should be a celebration." The good thing about the camera I had was I could point and shoot. I just rolled with it. I wasn't sober, I didn't care, I wanted to enjoy it as much as I was going to try to capture some good shots.'

Georgina also allowed herself to get lost in the atmosphere, 'I kept getting carried away with the crowds at times, as a fan. I had my camera on me the whole time anyway, so if there was anything that happened, I'd just try and capture it. So, it was kind of flitting between the two.'

Joseph was meeting seven people to photograph before the match, so he is probably the one who was initially more distracted by his craft. 'I was a little bit preoccupied in the morning, making sure that people were going to be meeting me when they said they would be, because I knew people were going to be pretty hard to get hold of when we were there. Some photographs were done before some beers, some were done after, but I couldn't really let go and relax into the occasion until I'd met those people and got those photographs. But then once we were in the ground, I started to soak it up a lot more.'

While Suri is also a West Ham fan, he had to maintain a stronger focus on his creative duties throughout the day and evening. He admits that was tough to do at times, 'There was that kind of tug of war going on in me emotionally between wanting to cut free of the film just to watch and enjoy the day and the game, and knowing that I also had a responsibility to document it – not just for West Ham supporters today but for the future generations.' He gives an example of what it felt like. 'Imagine if you had been asked to film your best friend's wedding. When you film it, you're not really in the wedding because you're having to document it. Well, imagine that scaled up a million times and you're in this event, but you're also having to record it and be so objective about it at the same time.'

While this book goes into great depth about the final game at Upton Park, it is brilliant that there are also others who have taken it upon themselves to document the beloved stadium's last match, or even season, from different perspectives. Having official documentation of the game is important, but fan-made media also undoubtedly has its place and is a great way of showing how much this meant to supporters.

This is the very reason that Gary Firmager was standing on his stepladder selling *Over Land and Sea* for so many years, while some supporters will have had a copy of the *Blowing Bubbles* magazine popping through their letterboxes and had bought 5Managers throughout the season on top of getting the official match programme. It's also why they watch fan-made YouTube videos and podcasts in their downtime and on the way to work or games. The players and club staff were obviously key to the evening's events, but so were the fans, and it is those very supporters who have helped to ensure the night and how it unfolded will never be forgotten.

Inside the ground

After years of doing it, walking through the turnstiles at the Boleyn Ground is something that so many of us completely took for granted for a long time. It was different now, though, as this became one of those previously small moments that suddenly appeared incredibly memorable. It was just sticking a ticket into a reader, waiting for the light to change and pushing through the gates, but the senses were on overload for plenty of fans as they did those simple tasks.

'I remember going through the turnstiles and touching the roof or something. I had never done that before and never done it at a stadium again. I just thought, "This is it, I'm never coming in here again,"' Daniel Hurley says. 'I sat in the Centenary Upper at the time, so above the away fans, and it genuinely felt emotional walking in and I wasn't really prepared for that. I thought it would be sad, but I guess I didn't realise how much it meant to me until I knew that was it.'

James Jones also reflects on how he felt walking in, 'Because of the crowds, we decided to get in a little bit earlier and that was purely because we thought if we leave it any longer, we're not going to get in before kick-off. It turned out to be a great decision because walking through the turnstile for the last time was emotional, it was hard. I think that was the first time it really hit me, I thought to myself, "That's the last time I'm going to do this in this ground."'

For all the emotions that had been stirred up on the way to the ground, the madness outside and the intense sense of anticipation, it is perhaps natural that this was the moment that realisation finally hit. After all, this is the point at which fans were actually inside the building that was the centrepiece of all the evening's sentiment. One phrase that was used throughout the day – and so will feature heavily in this book – is 'the last time'. There were so many things that took on a greater meaning because it was the last time they would ever be done, and this was arguably among the most monumental.

Joseph Fordham is one of the few who went back to the Boleyn on a later date, but he remembers his observations from when he entered for the stadium's swansong, 'I always entered through the same turnstile as a superstition, which was the Bobby Moore Stand, Gate 51. I'm a bit of a people-watcher, and I like to see what's going on around me. I perhaps wasn't focusing too much on how I felt, which I should have done; it was only afterwards that I thought more about how I felt about it being over, when I went back to the ground. I did my usual routine, straight up, I remember we used to get a beer in there if we had plenty of time before kick-off. In terms of how I felt about it, I wasn't really worried about the game, I just had a feeling we'd win it anyway. I was more worried about what everyone else was doing and taking the actual atmosphere in myself.'

Dan Lawless had a completely different experience to Joseph. 'It was weird because I was really aware and I was really present in that moment, thinking, "This is the last time you're gonna put your season ticket through the scanner, last time you're gonna push the turnstiles, walk up the stairs," all of that stuff and you're just trying to take it all in. Obviously, I'm filming at the same time – vlogging isn't something I usually do, but I just thought it was important that day. So, I'm walking up, trying to describe it but trying to take it all in at the same time. It was quite emotional knowing that this is the last time you're doing that walk to your seat.'

Once fans were inside, there were many who made a point of thanking the stewards they had come to know. 'My first game there was in 1994. So, I've been there that long, and I've been on the same stand all that time so little kids that started as babies, I've grown up to know,' Jacqueline Lange says. 'A lot of people came up to me saying goodbye because they weren't going to renew their season tickets at the new ground, elderly people I just knew I would never see again. I felt part of it because they were coming up to me and saying thank you for all my help over the years and it was really sad, but I did fulfil what I had to do.'

Freddie Bonfantini made sure to take in his surroundings and enthuses about them even when he looks back. 'It was great, I remember going through the turnstiles, walking in, going past the toilets, the little gates. It was amazing, as you walk up you see around, the noise was deafening already half an hour before kick-off. It was mad.'

It's funny what little things about the stadium can stick in people's minds. As fans, we never claimed that the Boleyn Ground was perfect, but it was ours and that makes it sacred. That is why something like the toilet in the Bobby Moore Upper that never stopped running is still amusing to me years later. If that had been anywhere else in the world, I wouldn't have given it a second thought – or at least not considered it with fondness.

'I miss the smell of when it's damp and the grass has just been cut and the dark of an evening game and then the floodlights come on and then the smell of that wet grass comes up,' Jacqueline Lange says. 'Silly little things as well like walking down the road and smelling the onions and the burgers on the stalls.'

While the imperfections made our home what it was, there were still plenty of fans who liked the idea of moving somewhere that was a bit more pristine. David Blackmore was one of those who had bought into the idea of moving, and he remembers the emotions he had as he walked through the turnstiles and went towards his seat, 'It felt like the end of one chapter and the start of another one. I think it's like when you leave your own home, the emotions that you feel about that, when you move out to university or when you finally move out of a house altogether, just anything like that. It's that raw feeling of leaving somewhere that you call home and something you've been used to for so long.'

For that reason, everybody who could possibly be at the Boleyn Ground did their utmost to find their way into the stadium. Tony Cottee was in his friend's box, which became a very different experience to usual games. 'Les was just continually going up and down the stairs getting his mates in and almost using the same tickets. I don't know how he was doing it but it was sort of give the guys the tickets, they come through the door, give the tickets back to Les, then he'd go outside give them to another two blokes, and they'd come in with the tickets. I think we counted 35 people in the box which is made for ten or 15 people. It was just funny. We had about 20 people on the balcony and then you had people standing in the doorway, other people standing on chairs in behind the glass looking at what was going on and it was a great experience. I think the club accepted that it was what it was and we were by no means the only box that were doing that. To be fair to the club, they did look after the ex-players.'

I had got into the ground very early, but even then, the concourse was a hub of activity. It felt as if there were so many supporters who simply wanted to make the most of every single second they had left in this stadium. James looks back on the concourse experience he had dreamed of, 'We managed to get a few beers at the bar, God knows how because you could hardly move down in the concourse. Suddenly my brother pops up and he's had his face painted full claret and blue, which was hilarious. Everyone was just singing and dancing in the concourse down by the bar. Some people were on their mates' shoulders, a guy had a curly haired wig on so obviously we were singing, "Oh Christian Dailly." He was in the middle and everyone was around him and there was beer everywhere and I think even then we almost forgot why we were all there. We forgot what the occasion was.

'That's why I look back now at those pictures with a lot of fondness because that's how we envisioned it being every home match. In reality it wasn't ever like that and it's the first time I've really seen it like that. It was a party atmosphere. That's the first time I've seen it at that scale at Upton Park and by this time I was already drenched in beer and my brother's on my shoulders and we're all singing and it was just a really, really incredible atmosphere. I don't think we'll ever experience anything like that ever again in terms of an atmosphere – not unless we go and do something crazy like winning the Premier League, which probably won't happen.'

There couldn't have been a greater gulf between the experiences in the concourse and the feeling of initially sitting in your seats – especially for those of us who got there very early. It was almost similar to being in the eye of a hurricane. Until that point where I stepped into the aisle, the experience had been absolutely chaotic, but in the best possible way. There was constant chanting, so much hustle and bustle, the bus incident and just an outward pouring of emotion from everybody who had come to say goodbye to Upton Park. It was completely different once I had got to the point where the main event was being staged, though.

The stands were pretty empty when I first sat down and it felt so quiet. I may have been sitting with my dad, but we didn't say a word for ages and it was almost like I was completely alone in the ground. I remember looking at the banners that had hung of Bobby Moore and Sir Trevor Brooking, wondering if there would be new ones at London Stadium. I also remembered the great (and not so great) times I had witnessed at this ground. My first game, sitting in the heavens in the West Stand as Lee Carsley scored the only goal in our 1-0 loss to Everton. Taking my nephew, Bobby, to his first game and how he had enthused about Payet the whole way home after seeing him score twice against Newcastle. Almost crying in the Sir Trevor Brooking Upper when a late equaliser robbed us of a win against Fulham in 2006/07, when my other nephew, Jake, told me it would be all right and was somehow correct. The play-off semi-finals, relegation battles that were won and lost, European nights, drab games and those that were more than I could have possibly imagined them to be.

I was only 20 years old, so there will have been plenty of people in those stands who have so many more Upton Park memories than I do, but to this day I'm grateful I have my own ones. Many fans stayed behind at the end to look around and think of the moments they treasured. That extremely humbling experience came before the 90 minutes for me.

Nigel Kahn thought of what the ground meant to him, as well as his loved ones, 'You're gonna sit there and think. I thought of my uncle who took me as a kid, he couldn't go into the game, but he was outside the ground before kick-off. I went to see him, not just at the football, I see him all the time, but it was good that I could go and see him outside the ground. It's hard because I lived a five-minute walk from the ground for about 15 years. We used to do our shopping at the Boleyn, so we used to be there on non-matchdays. When I went away from home, I could still go back to where I was as a kid because I was going to watch West Ham play.'

Roberta Moore was able to share the experience of being at the game with her family, something that was important to her. 'My kids have grown up all over the place. So, it wasn't until my son was about nine or ten that we moved back here, and we continued going backwards and forwards to Hong Kong for a long time. As we lived overseas, they didn't really understand the West Ham connection and the football connection that I have. Obviously, they're aware of who grandad was and when they came back to England and were going to school here and everything, they started to get more exposure.

'We get invited to West Ham when it's the 20th anniversary, it's the last Boleyn game, they come along and they start to experience it for themselves and it's like an extended family. We're always so welcomed when we're there. And people are always coming up to me and saying, "Oh, your dad was this and your dad was amazing, just wanted to say what your father meant to me," and I think the children have seen that over the years and it's wonderful. So, to go to something like that and for them to be part of it, and because they never got to meet my father, it's a way of me connecting them with him. It's almost a very tangible way of doing it, which brings great comfort and I'm very lucky that I'm able to do that.'

Of course, not everybody entering the stadium was there as a fan. Russ Budden recalls how different it was when he made his way into his DJ box, 'For a normal game, whether it was Upton Park or now at London Stadium, I get there four hours before, so this was totally different. I'd set up earlier and then I went back to court for jury service and came back. In terms of the routine we'd have a pre-match meeting usually and find out what's happening. For that last game we had an outside company come in to do the closing ceremony, so they were sort of taking over.

'When I got up to the box for the actual game, it was all a bit different. The company had basically knocked the windows through to put all the cabling down for the extra speakers and things like that because it was all feeding through the sound desk. The easiest way, because in theory they weren't going back there again, was to knock the windows out. It had almost been like a soundproof box where I stood, so for ten or 15 years I hadn't really heard any crowd noise, but I could hear everything for that last game, it was just mental.'

As a season ticket holder of 11 years, everything about the atmosphere that night – even before the game – blew me away. It is difficult to imagine how mindblowing it must have been to experience it on that scale as somebody who'd heard nothing for a decade or more. This will have only intensified as the stands began to fill up.

Whether fans were inside the ground or were among the stragglers still on Green Street and Barking Road, plenty of them will have been looking out for the team news, which eventually came through. Adrián had been West Ham's main goalkeeper throughout the 2015/16 season but picked up a calf injury during a 3-0 win over West Bromwich Albion, which kept him out for the final three games of the campaign. This meant that Republic of Ireland international Darren Randolph came in between the sticks. The 28-year-old was making just his second league appearance of the season, having been a regular in the FA Cup and Europa League qualifiers. Raphael Spiegel acted as cover on the bench.

'I never had any problems or worries with him going out there and facing Man United – that he'd be out of his depth or anything,' Phil Parkes says of Randolph. 'I always knew that he would probably do himself proud, especially with how important the game was to all the fans and everything else.'

Since Carl Jenkinson had returned to Arsenal after suffering from torn knee ligaments, Michail Antonio had largely been utilised as a right-back. That is where he continued against the Red Devils, being joined in the backline by Winston Reid, Angelo Ogbonna and Aaron Cresswell. New Zealander Reid had come back strong after two small lay-offs due to hamstring injuries, while Ogbonna and Cresswell had been regular features in the side leading up to this game.

Operating at the base of Slaven Bilić's five-man midfield was Cheikhou Kouyaté, with captain Mark Noble and Manuel Lanzini playing in central roles just ahead of him. The talismanic Dimitri Payet was fielded in his usual position on the left wing. Of this quartet, Lanzini was the only one who had been out of the team at all leading up to this game, coming off the bench at times, indicating the consistency Bilić was maintaining in his selections.

Diafra Sakho was primarily a striker, but the Senegal international was deployed on the right wing for this game, where he had been utilised with greater regularity since returning from a hamstring injury. This left Andy Carroll as the Hammers' sole front man, making his fourth league start in succession, having worked his way back from an injury of his own.

Alongside Spiegel, West Ham's bench was occupied by James Tomkins, Enner Valencia, Pedro Obiang, James Collins, Victor Moses and Emmanuel Emenike.

Manchester United were missing Luke Shaw and Bastian Schweinsteiger through injury, while Marouane Fellaini was suspended. Matteo Darmian and Ashley Young were also among those who missed out on a place in the squad.

David De Gea took his usual place filling their goal, with Marcos Rojo, Daley Blind, Chris Smalling and Antonio Valencia being the back four tasked with the job of protecting the Spaniard.

Louis van Gaal had opted for the same formation as Bilić, and it is Morgan Schneiderlin who was the deepest of United's midfielders. Ander Herrera and Wayne Rooney, who was their captain, operated ahead of the Frenchman, while Juan Mata and 18-year-old Marcus Rashford filled the spots on the wings. Anthony Martial, who was 20 years old and in his first season in a Man United shirt at the time, led the line for Van Gaal's side.

The away team's bench featured Sergio Romero, Phil Jones, Memphis Depay, Adnan Januzaj, West Ham academy graduate Michael Carrick, Jesse Lingard and Cameron Borthwick-Jackson.

Some fans won't think about the man behind the voice that makes the announcements, but Martin Godleman explains how much this role means, 'There was the guy who did the PA announcement before me, Jeremy Nicholas, who I took over from in October 2013. He'd been doing that job for 15 years, and yet I was the one who got the gig to sign off at Upton Park, and to sign on at London stadium. I sort of feel a bit sad for him because I know how amazing it was to be the person announcing the teams on that night.

'To think that me, as an 11-year-old watching West Ham v Chelsea, seeing Geoff Hurst, who was like James Bond for me, like a film star, to see him on the pitch, I couldn't believe he was 30 yards from me. Fast forward from that boy to then, if someone had stopped me as an 11-year-old and said, "When you are in your 50s, you are going to be reading the team out on the last night football is ever played with West Ham at this ground." Well, you just wouldn't believe that would you? And there I was.'

Away from on-pitch matters, one thing fans would have noticed when they got to their seat was the free t-shirt and bracelet that was on it. The club had organised for claret and blue tops to be placed in a certain order, so that patterns could be created in the stands, while the bracelets lit up to add to the atmosphere visually. Plenty of people put both of them on straight away, but I had opted to keep my top in its packaging and put it straight in my bag to keep forever. In fairness, I was wearing a retro claret and blue sweatshirt, so I like to think I didn't ruin the effect too much.

Those colours are something that Joseph remembers, 'It's quite a striking combination, I think, the claret and blue. So, when you see a sea of it, I guess it resembled the play-off final, that kind of thing, when you see so much of it in one place it's quite a beautiful sight. So that stood out more. I wore the colours, I wouldn't usually wear a West Ham shirt to games, so there's loads of people like me that wore a shirt for the first time in ages, albeit mine was white. It just seemed that there was a lot more of that evident on the night, so it was much more striking than it would have been for a usual matchday.'

The colours were also something that Randolph noticed when he warmed up following the initial delay. 'We went out for the warm-up – me, Woodsy and Raphael Spiegel – we were just about to start and Jamo ran out to say, "Come back, kick-off has been delayed." So, we went back inside and just kind of sat there talking. Then on our phones we could see what was happening outside. So, finally Man United got there and we walked outside and there was just claret and blue everywhere with the t-shirts everyone had and flags were everywhere. It was packed.'

The delay impacted plenty of people, including James Datson. 'I went upstairs to the press box and set my equipment up and I had my notes sellotaped to the desk. I sat on the end of a row, so I had a bit of a wall, because I was in the front row, so I could use a part of the wall to put my notes on because it was only a cramped press area, I just had a little desk really. It was very tight, you didn't really have much space.

'I thought kick-off was 7.45pm initially. Normally, I would go on to test it because some of my listeners would be in the stadium just prior to the announcement of the teams, so an hour before. Then we got some news about the time, so I went on to start just as we would normally have been kicking off.'

He was using battery-run equipment, rather than something plugged in, due to the fact there couldn't be a delay for the listeners. He explains, 'The equipment we use is very much like what you would get if you were going on a tour of a museum or something, and a guide was talking through a mic and you were listening on headphones as you walk around with the tour guide.'

Having packed enough batteries to last the night, spoken to his listeners about what happened with the bus incident and described what was going on before the game, James conversed with the fans, even though they couldn't speak back to him. 'I was asking their favourite memory, I remember saying, "Think back, when was the first time you came to Upton Park, the Boleyn Ground?" I would recall my stories of standing on the North Bank and things like that. I was just trying to give them a flavour of what it's like and trying to engage some of their memories.'

Even Sky Sports had to think on its feet, as Tony Gale recalls, 'Tony [Cottee] got a phone call that he didn't answer. I got a phone call at the same time and it was one of the floor managers from Sky and they were inviting some ex-players and they asked if I could do it because I work for Sky as well. I wasn't drunk or anything like that, but I'd been drinking and I thought, "Blimey, I had better sober up." Then I went downstairs and had an interview alongside Graeme Souness and Jamie Redknapp. They asked me one question and I went on for about ten minutes. Your speech tends to run away with you when you've had a drink. I never saw the interview funnily enough. People tell me it was okay, but I remember feeling like, "Christ, I can't stop talking.'

'It was great to be pitchside as well because the stadium was full up and the atmosphere was building and building. It was great to see a lot of the fans down there sitting in their normal seats that they sat in for many a year and going to say hello, signing things for them and just being part of it. I had the interview near Chavs' Corner – as they called themselves – and they were having a bit of a laugh there at my expense because every time I tried to speak, they were all drowning it out because they were singing to me.'

Being pitchside also made Gale think of his past memories at the Boleyn Ground, 'The ground had changed from when I started off at West Ham. I'd seen it develop into an all-seater stadium instead of the stadium that it was when I was there. Loads of memories come flooding back without a doubt. Not just from when I played there but from all the games I've commentated on there for Sky and for Capital Gold Radio who I've worked for since I finished playing. So all the memories come back and the great games I'd seen ever since I finished the game. Play-off games, cup games, league games, relegation, promotion – everything goes through your mind.'

The former centre-back wasn't the only one who couldn't help but think about the past. There was so much to appreciate about the Boleyn Ground that it was only natural for the mind to drift back to the times that had previously been shared there. However, everyone was soon to be nothing but present, as 'I'm Forever Blowing Bubbles' kicked off what would be an enthralling 90 minutes.

Singing 'Bubbles'

There are few songs, if any, in world football that are as synonymous with a football club as West Ham and 'I'm Forever Blowing Bubbles'. One of the big songs that comes to mind outside of that is 'You'll Never Walk Alone', but even that is played by multiple big clubs who all want to claim it as theirs. The only time you'll hear another club singing to the tune of 'Bubbles' is when they change the words in an attempt to mock the Hammers. You would be hard-pressed to find any West Ham fans who would be offended by anything using that tune, though, as it holds such a special place in the hearts of those involved with the club. It's so loved that it gets played twice before games – once when the players come out and again when the game kicks off.

West Ham's most beloved song had been chanted countless times throughout the day: on the streets, in the concourse, in the station, in pubs, people humming along to it or singing in their head. However, it felt even more special when it was sung for the first time with the backing music and everyone packed into the stands, with a mosaic forming on the East Stand that read '1904 – 2016'. Just before the players started walking out of the tunnel, that famed backing track began playing, hitting every fan in the Boleyn Ground with a wall of emotion.

It was enough to put a lump in Matt Datson's throat, and David Blackmore felt the same, as he says, 'I didn't sing it as I normally would. I just stood there, and I think it was the emotion getting the better of me. I remember standing there and being awestruck by everyone singing it as if their life depended on it, as if it was everything. I was really emotional about that to the point that I felt like if I did start to sing that my voice would probably crack, and I'd be bursting into tears everywhere. So it was probably at that moment that it really hit me.'

James Jones ended up being exactly the same as David would have been had he sung, 'I cried singing it and I found it very difficult singing it, I couldn't get the words out properly because I was crying. This one was different; we knew this was the last time we were singing this before a game. I remember tears rolling down my face. Mostly because I was sad that it was the end but a little bit because I'd had way too many beers at that point as well, so I was even more emotional.'

'That first time it really hit. I've only ever really felt it like that a few times before. We could probably count the amount of times on one hand,' Joseph Fordham adds. 'It would always give you tingles before a game anyway, because it's the curtain-raiser to every West Ham game and it was always an exciting moment. But that particular one went straight up there with the 2004 play-off final – when I also thought we were going to win, but we didn't. The atmosphere that day and that first "Bubbles", and then there will have maybe been a few league games over the years where it really kind of struck me and that definitely did.' Georgina Hunt was one of those who were listening in from outside the stadium's walls, but she had just as emotional an experience around the song. 'It's something that I'll never forget. It felt quite sad that I won't ever hear that in this place again.'

As powerful as it was, the first time was almost like the warm-up for the one that was to come when the game kicked off. Following that first big rendition, the players from both teams shook hands and got into position, with the men in claret and blue giving each other a supportive embrace. The mascots and captains had their pictures taken in the centre circle, Martin Godleman read out the line-ups again and the fans gave a rousing chant of 'come on, you Irons', while the songs about Carroll and Payet were also sung.

The bubbles machines were soon out again, though, even if they weren't the best ones, as Russ Budden kicked off a game with 'Bubbles' for the final time at Upton Park. The stadium DJ recalls, 'It's over 1,000 times I've played that song and it was very, very strange, but you could also hear all the atmosphere. Not even just Bubbles, because the bubble machines were really crap at Upton Park. You used to get a puddle of washing up liquid in front of them, but a few of them came into the box, and that was the first time ever, and I could hear the crowd and it was proper spine-tingling, but for me it was almost even more so because it was the first time I've heard the crowd properly at Upton Park for some time as well, so it was quite poignant.

'It's a real honour to do that job, to press that button, being a West Ham fan. I didn't realise until after I'd pressed it, after you hear them sing. It was really emotional. All you're doing is pressing play on a track on a CD. It's really emotional and obviously being the first person to press it in the new stadium as well. I'm not in the history books, but for me, my little personal history, I feel like I was still a part of what happened in that last game and I felt really humbled by it.'

The one thing that was so striking about 'Bubbles' this time around is just how much passion there was behind it. At that point in time, pretty much every West Ham fan in Upton Park had their hands in the air and chest puffed out, singing at the top of their lungs – if they could overcome their emotions enough to do so – ensuring this match got off to the start it deserved. 'It was ridiculous. I swear I could feel my legs shaking from the noise of it,' Daniel Hurley says. 'It felt like the noise was going through you. It's one of my biggest memories of the night, as I'm sure it is for a lot of people, how visceral the crowd was.' Joseph adds, 'It felt almost like there was a cackle. It was like a different kind of sound you could hear in the air, when you get that rippling applause combined with singing. It just seemed like someone had turned the sound up slightly too loud and the speakers couldn't handle it. That was something special.'

It was all of this that meant even those who usually wouldn't sing it, due to the role they fulfil on matchdays, couldn't help but get in on the action. James Datson is one of those people. 'I remember singing and I very rarely do because obviously I'm commentating. So as much as my regular listeners are West Ham fans, I have to be conscious that there will be some away fans listening to the service as well because we provide it for the away listeners too. So, in terms of hearing "Bubbles" I can remember thinking, "I've got to sing this, I've got to try and get some of the atmosphere for myself as well." But I remained professional in the sense that I didn't get too carried away because I had a job to do.'

Russ is another. 'I usually sing along but don't do it properly, but that last game I sang it because I could hear everyone and so you have to. You can't hear that song and not sing along to it. I proper belted it out that time. It was such a bizarre thing, looking back at it. It's silly, it's just pressing a button, but what that song means to West Ham and what it means to fans; it's such a synonymous song with West Ham and being able to press that button meant a lot to me because I knew what it meant to everyone else as well.'

Russ playing the track started off this most beautiful of renditions, but it was when the music cut out and the fans belted out 'fortunes always hiding' that the true power of this song could be felt. Dan Lawless remembers, 'It's that moment when the backing track cuts out, and you just hear the fans and I had literal goosebumps. The hairs on my arms were standing on end and the back of my neck, it was something I can't describe. You could tell everyone was belting it out as loud as they could and it just reverberated around the ground. It was unbelievable.' The fans sung that last part even louder, and it feels as though everyone wanted to make up for the fact there wasn't the backing track to enhance the volume.

At the time, there was the clear feeling that everyone wanted to get this one out perfectly, giving absolutely everything to make the final time singing this before a game as special as possible. The pure emotional intensity attached to the song in that moment meant we couldn't be anything but completely present. It was like a 35,000-strong orchestra working in perfect unison to create a moment in time that felt absolutely incredible and became totally unforgettable.

4
First Half

MIKE DEAN'S whistle blew to mark kick-off, but it was impossible for many outside the centre circle to hear it over the Hammers fans who bellowed out 'fortunes always hiding' as the backing track stopped. Nevertheless, the Boleyn Ground's final game did get started as Lanzini rolled the ball to Carroll. It was worked back to Cresswell, who hit a long pass up towards Carroll, allowing the big man to win the first of many aerial duels he would take part in throughout the evening. As the singing stopped and an extended war-cry of 'come on, you Irons' rang out across the stadium at a deafening volume, there was a large group of players from both teams competing for the ball, with Lanzini and Carroll right at the heart of the fight.

Former Hammer George Parris recalls the feeling around the stadium in the early stages, 'Usually, when a game has been delayed, people have the hump. No one had the hump, they were there for the evening. It was an electrifying atmosphere all evening.' Tony Gale adds, 'Delaying the game, it kind of built the tension up for the game all the way along. It wasn't the delay that you wanted it to be because some ex-players didn't manage to get there because of it, but it made the tension grow higher and higher.'

Looking at the atmosphere as a whole, Tony Cottee says, 'I think it would have been inspirational. I played in games where it was flat and I played in games where the atmosphere was incredible. Under the floodlights, as we always used to say at West Ham, it was always quite a hostile ground, the fans made it hostile for the right reasons as well because they wanted to get behind their team and try and put the opposition off. When the game kicked off, you could sense it was a special atmosphere. It was a full house and quite rightly everyone was up for it.'

The team in white eventually came away with the ball, after what momentarily resembled a playground bundle, but they didn't keep hold of possession for long. Herrera was put under pressure and forced to clear, allowing Ogbonna to sweep up with ease. Carroll was soon back in the thick of things as the ball was played back to Randolph who smashed it up the pitch. Valencia had tried to cushion the ball to Schneiderlin, but the Geordie got in ahead of the United midfielder and managed to win the game's first free kick. As would be a theme of the night, this act of selflessness was met with a giant roar of approval from the claret and blue army.

While all of that was going on, there was still some activity from those who had gone to the ground but couldn't get in. 'It started to empty out a bit. I think it was still quite busy down Green Street and outside the ground,' says John Newman. 'There was a lot of activity around the statue and there were people coming along and there were scarves around the West Ham players on the statue, all kinds of memorabilia was over there. That was lovely.'

The fans lucky enough to get in were soon singing about Payet as the talismanic figure was handed his first opportunity to deliver one of his world-famous free kicks. The chanting was so loud, even if it was far from in complete unison. It felt as though the supporters were so desperate to will the Frenchman on and show how much this meant. Payet declined the chance to put the ball in the box, though, opting to pass out wide to Cresswell. The left-back took one touch out of his feet and whipped the ball in towards Carroll, who managed to get his head on it at the back post but couldn't pick out a team-mate. Schneiderlin scuffed his clearance, hooking it high up into the air, and West Ham managed to keep the pressure on. There was even a shout for a penalty when Reid went down under pressure from Rojo, but Mike Dean showed no interest in giving it – there was still a roar of appeals from the stands.

The referee may not have condemned United to the worst possible start, but they still had another wave to overcome. There was a shout for a handball when the ball fell from the air and appeared to hit Blind's arm. It bounced towards Kouyaté, who maintained possession and got the ball to Antonio. The number 30 got a cross into the box and, once again, the away side struggled to clear their lines. The ball eventually hung over Lanzini's head, leading to the Argentine attempting an overhead kick which ballooned high and wide. His effort wasn't on target, but it did highlight his eye for the spectacular and a clear belief in his technical ability.

There was good reason for that, as West Ham fans had learned during his first season with the club. The Argentinian magician had come out of absolutely nowhere to fill the Boleyn Ground's stands with excitement, having signed on an initial loan deal from Al-Jazira in the United Arab Emirates Arabian Gulf League.

Lanzini was an unknown quantity when he arrived at Upton Park. Many fans of both West Ham and other clubs will have wondered who on earth he was and why the Hammers had gone to UAE to make a signing. The applause received after his acrobatic effort, despite it ending up nowhere near the goal, showed how much they now backed him less than a year later. This was also mirrored by the club's hierarchy and Bilić, who signed him permanently after the season's culmination. This was all earned, with the man wearing number 28 contributing eight goals and four assists in all competitions that term.

What is impressive about this tally is that he was able to contribute those goals and assists whether his team-mates were performing fantastically or miserably. The midfielder scored the opener just three minutes into a win against Liverpool when he snuck into the box and turned Cresswell's pass into the net, then he got a goal and assist after the 88th minute to secure a 3-1 victory over Crystal Palace, as well as smashing the opener past Thibaut Courtois from outside the box in a draw at Stamford Bridge. Alternatively, it was Lanzini who scored during the embarrassing 2-1 loss that saw the Hammers knocked out of the Europa League by Astra Giurgiu, while he was also the man who sent the ball flying past Hugo Lloris during the 4-1 away defeat against Tottenham.

Scoring and assisting goals weren't the only ways Lanzini excited fans though – as would be the case once again in this game. He had moments of trickery in his locker, and linked up with Payet and other team-mates brilliantly, while he also had the vision and technical ability to thread through wonderful passes. The midfielder's display against United was also enough to see him named among *Blowing Bubbles* editor David Blackmore's trio of stand-out players in this game.

It can be suggested that the Argentine was overshadowed by Payet's talents at times – as would happen to plenty of creative players lining up alongside the Frenchman – leaving him slightly under-appreciated. However, he was definitely a real asset for the Hammers and was capable of swinging matches in their favour, and getting fans on their feet while he was at it.

Lanzini had continued to thrive after signing on a permanent basis, especially after Payet's departure. The midfielder had done so well that he managed to get himself into Argentina's 23-man squad for the 2018 FIFA World Cup. However, he was forced to pull out after a horrific training injury before the tournament had started, which had left him with a ruptured anterior knee ligament. It wasn't until February 2019 that he would make it back on to the pitch for the Hammers.

While there were worries that he might not be the same player after this, Lanzini has had his big moments since then, including a sensational strike that saw West Ham draw 3-3 against Spurs, having been 3-0 down with 81 minutes on the clock. Even if the midfielder has rarely been seen as the main man, he certainly had the ability to come up with the goods when it mattered. So, while the acrobatic effort didn't end up being a spectacular one, Hammers fans knew it was only a matter of time before the man nicknamed 'The Jewel' provided his crowning moment in the Boleyn's farewell.

02:33

De Gea's goal kick led to a mini game of head-tennis near the halfway line, until Schneiderlin brought the ball down and played it to Herrera. Under plenty of pressure, the Spaniard won a throw off Kouyaté. Following the Hammers' blistering start, United took this as an opportunity to catch their breath and slow the tempo down, passing the ball around the back. The home faithful didn't need to slow down at all, though, as the first rendition of 'stand up if you love West Ham' rang out around the stadium.

It is moments such as this that may have had Phil Parkes thinking about his own playing days. He says, 'I joined in 1979 and left in 1990, so 11 years I was there – it's a long time. I had already been at QPR for nine years and I expected to be at West Ham for maybe three or four years maximum and then possibly move somewhere else or retire. Obviously, it never worked out that way, I ended up playing around 440 games in the end. I had never ever dreamt that I would play that many, but I'm glad I did because the atmosphere at Upton Park really inspired everybody, it just kept you going. You just wanted to be out there, especially in the evening games, it always makes it a bit special to play there.'

With the men in claret and blue stepping off Blind, after realising there were no other options, the Dutchman eventually tried to play a long ball forward to Martial. That was quickly snuffed out, though, as Antonio raced in to intercept and burst forward before losing possession. The fact United's first thought was to play the ball back to keep hold of it hints at the two completely different approaches the teams were taking. West Ham were gung-ho, harnessing the crowd's abundance of energy, while United were more considered in their play, as had been the case throughout Van Gaal's tenure.

The men in white did still show that they were bringing the fight to this game, refusing to completely sit back and watch West Ham play. Smalling broke the lines with a pass to Rashford, but Ogbonna was able to step in and stop the 18-year-old from getting in behind, immediately nullifying the threat posed. Ogbonna's tackle ended up going off the forward and out of play to earn a throw for the Hammers.

For a few moments, both teams attempted to get the ball forward but lost it immediately. That is until Rooney came away with it and passed to Rojo, who kept it moving left to Martial, allowing the Frenchman to get at Antonio for the very first time. This was a feud that would be played out throughout the majority of the match, but it was the man in claret and blue who came out on top this time. Refusing to dive in, he managed to keep Martial going wide until the ball eventually ran out of play. It turns out the ball flicked off Antonio's toe on its way out, but the Hammers happily took the awarded goal kick regardless.

After Randolph got the ball back into play, both teams showed a willingness to work for the result, temporarily missing the quality needed to make the most of that. Carroll had won the initial header with three men around him, but after the ball was worked out left to Payet, the Frenchman was tackled and West Ham were awarded a throw. There was another coming together of multiple men attempting to win possession, but once Herrera came away with it his attempted long ball to Martial went wayward and rolled harmlessly back to Randolph.

The Republic of Ireland international dropped the ball on to the floor before smashing it up the pitch. There was plenty of time for United's defenders to set themselves as the ball flew through the air, but they were no match for Carroll. The big man got up to win the flick-on, diverting the ball into Sakho's path. The attacker threatened to get through, but misjudged the bounce, allowing the ball to pop up and hit him on the arm, leading to Mike Dean giving the away side a free kick.

As had been the trend for United in the early stages, the ball was harmlessly passed around the back until Blind eventually tried to get it forward. This time, the Dutchman played a sweeping pass towards Mata on the right wing. United tried to work some space near the corner but failed to evade the West Ham pressure and Payet was able to nip in and win it back. However, Ogbonna's clearance didn't get too far and Rooney had the ball at his feet just inside the centre circle. More quality would have been expected of the United hero, who overcooked his pass and sent it flying out of play.

Antonio thrust the ball forward from the ensuing throw and Noble was able to come away with possession. There was a hum of subdued excitement from the stands as the Hammers skipper ran away with the ball, but Sakho was just unable to get on to his attempted through ball. Having won back possession, Van Gaal's men popped the ball around until it reached Rooney, who was taken out by Kouyaté – soon unhappy about a foul being given against him.

United played the ball around harmlessly for a few moments, going at a pedestrian pace. However the game quickened up as soon as Schneiderlin shanked his pass, which ended up at the feet of his compatriot Payet. The Hammers hero cushioned the ball to Lanzini, before the pair played a one-two and the Argentine started jinking his way closer to the Sir Trevor Brooking Stand. His pass to Sakho was wide of the mark, allowing United to clear, but their effort only got as far as Kouyaté, who made a first-time pass to Cresswell.

In those few seconds, Lanzini had floated into space, evading Schneiderlin's attention until it was too late. The number 28 spun behind United's back line towards the left wing, where Cresswell played a perfectly timed pass to him. It was like the fans knew something special was coming, because a murmur of anticipatory applause could be heard as Lanzini met the ball. He had been running away from the goal but had the presence of mind to hit a first-time low cross towards the penalty spot where Sakho was waiting, and also the quality to pick him out.

It initially seemed as though Blind had everything covered. The Dutchman had checked his shoulder twice and knew exactly where West Ham's Senegalese forward was. However, Sakho caught him and everyone else by surprise when he tracked back and flicked his left foot towards the ball. Blind did his best to block the effort, but all his intervention did was send the ball spinning into the bottom corner and out of De Gea's reach.

Sakho's effort was so nonchalant, and it was hard to believe that a strike hit with such a lack of intensity had managed to sneak past the goalkeeper. What made it even more difficult to believe was that the opening goal had come so early. This caused a delayed reaction from many, but as Sakho jogged towards the corner flag to celebrate, followed by his team-mates – who were ready to jubilantly mob the striker after he dropped to his knees – the Boleyn Ground absolutely erupted.

While ecstasy was the main emotion that filled Upton Park at this point, there were so many others attached to it in the stadium. Daniel Hurley recalls, 'I was scared that we wouldn't score, and our last goal would have then been an own goal in a 4-1 loss. I was desperate for us just to score, whatever happened, I just wanted a last goal so I was delighted.'

'It just reaffirmed what I'd already thought before the game that we were going to win,' Joseph Fordham adds. 'It seemed like a perfect start and if you could write one that would be it: nerves settled, 1-0 up with an early goal. It kind of helped to ease into the occasion a little bit more and enjoy it.'

The goal had a completely different impact on James Jones, though. 'I wasn't nervous at 0-0. As soon as we went 1-0 up, Sakho scored that goal, particularly so early on in the game as well, suddenly the nerves hit home. We were excited but nervous and people were hugging and looking at each other going, "We're going to do this, we're going to win our final game at Upton Park, it's gonna be a great send-off." That's what really kicked off the nerves but also the emotions as well, because you didn't know whether that was going to be the last goal. You were wondering, "Well, is that the last time I'm ever going to celebrate a goal here?"'

While there were plenty of contrasting emotions in the stands when the ball eventually hit the back of the net, there will have only been love for the man who scored the goal. Sakho had joined West Ham from FC Metz in the summer of 2014 and was unknown to the majority of Hammers fans at the time. Still, his record inspired some sort of excitement, as the Senegal international scored 43 goals in two seasons, helping Metz get successive promotions to Ligue 1.

While it was always unlikely Sakho would replicate these numbers after the massive step-up, he did make his mark in London. The striker had scored in each of his first six league starts, which equalled the Premier League record. He went on to score a total of 12 goals throughout the campaign.

A hamstring injury had heavily disrupted Sakho's season in 2015/16, but West Ham's number 15 still popped up with some truly important goals. The first of those showed that ice ran through the striker's veins. He was surrounded by Liverpool players, but was still able to find enough space to slot the ball beyond Mignolet's reach to make the score 3-0 at Anfield. Then there was the second in a 2-1 victory over Manchester City, with which Sakho highlighted his predatory instinct and willingness to put his body on the line to get the goal, as he ended up in a heap on the floor after converting. Maybe the most satisfying of the lot, at least until the Boleyn Ground's swansong, came at Goodison Park. Having worked his way back from the aforementioned injury, Sakho came off the bench with West Ham 2-1 down against Everton and 29 minutes on the clock. The striker then scored a header to bring the scores level before setting up Payet's winner with a deft flick.

Aside from the obvious contribution that Sakho made in front of goal, he also brought plenty of character to the West Ham squad. Martin Godleman says, 'I loved Sakho. He came, he wore this Joseph and the amazing technicolour dreamcoat when he was injured once; it was like a Batman cape with all these colours and the players were shaking their head – it was mainly the African players.'

Sakho would never have the same level of prominence at London Stadium as he enjoyed at the Boleyn Ground. During the first campaign at West Ham's new home, the striker made just four appearances due to injury, scoring another goal against the Red Devils as the Hammers earned a 1-1 draw at Old Trafford. He then didn't start a single match in 2017/18, before heading off to Stade Rennais at the end of the January transfer window.

There had been plenty of controversy and questionable decisions around Sakho's departure. Six months before he eventually left, his exit was stalled due to a day at the races. The Senegal international was set to meet with West Ham to declare that he wanted to leave, but was held up because his agent wanted to watch the horse he had bet on, Siege of Boston, in the 3.20pm at Chelmsford. The runner they had gone to see did win, but the agent later confirmed that 'off-field issues' had to be resolved before Sakho could complete his move away from London Stadium. People were also baffled by the forward's actions once his departure eventually became reality, as the forward left a Lamborghini worth £200,000 at West Ham's Rush Green training ground.

It would be easy for Sakho's decisions towards the end of his stay to cloud the judgements of his time in claret and blue as a whole. However, people shouldn't jump to hasty conclusions. While at Upton Park, Sakho put in plenty of effort on the pitch and also showed great ability in front of goal. Concerning arguably the most important point of all, the striker embraced the culture of the club. His crossed arms celebration often brought us Hammers fans even more joy after the elation of the ball hitting the back of the net.

10:25

As United got the game going again, David Blackmore was thinking, 'This is it, we're gonna take Man United to the cleaners, this is gonna be a fantastic night.' Looking back, he adds, 'It's just the ecstasy of feeling pure joy, but then straightaway as soon as I sat down again, I was looking at the clock going, "How long have we got to hold on for here?"' Meanwhile, the rest of the West Ham fans repeatedly belted out 'Diafra Sakho, he scores when he wants' at the top of our collective voices. Neither side was losing their concentration, though, as the away side put the pressure on immediately, with Herrera almost finding Martial just inside the West Ham box.

Looking back, Cresswell feels that first goal had a big impact on both the game and overall occasion, as he says, 'That early goal, I think, definitely helped us massively. Even the atmosphere, the tension, the passion, everything seemed to go on a notch again when we scored. It was kind of like the lads grew into the game more and that's what I felt helped us massively.'

Having just lost the ball, Herrera soon dispossessed Lanzini. After a few passes, Noble went flying into a sliding tackle on Mata, mercilessly going through the ball and man. Dean saw this as a free kick, much to the protestations of West Ham's captain and impassioned fans. There was no time to hang about and complain, though, as United swept the ball out wide with a quick free kick. Nothing came of it in the end. After scoring at the other end, Sakho had got between Martial's pass and its intended target, Rojo, to let the ball run out of play. Even though the reaction wasn't as loud as it had been a few minutes before, passers-by would have been forgiven for thinking there had been another goal on a normal day judging by the cheers. Even Randolph rushed out of his goal to shout some appreciative words to his team-mate.

The ensuing goal kick got the game going again, and the match's combative nature was highlighted again within a few seconds of the ball being back in play. Smalling won the initial header against Carroll, but Noble managed to get his own head on to the ball, though he could only divert it towards Rojo. United tried, once again, to release Martial, but Antonio managed to get his heel on to the ball when sprinting back, getting it towards Kouyaté, ready for the midfielder to set back to Reid.

This is where the Hammers showed the quality that had made them such a threat at times throughout the campaign. Reid fizzed the ball through the midfield towards Carroll, who dummied to go one way – fooling Schneiderlin in the process – and offloaded to Payet. The number 27 swiftly turned away from Valencia and slipped the ball towards Lanzini, who was bursting forward. However, the ball eventually strayed agonisingly close to the Argentine's outstretched foot, allowing Mata to get around and relay it back to the goalkeeper to clear. Kouyaté was able to chest the ball to Cresswell, but the left-back's quick pass forward could only find Valencia, who fired the ball off Payet and to the feet of Smalling who smashed it up the pitch.

West Ham weren't letting up, as Kouyaté's header fell to Herrera but he had absolutely no time. The former Athletic Bilbao midfielder was swarmed by claret and blue: Cresswell was first on to the scene, with Kouyaté, Noble and Lanzini helping him to win the ball back within a second. Shortly after that moment, Alan Smith, on commentary for Sky Sports, said, 'Well, Manchester United have got to get up to West Ham's level here. They're tigerish in the challenge at the moment, the home team.'

That statement was vindicated just moments later, when Reid's long ball up the pitch was met by a weak header from Valencia, under pressure from Payet. The Ecuadorian had shied away from it and ended up knocking the ball out for a corner. In typical fashion, this was met by ironic cheers from the West Ham faithful.

As Payet prepared himself to take the corner, Smith added, 'It's easy to cave in under these kinds of conditions. If you're a United player now you've just got to stand strong for the next ten minutes or so to try and get a foothold in this game.' They were strong enough from the resulting corner. Payet played the ball towards Noble, who fired a first-time volley from the edge of the box. His effort was eventually blocked and Ogbonna's follow-up failed to hit the target. When Noble realised he had hit the initial strike sweetly, he must have seen his name in lights.

The fans' excitement was palpable whenever West Ham were on the attack. When Reid won the header from De Gea's goal kick, Sakho was able to pick the ball up and flick it past Blind on the right wing. Even though he lost the footrace against the Dutchman, there was still an optimistic outpouring of anticipation from the stands when it started. Blind did well to turn away from the Hammers man before coolly offloading the ball to Rojo, who recycled it to Rooney.

Once again, the away side were unable to pass the ball up the pitch, and an underwhelming passage of play resulted in Smalling hopefully smashing it forwards instead. A less-than-convincing touch from Ogbonna made Herrera think he could steal the ball near the corner flag. There was no need to worry though, as the Italian got there with time to spare and cleared. United did get the ball back, though, as Noble was adjudged to have been offside before retrieving it.

United were looking far from their best at this point, perhaps struggling under the strain of West Ham's pressure – both in the sense of the players' intensity and the occasion. This was reflected as Mata made a rather pathetic attempt at a header from Rooney's lofted pass, which went out for a throw. There was an abundance of passion being shown by the men in claret and blue on the pitch, which was reciprocated by those in matching colours filling the stands. Sakho was constantly bustling about and after he lost the ball from the throw, the West Ham number 15 stepped in to win it back from Blind's header. This caused a ripple of applause from fans, as well as allowing Cresswell to recycle the ball back to Randolph.

With Carroll up top, the Hammers had the opportunity to get the ball from back to front quickly, causing an immediate threat. That was the case here, as the Republic of Ireland international smashed the ball up the pitch towards the 27-year-old, who found Payet on the wing with his flick-on. The Frenchman evaded Smalling with ease, finding some space to exploit further inside. However, once he broke into it, Payet was unable to find a team-mate, with his attempt at a return pass cutting through the defence but trickling harmlessly wide of the goal.

United's players struggled to get complete control of the ball after De Gea's goal kick. Just as Rojo was about to finally bring it down, Noble rushed in to steal the ball from his grasp. The men in white would be surprised by Mr West Ham in the same way plenty of times throughout the match. The captain may not have got the free kick he was expecting for this specific effort, but there was yet another appreciative roar from the stands, before slight contempt rang out towards Dean for not giving the foul.

It seemed as though United had identified Antonio as a weakness in the Hammers' back line. That is because they tried to get plenty of balls in behind him – perhaps feeling that he may not have had the best positioning, due to the fact he was not naturally a right-back. If that was the case, it was certainly a flawed plan.

The ball was worked around the back by United, until Rojo aimed a pass at Rashford that went flying out of bounds. United won possession from Randolph's goal kick and Rooney played another ball in behind Antonio. Martial was the intended recipient, but Antonio beat the Frenchman to the ball and passed it back to the goalkeeper, who once again hit a first-time strike up the pitch towards Carroll.

It was a rarity for the target man to receive a long ball under pretty much no pressure during the match, but this was one of those occasions. Carroll used the time afforded to him wisely, chesting the ball down and setting it back to Noble. The captain's pass was originally heading towards Payet, but the Frenchman saw Lanzini coming and selflessly stepped out of the way, allowing the Argentine to burst forward and surge through the middle, before playing a pass out wide to Cresswell.

The left-back was halted by Mata, but Lanzini was on hand to pick up the loose ball, which was worked around once again until it found its way back to Cresswell. He tried to play centrally, but in reality, it was a poor effort. Nevertheless, panic soon set in for United as Valencia slipped, letting Sakho retrieve possession on the edge of the box.

Again, West Ham worked the angle and eventually got the ball out wide to Antonio, who turned Martial and sent a left-footed cross in towards Carroll. He was able to chest it down, and rather than shooting, had the awareness to lay the ball back to Payet. It seemed certain that the talismanic figure would smash the ball into the top corner, but he wasn't having the best time so far and his half-volley was well hit but went straight at the goalkeeper, who dealt with it fairly easily.

United knocked the ball about, but there was never really any conviction in their play. Eventually, Blind was the man who once again tried to get the team going forward, but Herrera was swarmed by the home side as soon as the ball travelled in his direction. Lanzini was able to pick up the scraps before offloading the ball to Payet. Though when the Frenchman attempted to return the favour with a flick, the ball fell to a man in white. There was no harm done, as it was just smashed up the pitch, trickling through to Randolph.

With Carroll being such a big target man, there was always the temptation to use his aerial threat, as had already been done various times in this match. However, there were other ways to release him. Instead of hitting the ball up the pitch, Randolph opted to roll it out to Reid on this occasion. The centre-back took his time to assess his options, then played it to Payet – a pass that drew Smalling out from his previously deep position to pressurise the Hammers talisman. Smalling was immediately taken out of the equation, as Payet took the ball under control with one touch and passed to Lanzini with his next.

While those two touches had eliminated Smalling, Lanzini was able to take out Van Gaal's entire defence with one as he diverted the ball towards Carroll. Blind was miles behind the rest of his outfield team-mates, keeping the frontman onside in what was a truly disastrous and baffling piece of positional play. Lanzini was able to take advantage of this, releasing the frontman with a perfectly weighted pass.

Bearing down on the goal, only De Gea stood between Carroll and a 2-0 scoreline, despite the United defence sprinting back without a hope of getting anywhere near the ball. Maybe the amount of time was a disadvantage in the end, as Carroll hit an indecisive effort which went close to the goalkeeper's legs, allowing him to block the tame strike.

There was no sulking from the striker though, as just a matter of seconds later, he nudged Valencia off the ball after a Randolph clearance deep into the United half. Carroll then played the ball off the right-back to earn his side a corner. It was only when the ball was out of play that we got a glimpse of just how disappointed the Geordie was, as he looked to the heavens and shook his head.

From the resulting corner, Payet sent in a deep ball, which had appeared to be extremely wasteful at first. However, Noble was on hand to retrieve it and maintain the pressure. With the away team possibly taking it for granted that the ball was sailing out of play, the skipper had enough time to set himself and muster a cross that flicked off Martial's shoulder.

Antonio was on hand to head in at the far post, but the fans' celebrations, and his choreographed dance routine, were short-lived. The linesman had given a corner, adjudging the ball to have curled out of play and back in after striking the United forward. Given what had happened in the FA Cup, some in the crowd felt it was almost inevitable there would be a moment like this, as James Jones remembers, 'We weren't surprised because we're used to decisions like that going against us. It was sort of typical to have a goal disallowed against Man United.'

20:56

There were boos from the crowd, before we all started singing, 'We've got Payet, Dimitri Payet, I just don't think you understand, he's Super Slaven's man, he's better than Zidane, we've got Dimitri Payet,' as the Frenchman set himself to put in another corner. This was far from the first or last time that song would be sung. The Hammers were unable to make the most of the pressure this time around, though, as United cleared the ball after three separate deliveries into the box, eventually forcing Antonio to pass all the way back to Randolph.

He sent the ball straight back up the pitch, allowing Carroll to get his head on to it once again, diverting it towards the corner flag. Sakho was never going to reach the ball ahead of Valencia, who had a head start, but that didn't stop the Senegal international from pressurising the right-back. The ensuing clearance went as far as Noble, but West Ham's number 16 could only chest the ball out for a throw before jogging back to get in position.

The short break in play will have allowed some fans to take in what their fellow supporters were doing. Joseph Fordham was one of those, as he says, 'I tend to do some people watching. There used to be a kid sitting with his dad on the steps and I always used to look at them. He was so young the kid, he must have been about eight, always in his kit, even in the winter. He would turn up, take his jacket off, just sit there in his full kit and his dad would be putting it on. I just used to watch and think it's really sweet and what's that kid thinking today.'

They hadn't managed it many times up to this point, but United worked the ball through the thirds well following the throw. It was eventually moved between three men in white near the left flank, which opened the space for Rojo to play the ball to Rooney. The 30-year-old was no longer the goal machine he had once been, now operating in a deeper midfield role. However, there will have been much more expected of him than an effort from outside of the box that ballooned high and wide – getting closer to the Bobby Moore Upper than Randolph's goal. He may not have been able to make the most of this opportunity, but the space Rooney was able to find did offer a small indication of the increased level of influence he was having in the game.

In the minds of many Hammers fans, Rooney will have come into this as public enemy number one. The striker-turned-midfielder had a knack for winding up opposition fans, as he proved when he kissed the United badge twice at Goodison Park, infuriating the very Everton supporters who had once adored him. West Ham fans also hated the sight of him as he had a habit of scoring against the Hammers.

Before this game, in 19 matches against, Rooney had recorded 14 wins, three draws and two losses. He also managed 12 goals and four assists during that time, showing just how much of a pain he had been for West Ham defences to deal with. The tone was set in his first match at Upton Park as a United player, in 2005, as he got a goal and assist to overturn the lead secured through Marlon Harewood's opener.

In addition to that, he scored a hat-trick to turn the game around when United had been 2-0 down at half-time in

2011, his goal knocked West Ham out of the FA Cup in 2013 and he embarrassed Adrián from just inside his own half in 2014. Rooney would have loved nothing more than ruining another, and far more important, game for West Ham fans, especially as this match was so vital in United's attempts to secure Champions League football for the 2016/17 campaign.

23:09

Randolph sent his goal kick flying up the pitch, but not even Carroll could reach this attempt at a pass as it went wayward and straight to an area completely devoid of claret and blue. As had been the case so many times throughout the game's first quarter, United knocked the ball around deep in their own half. This time, having drawn out the Hammers midfield, Valencia played a pass down the line for Rashford to run on to. Ogbonna was there for close company, though. The teenager managed to create a tiny bit of space before finding Herrera with a pass to the edge of the box. However, the midfielder was crowded out by the Hammers and was dispossessed before Cresswell smashed the ball all the way to De Gea.

The away side came forward again, as Rooney switched the ball out to Rojo, who touched it down to Martial. The Frenchman was put under immediate pressure by Noble, while other West Ham players soon came to help their captain out. The United man quickly offloaded the ball to Rooney and the Red Devils captain played it back out wide to Rojo, leaving him with plenty of space. The Argentine played a pass to Rashford in the box, but the youngster stepped over it thinking a team-mate was behind him, only for the ball to roll through to Lanzini. He played the ball to Kouyaté, but once again West Ham weren't able to keep possession as a throw-in was eventually conceded.

United had begun to control the ball and pace of the game more in the last couple of minutes. However, they still hadn't carried any real threat to Randolph's goal, with the Hammers standing strong defensively. That threatened to change when they switched gears to quicken up their passing after slowly playing the ball around. Smalling popped the ball in to Herrera, who played a one-two with Valencia before clipping an effort forward for Rashford to run on to. This put the teenager into a direct race with Ogbonna, who was able to reach the ball ahead of his opponent, before getting his body between man and ball to usher it out of play. After getting the better of a player much his junior, Ogbonna had the look of a man who knew he'd done his job well when strolling back into position with a slight grin making its way on to his face.

Randolph's goal kick was flicked on by Carroll, but there was nobody to get on the end of it, allowing Blind to control the ball with ease. Perhaps looking to continue United's momentum, while also aiming to make the most of a rare period in possession without being pressed, the Dutchman attempted an ambitious pass. However, all this did was put his team on the back foot once again, as the ball cannoned off Kouyaté's chest to Noble, who played it out wide for Sakho to get on the end of. He tried to get past Smalling, but after an attempt to push the ball past the defender rebounded back to him, West Ham's number 15 played the ball inside to Lanzini. The Argentine took one touch and smashed an effort from just outside the box, which had De Gea worried, but eventually fizzed past the post, getting close enough for a collective 'ooh' to ring around the Boleyn.

Under Van Gaal, a lot of United's build-up was methodical and that was highlighted in their play from the resulting goal kick. De Gea passed the ball short to Blind, and United moved it around, slowly working their way up the pitch, before Rooney played it wide to Valencia. The right-back passed to Martial, who managed to get the ball back to him despite the attention of three Hammers. Valencia then got a cross into the box towards Mata, but Reid was in charge of the situation, getting his head on to the delivery despite a push from the United man, which was adjudged to be a foul. Even if the foul hadn't been called, Rojo's effort at the back post was a wild one and went well wide.

This gave David Blackmore a chance to take in his surroundings, as he recalls, 'I probably spent more time than I should have looking around me and just honing in on different aspects of the crowd. I'd try to pick people out and because of where I sat, I could only really see the Bobby Moore Lower and Upper. I tried to look over to the Chicken Run as well. Looking across and seeing all those light blue shirts is probably the most memorable moment I had from that night.'

Following Randolph's long free kick, there was a full minute where the play verged on the bizarre. Neither team seemed capable of holding on to the ball, even for a couple of seconds, as possession switched hands quicker than the programmes outside had done. This was all nearly topped off when Rojo made a poor attempt at playing the ball forward, which harmlessly followed through to Cresswell. The Hammers left-back tried a first-time pass of his own, but it rebounded off Herrera and back towards Randolph's goal.

There didn't seem to be much concern as Ogbonna casually jogged back and passed the ball to his goalkeeper. However, Randolph took a poor first touch, which Rashford saw as an opportunity to try and nick the ball away from him. The Republic of Ireland international wasn't spooked, though, and had the quickness of both feet and mind to drag the ball away from danger with his right foot, before picking out Carroll with his left.

Randolph certainly showed a cool head in this moment, which will have been vital coming into such a big game. The 28-year-old was largely seen as Adrián's understudy throughout the campaign but started the game due to the Spaniard's injury. While it is always good for a club to have their first-choice stopper in goal, this didn't necessarily cause great concern for many fans as Randolph was also trusted between the sticks. After all, by this time, he had been included in various Republic of Ireland squads, getting on to the pitch eight times for his country.

Phil Parkes is definitely somebody who had faith in him. If it wasn't for the 1981 Hammer of the Year winner, the man who would celebrate his 29th birthday a couple of days after the match might not have ended up at the Boleyn Ground at all, let alone appear in such a historic match. Parkes explains, 'I had to go and watch him for David Sullivan. They sent Bobby Moon to look at him and Bobby Moon said he was no good, don't even bother with him. So, he [Sullivan] said he wanted me to go and have a look as a second opinion. I saw him play a couple of times when he was at Birmingham and he didn't have a lot to do in the first game he played, but the second game he played at Watford and he played really, really well. I said to David Sullivan, he's on a par with Adrián. For me, they were good competition for one another. I always knew that he was a capable goalkeeper.'

Randolph would go on to leave West Ham in 2017, joining Middlesbrough in the Championship, so that he could become the first-choice stopper once again. Having established himself as the Republic of Ireland's number one, Randolph earned cap number 50 in November 2020, keeping a clean sheet in a 0-0 draw against Bulgaria. He had also returned to London Stadium by this time, coming back in January of the same year to help the club deal with Łukasz Fabiański's injury after Roberto Jiménez had made a complete mess of it. So, while Randolph isn't the biggest name, he has come in and done the job well at vital times for West Ham.

The final game at the Boleyn Ground was the biggest example of this. It takes a lot of confidence for a goalkeeper to show authority in a match like this one, and Randolph showed how much he possessed with that flick under pressure from Rashford. Looking back on that night, the stopper says, 'It was just a special night to be a part of; the way the game went, it's one of those special nights that's definitely up there with my top nights in football.'

28:59

Carroll was able to bring the ball down and it was worked to Reid, but the New Zealander's long pass went out for a throw. The ball was moved from left to right by United, before Mata attempted a long delivery forward that was headed away by Ogbonna, but the Hammers had conceded another throw seconds later as Kouyaté's pass went over Cresswell's head. Possession switched hands quickly as the two sides attempted to force the play, with Rooney ultimately sending an attempted switch straight to Antonio. The right-back was able to find Sakho but the forward was unable to bring the ball under control and it went through to De Gea.

The stopper rolled the ball to Blind, who nonchalantly roamed forward with it at his feet. The 26-year-old only came under any real pressure when he got to the halfway line, which forced him to pass out wide to Martial, who was driven back by Antonio and played the ball to Smalling. Every man in claret and blue had stepped off slightly, giving the away side time to think. That is until the ball was rolled back to Martial and Noble pounced into action. The Hammers captain read the Frenchman's mind and stole the ball away, before the United man slipped and was left crumpled on the floor in Noble's wake.

Noble wasn't waiting around and drove forward with the ball at his feet, drawing both Smalling and Schneiderlin towards him. Once the defenders were in a position of no return, Noble rolled the ball left to Payet, who had the freedom of Upton Park. Payet jinked to the right and tried to curl the ball past De Gea. The 29-year-old got it horribly wrong, though, and the ball went high and wide, far from that top corner he had found so elegantly on plenty of occasions throughout the campaign. Bilić couldn't hide his frustrations, holding his head in his hands before screaming at the heavens. This summarised how pretty much every West Ham fan felt.

While the Frenchman had fluffed his lines, the play before the effort felt like a microcosm of Noble's entire game. He was absolutely everywhere, was constantly harassing the opposition, made good decisions and showed quality on the ball. This shouldn't have been too much of a surprise to onlookers, though, as you don't get a nickname like Mr West Ham without turning up for the club when it matters. As Daniel Hurley puts it, 'Noble had been great all year. In that game it almost felt like there was two of him. With Noble, you knew he'd have a good game, it demanded it from him that night and he was exceptional.' This game was as important as any most fans in the stadium will have ever attended, and it felt as though Noble felt exactly the same way. Ultimately, that's because he was also a Hammers fan, as well as the club captain.

'It's a very proud history of bringing academy kids through – that goes well before me, we're talking the World

Cup winners and before that in the 50s. So, it's always important that we've got kids coming through,' Tony Cottee says. 'It's great that Nobes had the honour of captaining the team for the last game and then obviously the first game at the new stadium and he got to do all the speeches on that night. He's been such a great servant.'

Noble was born in Canning Town, living a stone's throw away from Upton Park. The midfielder then ended up signing for his boyhood club and becoming the youngest-ever player to turn out for the reserves. At just 17 years old, he went on to make his debut in a 2-0 League Cup win against Southend United in 2004. What happened in the 12 years following that game meant Noble already held a very precious place in Hammers fans' hearts.

The midfielder's league debut came in 2005, when West Ham were fighting to get up from the Championship. It was at the end of this campaign where we all got our first iconic Noble moment, where his inner fan came out as Bobby Zamora scored the play-off final winner against Preston North End. He had been warming up behind the goal and went absolutely mad when the ball hit the back of the net, jumping on Zamora's back in jubilation.

After short loan spells at Hull City and Ipswich Town, the then-teenager was back at Upton Park and ready to make his impact. Noble's first goal came in the FA Cup against Brighton & Hove Albion, but it was in the league campaign that he had an even more memorable strike. The Hammers eventually lost 4-3 at home against Tottenham, but the team put in a great performance that was started by Noble smashing his effort past Paul Robinson from the edge of the box. This culminated in the Greatest Escape that ended with Noble and his team-mates celebrating on the Old Trafford pitch.

There have been so many other ups and downs during Noble's time with the club. For example, the midfielder was part of the side that finished bottom of the Premier League under Avram Grant in 2010/11. There were to be very different emotions at the end of the following season, though, as Noble was right in the thick of the celebrations after Ricardo Vaz Tê's winner at Wembley against Blackpool in the play-off final.

As time went on and West Ham carried on playing in the Premier League, Noble's importance to the squad and wider club only grew. That was marked in two massive ways during the 2015/16 season, way before the final game. The first was that the boyhood Hammer was handed the captaincy following Kevin Nolan's departure. Then there was his testimonial, which had a plethora of fan favourites from down the years playing, including Paolo Di Canio, Julian Dicks and Luděk Mikloško.

Freddie Bonfantini, who was taking photographs for his book *Long Live the Boleyn*, was allowed in the changing rooms for the testimonial. He shares his big takeaway from that experience, 'To me, the best thing to happen was actually seeing what Mark Noble means for the football club, which is something that many, many fans I don't think realise. He is pretty much completely involved with how the club is with the day to day and how much he cares. I give him a hard time when he plays because he tries to do his best but sometimes he just hasn't got the legs anymore.

'But that man is honestly so important and crucial for the dressing room, for the structure of how the club is run and everything and he's such a nice man. To me, that was what really came out of the experience: how we're a very lucky football club to have a person like that in the team. I remember being there, and he was literally shaking everyone's hand, shook my hand, he was there with his kids and he was just such a nice man. During the testimonial, I understood then, and you can understand why all the managers want to play him, because they're there day in, day out. They see how important it is.'

Suri Krishnamma echoes that sentiment, as he looks back on speaking to Noble as part of *Iron Men*, 'He was a very engaging person, a very welcoming and inviting person. We went to his house and his home and managed to film in the car with him. We had some good conversations with him about penalty taking in particular and why he tends to never miss from the spot.'

The 29-year-old had also shone that term through his performances, with this arguably being the best season of his career. Linking up with Payet and the motivation of the season's status will have played a part, but Noble deserves full credit for how much he turned up when it counted. This happened to the point where many Hammers fans felt it was criminal that he didn't get to represent his national team, with 'too good for England' often ringing around the Boleyn Ground.

On the final night at Upton Park – which was actually two days after Noble's birthday – it felt as though everything that had come before was designed to prepare that boy from Canning Town for the night he would write his name in the history books, becoming West Ham's last-ever captain at Upton Park. He certainly didn't disappoint and there was a real sense of pride in seeing him completely boss the game. Looking back on the skipper's performance, James Jones says, 'It summed up his season in West Ham colours, and his entire career. He was on the pitch but obviously felt every single emotion that all the fans were feeling around him, and he played exactly like that. He knew that losing wasn't an option and he made sure of it.'

It was easy to think that Noble and his team-mates could make anything possible, with the captain ensuring that absolutely everything was all right. Immortality isn't reality though, and as West Ham's time at London Stadium went on, it became clear that not even Mark Noble was enough of a remedy for the problems faced at times. However, the skipper was always standing at the forefront whether the times were brilliant, dismal or anything in between. Mr West Ham has led the club with pride and passion during any game in which the captain's armband has adorned his arm – and many more before he had the privilege of wearing it. As David Blackmore puts it, 'He will run through brick walls for you and I think that night was the epitome of it.'

31:36

It wasn't long until West Ham had the ball again, as Antonio was afforded plenty of space to comfortably bring it down. He then passed to Sakho who ran forward, but the Senegal international wasn't on the same page as his fellow attacker. Sakho had played the ball in front of Carroll who had already stopped, expecting a ball to feet. There was a collective groan as Valencia came away with the ball and cleared it up the pitch, eventually winning a throw for the away side.

United had tried working the ball through the middle, but it was only when Rooney sprayed the ball out wide to Martial that any sort of danger seemed to arise. The United number nine menacingly made his way down the left wing before trying to make a pass. He attempted a one-two with Mata, but the Spaniard's pass was cut out by Noble. For a second, it seemed as though Martial had luckily got through on goal as the captain's interception ricocheted off the attacker. That wasn't to be, though, as a shout of handball from the players and supporters was validated by the sound of Dean's whistle.

Another Randolph hit up the pitch, another takedown from Carroll. This time, the big man even added a pirouette on the ball. He did lose it eventually, though, as Herrera stepped in to poke the ball away to Rojo. United were passing the ball around the defence, with a backdrop of Hammers fans chanting 'stand up for the Boleyn Ground'. So, while this was another lull in proceedings on the pitch, it was difficult not to get goosebumps from the thousands of supporters standing with their arms out wide, showing appreciation for our true spiritual home. There was also a ripple of applause that accompanied the chant.

Us fans worked our way through the entire songbook throughout the day and into the night. During the game, there was very rarely a moment of silence, as we sung about the players on the pitch, our love for the Boleyn Ground, players from the past and even broke out into random song at times. It was exactly how we would have loved every game at our beloved ground to have been. This was one of Upton Park's best-ever nights, and a part of that is definitely down to the atmosphere all of that singing and chanting helped to create.

The ball eventually came to Rooney and he popped it off to Herrera. The Spaniard then attempted a through ball to Rashford, who was running down the left wing, but Reid sprinted across and was able to clear for a throw. Once the ball was back in play, the men in white managed to work a crossing position for Martial. His delivery into the box could only find Ogbonna, though, and the former Juventus man flicked it away with his head, but only as far as Valencia. United's number 25 played a pass back to Rooney, who whipped a curling cross towards the front post, but Rashford was unable to get on the end of it, allowing Antonio to chest it out for a corner in an unorthodox but effective fashion.

Blind's ensuing corner could only find Sakho, who teamed up with Noble to get it away to Lanzini. The Argentine tried to spring an attack, sprinting forward before flicking the ball towards Kouyaté. However, Schneiderlin got across to dispossess the Hammers man, with Mata reaching the loose ball and playing a first-time pass back to De Gea to prevent any danger from unfolding.

The Spaniard released the ball to Rooney, who was acting as the team's main creative hub in this game. He switched play from left to right, picking out Mata, but West Ham players swarmed him and Noble was able to get his head on to an attempted pass. Payet then cushioned the ball to Lanzini and the Hammers were immediately looking to get up the pitch, as Cresswell played long towards Sakho.

Smalling eventually won the duel, but once again, it was West Ham who picked up the second ball. Payet won possession and lent it to Noble, who played the ball back to West Ham's talisman. Payet soon ended up in a heap on the floor as Valencia went through him to get the ball. Hammers fans began jeering for the game to be stopped, while Blind and some other United players protested that the game should carry on. Herrera stood with the ball at his feet for a moment, clearly conflicted about what to do. In the end, he passed the buck to Valencia, rolling the ball towards the right-back, who flicked it out of play so that Payet could get treatment. After all of that, Payet didn't even end up getting any medical attention.

Once the ball had been returned to De Gea so the match could continue, United slowly built the play again. They moved the ball forward but ended up bringing it back to the centre-backs, unable to find any meaningful space further up the pitch. Rooney dropped deep and pinged a ball to Rojo on the left, and he swiftly offloaded it to Rashford. Noble showed his usual dogged determination and wrestled the teenager off the ball, even managing to earn a foul for himself – much to Rooney's disdain. Us fans were certainly impressed, though, as we gave the captain an encouraging cheer, then began chanting that he was 'too good for England'.

Sometimes, watching Carroll win headers is something to behold in itself. This was one of those moments as the frontman seemed to contort his body over Valencia, while nudging the Ecuadorian out of the way, to connect with Randolph's delivery up the pitch. Unfortunately for Carroll and West Ham, there was too much on his connection and the ball went out for a goal kick.

United played a fairly risky game as they passed the ball around their own box under pressure. It worked, though, as Rooney received possession in the middle of his half with acres of space to pick out a team-mate. He eventually got the ball to Valencia and played a couple of passes on the right wing before Cresswell stepped in to concede a throw. Once again, United tried working the ball backwards to then go up the pitch, but Blind's attempt at a threaded pass evaded everyone and rolled through to Randolph. The goalkeeper grasped the opportunity to take any heat out of the situation by holding on to the ball for a bit.

Smalling won the header from Randolph's clearance this time and Blind was able to switch the ball out to Valencia. Lanzini picked the ball up after a loose touch from Herrera and broke forward, threatening to cause some real danger to United's defence. That was until his attempted pass to Sakho crept under the Senegal international's foot. It ended up trickling through to Dea Gea, who hit a pinpoint pass to Martial. The ball was recycled back to Blind, then passed to

Rooney and switched out wide to Valencia. The Ecuadorian then popped it off to Herrera, who played it first-time to Mata.

This had opened up space for the Spaniard, who attempted a cross, but Reid was able to throw his head at it, deflecting the ball towards the corner flag. Cresswell reached the ball before it went out of play, getting it to Payet. However, the Frenchman's first-time pass was loose, allowing United to regain possession near West Ham's box.

The away side were playing quickly now, bringing out one-touch passes in an attempt to move the ball and Hammers defence around. Bilić's men were incredibly organised, though, and were able to force them back, with the ball landing at Rojo's feet near the centre circle. He played it out to Martial, who attempted a one-two with Mata, but was unable to keep hold of the return pass, allowing Noble to get a foot in before sliding in on Rojo to force the ball back to Rooney.

Perhaps trying to force the issue, Rooney attempted another one of his big switches to Valencia, but Cresswell read the danger again and was able to head the ball to Payet. The play was initially slowed down, but the ball ended up with Ogbonna and his big switch was a lot more successful than Rooney's. Antonio was able to control the bouncing ball before squaring up to Rojo. He invited the Argentine to make a challenge and knocked the ball past him, the bait was taken and West Ham had a free kick.

Payet delivered the ball into the box, but Smalling was just able to get ahead of Carroll, flicking the ball backwards where Reid was waiting. The West Ham number two twisted and turned to try and get enough space to cross it in, but eventually settled for keeping possession by passing back to Cresswell. The left-back took a touch out of his feet and sent a cross into the box from deep, although it fizzed agonisingly close to Antonio's head, allowing Smalling to head it away again, but only as far as Ogbonna.

There was another wave of pressure for United to endure. The Italian rolled the ball to Lanzini, who skipped away from Blind and passed to Sakho just inside the United box. He was initially crowded out and dispossessed, but the forward recovered the loose ball and played it to Antonio, who was in a central position. Antonio scuffed his shot a bit but still managed to get a corner from Valencia. After hanging on outside their own box, the fact that the Hammers had worked their way up the pitch so quickly was clearly appreciated by the fans, as calls of 'come on, you Irons' rang out.

Payet drilled his corner into the box, but while Sakho was able to get his head on it, he couldn't keep the ball down. Sakho clearly felt he should have done better, as he turned away and shouted in frustration, but there was a ripple of applause from the stands regardless.

De Gea's ensuing goal kick was just about kept in by Valencia, who headed it to Rooney. But having been dispossessed by Sakho, the United captain could only take the West Ham man down, giving Dean the easy decision of rewarding a free kick. Perhaps fearing that a yellow card would be flourished, Rooney nudged the ball away and jogged back into position while doing everything in his power to avoid eye contact with the referee. The yellow didn't come.

There must have been a temptation to launch the free kick in from just inside the United half, especially when Carroll was hanging around the back with his arm in the air. However, Noble opted to play the ball short to Payet, who then passed it on to Antonio near the touchline. He twisted his way to get some space from Martial, before swinging a left-footed cross towards Carroll, but the big man's acrobatic attempt went flying out of bounds. Much to Carroll's frustration, Dean gave a goal kick despite it seeming as though the ball had gone out via a deflection off Valencia. The crowd joined in with Carroll's protestations, but the referee was not to be swayed.

There was a battle for the ball after De Gea's goal kick until Kouyaté rushed in and headed it out for a throw. After United had knocked the ball about a bit, Rooney found some space near the centre circle. As he had done so many times already, he used this to turn and play a long ball out wide, with Valencia, once again, the target, having roamed up the pitch. This time, the Ecuadorian cut inside Payet and gave it back to Rooney, who had floated near West Ham's box and clipped the ball towards Martial with a dinked first-time cross. However, Reid was able to get in and distract him, preventing the 20-year-old from taking the ball out of the air cleanly.

It bounced to Ogbonna and the centre-back instinctively cleared his lines, directing the ball towards Carroll, but the striker was unable to get anything on it while attempting a first-time pass. Smalling prevented any potential danger by passing back to De Gea, who started another United move by sweeping a pass out to Rojo. When the ball reached Mata, the Spaniard tried to release Martial with a pass behind the West ham defence, but for the second time in a matter of moments, Reid was there to intervene.

After a couple of passes, the ball was back with the New Zealand international, who picked out Sakho with a pinpoint pass that cut through the midfield. A short tussle with Blind followed, and the Hammers forward lost out, laying on the floor in frustration for a moment before getting back to his feet. Meanwhile, United were moving up the field again.

The ball was worked to Martial, who played a one-two with Rashford and attempted to run behind Antonio. Once he got into the box, the Frenchman fell to the ground after minimal contact and looked to the referee, while Rashford's ball rolled harmlessly through to Randolph. West Ham fans made their feelings known towards the United man as boos and jeers rang out around the Boleyn Ground. Nothing was given, much to the frustration of the men in white, as Rooney led his team-mates in telling Dean that he should have given them a penalty. Antonio gave a dismissive shake of his head while walking up the pitch and into position.

The away side had to recapture their concentration pretty quickly, though, as the ball was launched up the pitch and West Ham tried to get one last attack in before half-time. Smalling's header from the initial long pass only went as far as Noble, who played it to Lanzini, allowing the number 28 to spread play out wide to Antonio, who was one-on-one with Rojo again. Antonio tried to put it past him, but the defender stretched out a leg and managed to get his knee to the ball and cleared, though it only went as far as his compatriot, Lanzini. However, United were given respite from the pressure they had endured as Dean signalled for half-time. To many, it felt like nowhere near enough time had gone past for the whistle to be blown, but it could still be heard around the stadium.

The 1-0 scoreline indicated that West Ham had only just edged it in the first half, but there will be plenty of Hammers fans who will argue that their team completely dominated. 'I think it's almost under-spoken about how well we played in that first half. As good as Liverpool and City are now, I think they would have struggled to live with us in that first half of the game,' says Daniel Hurley. 'I think the pace we moved the ball at and how we were getting into the ball and tackling and stuff was unbelievable. That wasn't a bad United team, but they couldn't get near us. The first half is, I think, as good as I've ever seen a West Ham team.'

Most Hammers were on a high after such a magnificent performance and occasion so far. There will, however, have been others who were fearful that the likes of Carroll and Payet missing good chances could come back to haunt the team.

5

Half-Time

HALF-TIME IS sacred in football. The benefits are plentiful as managers and coaches can make tactical tweaks, while there is also an opportunity for the players to take on fluids and have a break. This period that sits between the two 45 minutes filled with action is also important for the fans, whether they are in the stands or elsewhere. Those sitting in pubs can make a trip to the bar, while those sitting in their armchair or on the sofa at home can get the kettle on without risking missing a goal.

Those in the stands are often able to treat this time very differently. Some have a natter about general life, while others dissect what they have just seen, figuring out what their manager should do to secure three points. There are also plenty who pile into the concourse to get a pint, a hot drink, some food or to nip to the toilet. As fans, this time isn't something we usually think about or cherish that much, but as the second half kicks off and you have a chicken balti pie or hot chocolate in hand, or have managed to down a pint or two, you'll often feel thankful you had it.

'It was like before the game down in the concourse. We were partying, we were drenched in beer and we were just trying to make every single second count in that ground,' James Jones recalls. 'We knew we had 45 minutes left of football there, then obviously we had the thing after but we knew that this was it. Everyone down there was just looking at each other and hugging and beers were flowing and people were on each other's shoulders again and the amount of times I sang "oh, Christian Dailly" that evening was probably a record in one night. It was just a great atmosphere and a couple of my mates didn't go down; they wanted to stay up by their seats at half-time, just soaking the atmosphere up there and to be out by pitch side for as long as they possibly could, which is fair enough. Everyone was in a great mood and you know what, looking back, we could have been 5-0 down and I still reckon everyone would have been in a great mood.'

For a game as intense as the final fixture at Upton Park, above all else, plenty will have just been grateful to move back from the edge of their seat and relax a bit. To make the most of the time, some people stuck to their traditions, while there are others who did something on the spur of the moment.

Joseph Fordham was very much in the former category. 'One of the lovely routines about Upton Park, that I miss a lot, is my brother used to sit just slightly away from us, about five rows in front but the other side of the aisle. At half-time, the woman that I used to sit next to, she would always go downstairs for half-time, and he would just come up and stand in the place, and we would just chat and then when they came up for the second half, he would go back down. I wouldn't say it was different to most half-time breaks for us, but in the best possible way, because I used to love those moments where he would come up and chat.'

James Datson recalls what it was like for him, as well as the other commentators and journalists in attendance, 'The press box at West Ham was very tight, you're crammed in, so I remember at half-time there was never enough time to go back downstairs, so we were all trying to hover to grab a sandwich and nine times out of ten you can't get there.'

For those who stayed in their seats for half-time, there was some entertainment, including a brass band that led yet another rendition of 'Bubbles'. As half-time drew to an end, people would have noticed a figure in white standing by the touchline ready to come on to the pitch. That man was Michael Carrick, who was replacing Schneiderlin after the Frenchman had endured a tough time during the first period.

There will likely be those who were disappointed not to see the 34-year-old starting on such a historic night due to his links with the Hammers. He had been part of the West Ham team that won the 1998/99 FA Youth Cup, alongside Joe Cole. Having made his first-team debut during a 1999 UEFA Intertoto Cup draw against Finnish side Jokerit, Carrick went on to make over 150 appearances in claret and blue.

He was part of the 2002/03 squad that criminally got relegated, doing so with 42 points – the highest total for a side facing the drop in Premier League history. Fellow youngsters in that team included Cole, Jermain Defoe and Glen Johnson. There is one thing that sets Carrick apart from the others and earned him great respect among the Hammers faithful. While the aforementioned trio immediately fled Upton Park to continue in the Premier League, Carrick stayed.

He ended up getting into the PFA Team of the Year for the First Division that term but was unable to earn promotion. West Ham had finished fourth, then got past Ipswich Town in the play-off semi-final. However, defeat awaited at the Millennium Stadium as a tap-in from Neil

Shipperley was enough to win the match for Crystal Palace. After one campaign in the second tier, it was time for Carrick to return to the big time with the blessing and appreciation of Hammers fans – even if it was a shame that he ended up at White Hart Lane.

The midfielder had shown great loyalty before going off and achieving success, with his Manchester United trophy haul including five Premier Leagues, a Champions League, a FIFA Club World Cup, two League Cups and an FA Cup. Therefore, it was fitting that he was able to get on to the pitch for this historic match – even if he was on the opposing team.

Not all of the attention will have been on the former Hammer, though, as David Blackmore recalls, 'The thing I can remember is that not many people around me were sat down. Normally when it gets to half-time people sit and they flick through the programme or they dash to the loo. It just seemed like people didn't want to leave their seats, it was the same at full time as well. At half-time, the vision I've got is people in their light blue shirts all milling around, all chatting away. There was definitely more of a buzz that evening, in terms of energy around the stadium at half-time, that you wouldn't normally expect at any ground, because people go to the loo, get a beer, a pie or whatever. People were up for it that night, and it made for a special "Bubbles" when they came out again for the second half.'

6

Second Half

THE SECOND half got started with West Ham's famed 'Bubbles' chant reverberating through every nook and cranny of the Boleyn Ground. The 'Bubbles' before kick-off is more often remembered, but this one was also spine-tingling. This time it was United who restarted the proceedings, with Rashford rolling the ball to Herrera, who played it back to Smalling for him to hit long towards Martial. In case anyone had forgotten, West Ham were reminded that they still had to go out and get the win. Martial beat Antonio to the initial header before Rashford drew a foul from Reid near the box to immediately put the home side on the back foot.

The situation's severity could be seen through Randolph's intensity when setting up the defensive line. The box was a hub of activity as Rooney put in a ball that could easily have been hazardous, but Sakho managed to get his head on to it and clear. Carrick was able to retrieve the ball, but uncharacteristically his first pass of the game was wayward, sailing out of play rather than to Rooney's feet. This earned the former Hammer an ironic cheer to go with the genuine one provided upon his introduction to the action.

Perhaps recognising the early pressure and looking to calm things down, Antonio slowly jogged over to retrieve the ball. Once he had it in his hands, the West Ham number 30 hurled it up the line towards Carroll, who returned the favour. A long pass was played in behind the United defence for Sakho to run on to, but it was slightly overcooked and went through to De Gea. Sakho took his opportunity to remind Smalling that he was there, though, pushing the centre-back as the West Ham man's route to pressurise De Gea was blocked off.

The Spaniard threw the ball out wide to Valencia, who almost put Smalling in trouble with a pass back to the centre-back as Sakho sprinted to shut him down again. While Smalling was able to prevent a disaster, he smashed the ball up the pitch and lost possession as Ogbonna was able to coolly chest down to Cresswell.

The ball was played back to Randolph, with West Ham having a more measured start to the second half than had been the case in the first. However, that didn't mean they were taking their foot off the gas as the Hammers played the ball quickly and precisely after Carroll brought down Randolph's long pass. It eventually reached Lanzini on the halfway line and the Argentine popped the ball in to Sakho, who flicked it first-time to Antonio. This gave Antonio the chance to get at Rojo, which he took and sprinted past the defender. In the end, having already beaten him twice, he tried to do it again and slipped, allowing Rojo to steal the ball away before Herrera got hold of it.

United weren't able to get out, though, as Kouyaté rushed to meet Herrera's pass ahead of Martial. The ball went straight to Lanzini's feet, then Payet had it and tried to return it to the Argentine, but Lanzini was hit by a robust, yet fair, sliding tackle from his compatriot Rojo. Martial retrieved the ball and immediately raced up the pitch to start a counter-attack for the away side. However, by the time he offloaded the ball to Mata, West Ham had already managed to get numbers back. The Spaniard played a pass to Valencia, who had run past him on the overlap. He tried to cross it first-time, but the effort careered off Cresswell's chest and behind for a corner. While United's players and fans had their arms in the air calling for a handball, wanting a penalty, the referee had absolutely no interest at all. Dean even rolled his eyes, shook his head and dismissively muttered, 'Jesus Christ.'

Martial stretched enough to get his head on to Blind's deep corner but wasn't able to get a convincing contact on it. This meant the ball tamely hung in the air, allowing Sakho to chest it down and spring an attack of his own, playing through to Kouyaté. Rooney was able to get back, though, tackling the Senegal international to concede a throw near the halfway line.

Antonio's throw led to a very strange game of football tennis where both sides seemed merely to be smashing the ball away as far as they could. It was almost like the players didn't care where the ball was on the pitch, or who had it, as long as it was as far away from their goal as possible. That is until Reid cleared it right into the corner, setting up a foot race between Sakho and Blind. The West Ham man was able to get there first and keep the ball in play, forcing the Dutchman to do something. He tried to copy what others had managed, but when Blind put his foot through the ball, it skewed towards his own box rather than up the pitch, forcing Carrick to attempt to head it upfield under pressure from Carroll.

The ball only got as far as Payet. The Frenchman, who had shown plenty of times throughout the campaign that he was capable of the spectacular, set himself to pull off something special once again. He watched the ball drop and went for a volley but was just unable to get his angles right, sending his shot wide. There was a round of applause from the stands, as Smith said on the Sky Sports commentary, 'For most people, you'd say it's ridiculous taking this one on, but maybe not with Payet.' Even if Payet's talents vindicated the decision to take the shot on, the effort turned out far from how he would have wanted it to.

There was a short break in play following Payet's effort – not because the ball had gone over the stands, but because it was stuck in one of them. While De Gea pleaded with the supporters in the Bobby Moore Lower to give the ball back, they threw it among themselves, cheering every time. Eventually, another one was given to De Gea from the benches and it was only as the Spaniard was about to take his goal kick that the fans behind the goal mockingly threw the ball back on to the pitch.

Frustrated at having his time wasted while behind, the Spaniard smashed that ball towards the dugouts before hitting the other one up the pitch for his team-mates to battle to win. That strike sailed over Cresswell's head under pressure from Mata, allowing Rashford to run on to it. The teenager then passed to Mata, who had rushed into the box and was met by Ogbonna. He was able to get away from the Italian, though, faking to pass before heading towards the touchline and pulling the ball back into the danger area.

Randolph, Reid and then Antonio all came agonisingly close to cutting out the pass, but it rolled menacingly past all of them until it reached Martial, who couldn't have missed. The Frenchman wasn't taking any chances, though, as he put the ball into the empty net with conviction, before running behind the goal towards the celebrating away supporters. Martial embraced the man who had set him up, before jogging back with his team-mates as they continued to hunt the win that would help them secure Champions League football. Large sections of the Boleyn Ground were almost silent, while the away section erupted.

There was plenty of excitement around Martial, who was still in his first season as a Manchester United player at the time. Initial questions had been asked from other fanbases about the logic of spending so big on someone who was still 19 years old as the Frenchman had cost an initial £36m, with the fee potentially rising to £58m.

That immediate outlay had made him the third most expensive signing in the club's history behind Juan Mata and Angel di Maria – he was also now the most expensive teenager in world football. The signs were there that Martial would fare better than either of United's other top three signings as he went on to record 17 goals and ten assists in 49 appearances across that first campaign.

The forward had announced himself in style when he came off the bench to make his debut against Liverpool and marked it with the final goal in a 3-1 win. On that day, he had picked the ball up on the left and driven past Martin Škrtel before placing his shot into the far corner, showing how deadly he could be in the opposition box. His equaliser at Upton Park didn't take as much skill as the one that opened his account with the Red Devils, but it was another example of the Frenchman stepping up on a big occasion.

While there was frustration from the West Ham fans in the stands, there wasn't too much concern from some at this point, as James Jones says, 'Man United are Man United, they always score. So, it wasn't a great shock. I mean, it was a good goal. We were a force that year throughout, particularly against teams in the top six. So, at 1-1, I genuinely felt we've still got it in us to get a result.'

51:33

As was previously mentioned, there were fears that, having performed so well in the first half, West Ham could have been punished for not going into the break with a lead that was greater than one goal. Looking at Bilić's face as play was restarted, it seemed clear that he was aware this situation should not have been allowed. However, this was West Ham's big day, and there was no way the team was going to lie down now – the fans wouldn't have let the players do that even if they had thought about it. There was a rallying cry of 'come on, you Irons' repeated as play resumed, and it was only a matter of seconds until Carroll won yet another free kick for his side, just ahead of the centre circle this time.

Noble played the ball short to Cresswell, who took a touch out of his feet and whipped it into the box, though Blind made a strong header to clear. Ogbonna got to the loose ball first as he nudged Rashford out of the way, before attempting a pass forward to Noble. Rojo got there first and knocked it out of touch. The strength of United's protestations when West Ham were given the throw offered an indication of the boost that goal had given them. It would have felt as though a whole half in which they were outclassed for pretty much the entirety was now erased after about five minutes, as they were back on level terms.

This now felt like more of a true duel than it had done at any other point of the night. Antonio's long throw into the box was headed away by Rojo, but only got as far as Lanzini, who had been lingering just outside. He lost the ball quickly, though, as Martial stepped in to intercept the Argentine's attempted pass. The Jewel didn't give up on it, and he was one of a trio that crowded Martial out before sliding in on Herrera to prevent anything dangerous from flourishing at the expense of a throw.

The Hammers immediately won the ball back once it was in play again. A series of first-time passes later and the men in claret and blue came so close to getting in as Noble played forward. The effort was inches away from Sakho's head, while Smalling just managed to reach it ahead of Carroll. Martial was clearly full of confidence after his goal, but the Frenchman attempted to chest the ball down and messed it up, as it went out of play.

This epitomised how the game momentarily plummeted into a scrappy affair. That continued as United won the header from Antonio's throw and got the ball to Martial. The Frenchman did a few kick-ups before flicking the ball over Antonio's head, attempting to release Herrera. However, Antonio raced ahead of the Spaniard, bringing the ball down and holding him off. Herrera kicked the back of Antonio's leg before the Hammers man attempted a pass that rebounded off Rashford and into touch, leading to the referee giving a foul as there was no advantage to be had. Both Antonio and Bilić looked disgusted by the tackle, with the Croatian letting the fourth official know exactly how he felt. Meanwhile, Antonio waved his hands in the air and gesticulated towards the referee.

Reid's ensuing free kick found Carroll, who stretched to get his head on it. After the header ballooned up into the air and slowly came down, the striker managed to win it again, chesting it down before falling to the ground under pressure from Smalling. Even when he was on the floor, the frontman managed to knock the ball in Payet's direction, offering the Frenchman a chance to show his supreme talent, breaking up the disjointed play that had preceded this moment. He confidently strode up to the ball and struck it with the inside of his right foot, sending it spinning towards the bottom corner while De Gea sprawled across his goal line. However,

Payet was inches off and hit the side-netting. The number 27's frustration was clear, as he lifted his shirt over his head before looking around with a grimace on his face – there were plenty of fans who will have been just as disappointed, having jumped up believing the shot was destined for the bottom corner.

United built their attack down the left following the ensuing goal kick, with Rojo running down the line before playing a one-two with Martial to get into a crossing position. However, Randolph came out to confidently catch the defender's delivery into the box, showing that he hadn't been impacted by the goal conceded. Meanwhile, West Ham supporters started booing the away fans as United got into full voice, something that had been a rarity up until that point. After assessing his options, the stopper smashed the ball up to Carroll, who had Smalling climbing all over him in an attempt to win the ball. The centre-back had got away with this tactic a few times, but he made it incredibly obvious on this occasion, forcing Dean to give West Ham a free kick.

Somehow, United still managed to take exception to the decision. Mata decided to grab the ball to stop West Ham taking the free kick, in addition to remonstrating to Dean about it apparently not being a foul. It was clear that Hammers fans weren't impressed by this. As all of that went on, Van Gaal was deep in discussion with Bilić, who seemed to find the Dutchman's protests amusing. The Hammers manager laughed, shook his head and, when the United boss came back to make another point, Bilić jokingly grabbed the back of his hair while chuckling further.

When he was finally able to take the free kick, Payet put in an extremely dangerous delivery. It was perfectly placed between the United defence and De Gea, meaning everyone seemed to stop in the hope that others would be able to sort out the issue. Sakho was right in the middle of all of this, though it seemed he was also in a state of confusion. As the ball approached the forward, bouncing just in front of him, he was indecisive about whether to go at it with his head or foot. In the end, he chose to go with the former, which proved to be the wrong decision as the ball bounced off his shoulder and soared over the crossbar. There was a collective release of disappointment from the stands, as the supporters had expected to see the net in front of the Bobby Moore Stand bulging – some had near enough started celebrating before Sakho even connected with the ball.

West Ham immediately won possession back following De Gea's goal kick, as Antonio made the initial header, before Sakho played the ball off Rooney to win a throw. This was seen as an opportunity for the Hammers to get their foot on the ball for a bit, but a wayward pass from Payet forced Kouyaté into a 50-50 challenge with Martial. The Senegalese midfielder came away with the ball and was sent flying, winning a free kick, while the United man got some pain of his own and a yellow card for his troubles.

Martial hobbled back to get into position, but West Ham weren't about to wait around for him to get there. The ball was played short to Payet, working a better angle for him to cross towards the likes of Carroll and Kouyaté. However, De Gea rushed off his goal line and collected convincingly, taking it right off Carroll's head after the big man's eyes must have lit up.

The ball was back with Carroll within seconds, though, as United's long clearance was intercepted by Cresswell, who picked out the striker in a wide position. Carroll even got himself a big cheer from the crowd as he twisted and turned to send Smalling for a hot dog, then jinked past Valencia and played the ball back to Lanzini. It was then popped off to Cresswell, and while the left-back did manage to take on one man, Valencia made things right and got the tackle in, giving away another throw. A few seconds later, Cresswell had won a corner, which was just waiting for Payet to put in one of those lauded deliveries.

He provided the ball in and despite Smalling incessantly grabbing Carroll, as well as Rooney jumping into him, the striker managed to get his head on the ball. The big man couldn't keep his effort down with all of that pressure, however. It was clear to see what Carroll thought of the attention that he had received as he began gesticulating and shouting towards Dean to demonstrate what had been happening. Even Martin Tyler, who was commentating for Sky Sports, described how the Geordie was 'being a bit man-handled'.

Carroll had initially signed for West Ham on loan from Liverpool in 2012, before making his move to east London permanent for £15m during the summer of 2013. There was a fair share of injury frustration during his time at the Boleyn Ground, but Carroll also earned a lot of respect for the effort that he constantly put in – while there was a skill level that could be under-appreciated by many.

Carroll's fight was on show in this game, perhaps more than any other, from the first whistle to the very last. Within two minutes he had won three headers – two of which were in the opposition box – got a free kick for his team and also come out on top in a 50-50 challenge on the ground. West Ham's energetic start laid the base for their entire performance and he was central to that.

One of the game's biggest match-ups was Carroll coming up against Smalling. It seemed that whenever the ball was anywhere near the Hammers striker, Smalling was all over him, grabbing at his shirt and just generally clambering all over him in an attempt to nullify the aerial threat posed.

Bobby Zamora feels the United centre-back made the wrong decision in trying to go toe-to-toe with Carroll. 'I played with Chris Smalling at Fulham, so I know him quite well. I know he's quite a handful, always trying to win the ball, every single time. That's probably his downfall, he doesn't let off. He should pick and choose his players and Andy's probably one that you shouldn't, because that's what Andy wants, he wants somebody to fight him. He's a big strong lad and he put himself about. Andy did great, that's what you want to see from him.'

There is certainly a strong case to be made that Carroll came out on top in his individual battle as he won nine aerial duels throughout the match – more than any other player on the pitch. He also impressed outside of that, showing some tidy footwork, tracking back in the place of Sakho at times, putting the United defence under constant pressure and dealing with the extremely close attention being paid to him well.

So, even if he didn't hit the back of the net – having one effort saved by De Gea and a header cleared off the line by Martial – Carroll ensured his impact on the game was felt. His run of six goals and an assist in the seven games before this one had got him in the conversation for England's squad to compete in the 2016 European Championships. The numbers alone are impressive, but these weren't just any old goals. The sequence had started with a well-taken finish to beat Thibaut Courtois and score West Ham's second goal in a 2-2 draw against Chelsea. It also included a hat-trick in a 3-3 draw with Arsenal, featuring a brilliant acrobatic effort for his second.

The truly impressive nature of the big man's form can be seen in the fact that he recorded nine goals and two assists all season. In the end, he wasn't selected, but as Tyler said during his commentary of this historic match, 'You can't ignore him, at least tonight.'

Carroll stayed at West Ham for three years after the club left for London Stadium, before he returned to Newcastle United. While his influence declined over time, largely due to various injuries, he still had some big moments in claret and blue. There was his brace to secure a 3-1 win over Middlesbrough, another pair to help earn a vital 2-1 victory over West Bromwich Albion and his final goal for the Hammers, a header to get past Birmingham City in the FA Cup. There were so many qualities in Carroll's game outside of just goalscoring, and they were all on full display against the Red Devils.

59:04

United were able to get their foot on the ball following the goal kick as they had won a throw, from which the ball was played back to Smalling. West Ham sat off and let him have it, which was a bit of a rarity. The centre-back used this time well, pinging a ball across the field that Rojo was able to get his head on to ahead of Antonio. Rojo's efforts in maintaining possession were futile, though, as his header went straight to Reid. The New Zealander couldn't keep hold of it either, as Rooney stepped in to intercept his attempted out-ball, before Martial took over. The Frenchman had no chance. As he had done so often throughout the night, Kouyaté was able to step in and win possession back before clearing it upfield – putting United back in pretty much the exact same position as their previous throw.

As was often the case due to Van Gaal's methodical style of play, United played the ball around the back. Blind slipped up this time as he allowed Smalling's pass to roll underneath his foot and straight into Sakho's path. There was suddenly a hum of excitement in the stands as the Senegalese forward fronted up the Dutchman, but he was ushered towards the corner. Blind managed to nip in and steal the ball away, but his touch only got as far as Noble. Mr West Ham worked some space from Rojo and passed to Lanzini who played it backwards, ready for Reid to revitalise the move by spreading the ball out wide to Cresswell.

It was then worked back to the right, where Antonio was waiting to release Noble with a first-time pass, but Blind reached it before the Hammers skipper and cleared. It seemed as though Rashford might pose a problem for Reid, who was isolated against the teenager and would have been left for dead if he had missed the floating ball. The more experienced head came through, though, as Reid eased the United forward out of the way and played the ball to his centre-back partner. Martial raised a hand to suggest it should have been a foul, but Dean didn't even consider it. Just seconds after feeling they should have had a free kick of their own, United gave one away as Herrera brought Cresswell down when trying to get ahead of him to intercept Ogbonna's pass. The Spaniard was quick to pick Cresswell up before pleading his innocence to Dean, likely fearing the yellow card that never came.

The ball was knocked about after a short free kick, until it once again reached Cresswell, who played it down the line to Lanzini. The Argentine initially did well to hold off Valencia and turn away from him, but the West Ham man went down when the Ecuadorian pulled on his arm. Dean had no interest at all in giving a free kick, much to the frustration of Lanzini and the fans in the stands.

Maybe inspired by this moment of annoyance, Hammers fans started singing 'Bubbles'. The rousing rendition seemingly spurred Cresswell on as he stormed in to steal the ball away with his head shortly after United's throw. Sakho drove forward with the ball at his feet until Smalling forced him to turn back. The move didn't stop there, though, as he played the ball to Noble, who flicked his foot to hit a pass that made its way through to Lanzini courtesy of two attempted headers by men in white.

The Argentine returned the pass to his captain, who sprinted down the line, then chopped the ball away from Herrera's attempted slide tackle – opening up some space for himself on the corner of United's box. Spotting Carroll running towards the back post, he played a deep cross and despite Rojo pulling on the striker, he managed to stretch and connect boot with ball. There was a collective 'ooh' from the stands as the ball went towards the edge of the six-yard box, where Sakho would have been on hand to finish the move off. However, Blind got there first and headed it out for a throw.

Antonio launched the ball into the box, and it was flicked on by Sakho, but United were able to make a clearance that landed straight at Cresswell's feet near the centre circle. The Hammers left-back launched the ball back towards where it had come from, and while Antonio was able to get his head on it, he could only direct it back towards the Bobby Moore Lower. While the pair's efforts didn't come to anything, they were appreciated as a big round of applause went around the Boleyn, followed by a rallying cry of 'come on, you Irons'. Antonio gave Cresswell a thumbs-up for the idea and ball he had sent over.

It was easy for the left-back to go under the radar at times, potentially due to the position he played in, but he was a vital part of this West Ham side. The defender, who was born in Liverpool, moved to Upton Park in 2014 and had been the main man in his position ever since. It can be argued that there had previously been a struggle to find someone who could convincingly hold down the left-back position before his arrival.

Despite making a step up from the Championship with Ipswich Town, Cresswell immediately became one of the first names on the team sheet at Upton Park. At the end of his first season, he walked away from the Hammers' awards evening with both the Hammer of the Year and Players' Player of the Year accolades. If this wasn't enough of an indicator into how highly the defender is regarded, Cresswell was also included in the club's top ten players of the 2010s on West Ham's official website.

It was the mixture of his defensive and attacking capabilities that had made the 26-year-old such a popular figure among his team-mates and supporters alike. Looking at the defensive side of the game, he had good discipline, awareness and wasn't afraid to commit to a challenge.

Cresswell also had a wand of a left foot, which was a threat from open play and set-pieces – though his quality in the latter category wasn't used as often in 2015/16 due to Payet's presence. In total, Cresswell got two goals and four assists that term. His assist tally included a pass to set up Lanzini for the opener away against Liverpool and the delightful cross that Carroll headed in to secure a win against Chelsea.

Then there are the goals, which truly showed just how lethal that left foot of Cresswell's is. There was his strike in the 1-1 draw away against Aston Villa, when he picked the ball up outside the box and sent it flying into the bottom corner. His second of the campaign was even better, though, coming in a 2-2 draw against Leicester City. The King Power Stadium played host to some pretty remarkable moments that term as the Foxes went on to win the Premier League, but that ground won't have seen many goals that showed more quality than Cresswell's. Danny Simpson had failed to convincingly head Antonio's cross clear, only managing to divert the ball towards Cresswell, who chested it down, set himself as the ball bounced and sent it fizzing right into the top corner, giving Kasper Schmeichel absolutely no chance.

The defender immediately had personal struggles as the Hammers began life at London Stadium. He suffered a serious knee injury in a pre-season friendly against Karlsruher that kept him out until October. Despite this, Cresswell has had plenty of big moments since that to display the supreme quality he is capable of producing. The man who came through at Tranmere Rovers recorded a brilliant seven assists during the 2017/18 campaign, while he later scored goals such as an unstoppable free kick against the Red Devils and a strike with his right foot to beat Chelsea at Stamford Bridge. This sort of quality renders Cresswell a revelation of a signing for West Ham and an absolute bargain. It is also why he was able to play a key role in the Hammers' performance on this historic night.

It's clear that this was also a very special night for the left-back, who says, 'I remember even Nobes and I, we used to speak about the pressure and even still to this day, we find ourselves talking about how good of a day it was. If there's one game that I could go back to and actually relive that game and the atmosphere and the things that I'd do now looking back, what I'd take in, it would be that one. I'm just gutted I didn't get footage to look back at it or video anything or take pictures with the lads or whatever. I know there's still loads of stuff out there. It's the best atmosphere I've ever played in. I think if you ask most of the fans, everything was kind of perfect.'

63:20

Martial had already caused frustration for those of a claret and blue persuasion, and he did so again when the ball was worked to him after De Gea's goal kick. The Frenchman received the ball near the halfway line while backing into Reid and won a free kick. United didn't take the chance to go direct, though, as Carrick fed Smalling so they could build from the back again.

The ball was played around the halfway line until it found its way back to Carrick, who looked forward. He did what so few in white had managed by breaking West Ham's midfield line with a pass into Rashford's feet, which opened a bit more space as United continued to methodically move forward while ensuring they maintained possession. Following that ball in to Rashford, each United pass seemed to carry a greater threat that they could break through the defence. However, after all of that, Martial messed up his flick near the edge of the West Ham box and barged Reid over, though Dean didn't deem this to be worthy of a free kick.

The Frenchman sprang into action when he realised a foul wasn't being given and got the ball to Rashford. United were in the Hammers' box, but the teenager was crowded out by four home men and his attempted pass deflected off Noble. Rooney was able to pick it up, though, swiftly taking a touch out of his feet and pinging the ball out to the right wing, putting Valencia one-on-one with Cresswell. He got the ball to Herrera, who, just like Rashford, was crowded out. Again, the ball fell to a United man as Mata got it and passed to Rooney, who rolled it across to Rojo as Mata continued his run in an attempt to get behind the defence.

Perhaps running out of patience after seeing his team-mates fail to breach the defence, Rojo took it upon himself to try to pick the Spaniard out. Reid read the danger and was able to cut the pass out with relative ease. He cleared towards Carroll, but the striker was extremely isolated, and the ball was back in United's possession as quickly as it had been taken from them.

The away side were really beginning to build pressure, which could be felt from the atmosphere in the stands as Carrick quickly got the ball back to Martial in a wide area. Reid had followed the forward out and was all over him, desperately trying to reach the ball, but the United man managed to turn and get it to Mata once again.

The Spaniard had plenty of space to exploit, something that had been pretty much non-existent anywhere near the West Ham goal before then – even the equaliser had been created in tight spaces. Mata spotted Rashford running behind Antonio towards the corner of the six-yard box and picked him out, before the youngster aimed a back-heel towards the back post where Herrera was waiting.

The ball rolled menacingly across the goal face towards the Spaniard, with Ogbonna and Randolph unable to do anything but look on helplessly and hope he wouldn't reach it. However, Cresswell was able to recover, nudging Herrera off the ball and allowing it to run out of play. As the away section erupted with calls for a penalty, West Ham fans let out a mocking cheer towards them and Herrera, before taking a collective breath having seen their team withstand such a serious and sustained bout of pressure. It turned out that it should have been a corner as Rashford's back-heel went off Antonio's foot – something the youngster made sure to tell the referee. However, a goal kick was eventually given.

When Randolph cleared up the pitch, Carroll was able to distract both Rooney and Rojo enough to stop either of them getting their head to the ball. Both teams struggled to gain control with a few successful tackles coming in quick succession until Rojo dispossessed Sakho by kicking the ball out of play. On commentary, Martin Tyler said, 'It's such a good contest that you're tending to forget what's going to happen afterwards with the ceremony and the ground being knocked down.' As the camera panned to the fans wholeheartedly singing 'Bubbles', he continued, 'They know their football here and they're trying to inspire their team. A magnificent example of a community coming together as West Ham have grown through the last century.'

While being serenaded with that especially loud and proud version of 'Bubbles' by their supporters, the West Ham players took the chance to get their foot on the ball after Antonio's throw. It was knocked harmlessly forwards, back and sideways until it arrived with Reid, who saw an opportunity to step out and hit a pass into Lanzini's feet. He did just that and the Argentine quickly popped the ball off to Carroll. Blind was able to stop the striker's attempted pass to Sakho, but Kouyaté came racing forward to retain possession and continue the attack down the right. The ball was played to Antonio, whose cross was blocked by Rooney and went out of play. The crowd and players called for a handball but had to settle for a corner, as Dean shook his head and repeated the words 'too harsh'.

Even though the Hammers weren't awarded a free kick, given the aerial prowess within the team and the quality of Payet's delivery, there was still a threat to be posed. That proved to be the case as the Frenchman's corner was met by a strong Carroll header near the penalty spot. Martial did his job on the back post, though, earning one big collective groan from the stands as he cleared off the line, while Carrick got an extra flick on the ball so it went out for a throw.

Lanzini quickly threw the ball to Noble and got it back before driving up the left wing. He was eventually met by

Valencia and Herrera, but the Argentine was relentless in his desire to keep possession and work an opening. He ended up twisting and turning to get his body between the ball and the two men. In an attempt to win the ball back, Herrera stuck out a foot and tripped up the Jewel. Thanks to that, the Hammers had a free kick in the perfect position to deliver a cross into the box.

There was never going to be anyone other than Payet taking it. As West Ham's talisman trudged over to the ball, he was given a high-five by Carroll, while the supporters clapped in unison and shouted 'West Ham'. Payet struck the free kick towards Carroll at the near post. As had been the case so often throughout the match, Smalling was all over him, and this time it worked as he headed the ball away – much to the frustration of West Ham's number nine.

United weren't standing around to listen to his protestations, though, as they immediately began working the play up the pitch. West Ham fans thought Rashford had run the ball out of play, but the throw wasn't given and he just managed to keep hold of possession by playing a one-two with Valencia. There was a bit of luck involved for the youngster as the ball rebounded off his back foot following Noble's tackle and ran back into his path.

When the ball was eventually stolen from him, Mata was on hand to take it back and continue the United attack, offloading it to Valencia. United's number 25 was hit by a big tackle from West Ham's captain but somehow the ball didn't move from underneath his right boot. A pass was played back to Rashford, who had hung back and then played it to Martial. The Frenchman spotted Mata running into the West Ham box and attempted a through ball to the Spaniard.

Ogbonna slid in on the edge of the box to prevent it penetrating the defence, with the ball landing at Antonio's feet for him to smash away. The clearance had initially flown over Blind's head but the Dutchman showed composure and skill to deal with the danger and turn away from Carroll. The frontman didn't give up on his cause, though, sprinting back to put him under pressure and committing to a hard sliding tackle – it turned out to be late as Blind had just given the ball to Rooney.

It was an obvious yellow card for Mike Dean to give the big man, as highlighted by the fact Carroll accepted it with an apologetic flick of the wrist. It wasn't the most advisable piece of defending, but Hammers fans loved the determination on show. We let Carroll know by applauding him and chanting his name over and over again – even Noble gave the striker a small round of applause. It's hard to imagine that Blind was as pleased about it as we were.

Carroll could have perhaps done with taking some tips from Ogbonna, the man who had prevented the Red Devils from carving out a clear chance moments earlier. The Italian was a master of timing his challenges, something that had saved West Ham on many occasions – in this game, those that had come before and plenty more that followed.

He had signed for the Hammers from Juventus for a fee of £10m during the summer of 2015. Earlier in his career, Ogbonna had been a rising star at Torino, with plenty of excitement attached to his name. However, the defender struggled to find consistent game time with the Old Lady, which ultimately led to him leaving for east London. With that said, you don't manage to get into the Italy national team as a defender without having some class.

The move definitely turned out to be beneficial for West Ham as Ogbonna was just as cool on the pitch as he looked off it. He was also a man for the big occasion, as was shown through his only goal of the season. The Hammers were drawing their FA Cup tie against Liverpool, with the game seemingly destined to go into penalties. West Ham had one last throw of the dice in the 120th minute as Payet was lining up a free kick from the right wing, halfway inside the Liverpool half. Liverpool players had been grabbing and pulling Ogbonna, but he used his intelligence and experience to find the space needed to get up and reach the cross with his head. The Italian then provided the quality required to guide the ball across Simon Mignolet and into the back of the net, giving the Belgian absolutely no chance.

While the defender spent a little bit of time on the bench during his first term with the Hammers, he was an important part of the team. All of the traits that made this the case were shown during the Boleyn's final game: an ability to make good judgement calls in tough situations, the anticipation to pick out opposition passes, quality on the ball and the fight not to be overawed by top-level attackers. He kept hold of the ball brilliantly in this game, completing 85 per cent of his attempted passes – Blind was the only starter who had a higher success rate.

Despite requiring knee surgery during the first season at London Stadium, Ogbonna has largely been a trusted member of the defence throughout his time in claret and blue, no matter who the manager has been. Tony Gale, the centre-back who played 359 games for West Ham, says of Ogbonna, 'He's got better and better since he's been at West Ham. I do rate him as a player. Anyone who lasts as long at a football club as he has is classed as a good signing.' While the Hammers couldn't keep a clean sheet on the night, Ogbonna showed enough ability to highlight why so much faith is placed in him on a weekly basis.

69:10

West Ham were able to win the ball back soon after the free kick was taken, as Reid rushed in to nick it away from behind Rashford. Lanzini and Kouyaté paired up together well, playing one-touch and two-touch passes between them in a way that allowed them to slowly bring the play forward. That sequence ended when Kouyaté managed to get the ball to Payet with a first-time pass before being taken out by Valencia.

Spotting the threat West Ham were carrying, Dean allowed play to go on as Payet drove forward. Also seeing the situation's urgency, Herrera decided to foul the Frenchman on the edge of United's box. The Spaniard quite literally had his pants pulled down by the Hammers attack, as he had to pull them up when he was on the floor. Not forgetting Valencia's unlawful intervention a few seconds earlier, the referee gave him a yellow card.

It had always felt as though pretty much any blade of grass on the Upton Park pitch was 'Dimitri Payet territory'. As Alan Smith stated on the Sky Sports commentary, this really was a prime location for him – slightly outside the box, fairly close to being in line with one of the posts. Showing just how much of a threat he was from this sort of position, Herrera decided to stand on the post, pleading with De Gea to let him stay there and help keep out any effort on goal. However, as he realised this meant the likes of Carroll and Antonio would then be able to get near the goalkeeper, the midfielder ran out to stand next to the wall. The Boleyn Ground was full of expectation as the Frenchman approached the ball. They were left disappointed though, as after all of that build-up, the shot sailed harmlessly over the crossbar.

Once again, De Gea had to wait to get the ball back from the Bobby Moore Lower as fans threw it about among themselves. Whether they meant it or not, whoever did give it back added a little more frustration for the stopper while getting a cheer from everyone else. That is because they got it on top of the net, seemingly leaving the Spaniard confused for a second.

When he finally had the ball in his possession, De Gea passed it to the left of his box towards Blind, who gave it back to him. With West Ham's attackers closing off his easy options, the goalkeeper attempted a pass towards the halfway line but made a complete mess of it, only managing to find the head of Kouyaté. However, after the two sides had struggled for possession with plenty of 50-50s for the ball, it was Rooney who came away with possession.

Kouyaté tried to steal the ball back again, but the United captain just managed to get in ahead of the Senegal international, diverting it towards Rashford. The youngster played it out wide towards Martial, allowing the Frenchman to single out Reid and push past him, breaking into the box. Randolph had taken a step out, presumably looking to cut out the return pass to Rashford at the back post.

Whether he meant it or not, despite falling over, Martial was able to exploit the space that was being left by the Republic of Ireland international, squeezing his shot just inside the far post. It was so hard to believe the ball had nestled inside the net from that angle. The moment of realisation was truly gut-wrenching, as Dan Lawless says, 'I felt sick to my stomach. I just felt that sense of dread like, "Oh no, after all of that good feeling and everything, you're telling me this is how it's gonna end." It was horrible.'

As Reid looked at his goalkeeper perplexed, Ogbonna stood with his hand on the post in disbelief, Antonio lay on the floor and Cresswell held his head in his hands. Meanwhile, Martial ran off behind the goal to celebrate with the jubilant United supporters before being mobbed by his team-mates. De Gea wasn't afraid to celebrate either, as he looked back at the Bobby Moore Stand shouting 'VAMOS' at the top of his voice.

Joseph Fordham recalls, 'De Gea was goading us in the Bobby Moore Stand. We were in line with the edge of the six-yard box on the right-hand side as you look down at the pitch. He was giving it a little bit. He was enjoying it and he was getting stick from the fans in the Lower.'

Joseph also remembers the celebratory roar from United's section in the Sir Trevor Brooking Lower, 'There was a deafening silence apart from that distant roar you get from the away fans – that's one of the best and worst noises in football if you ask me. If you're at the other end of the away end and you just hear that distant roar, you think, "Ahh, fuck off," because they look so happy. It's one of my favourite sounds at a football match, but it usually comes with bad news: you've let in a goal. I remember everyone apart from them being very quiet but everyone around us was like, "Oh, that's not what's supposed to happen, this is not part of the plan."'

Daniel Hurley was far closer to the away fans, sitting in the Sir Trevor Brooking Upper, so that noise was far less distant. 'It was pretty much the only time in the game you could hear their fans. Obviously, I was sitting above them, but they were doing that Anthony Martial song. They were singing that over and over again. I just thought, "Oh God, this is the last 15 minutes of our time being here and I'm gonna be hearing this bloody Martial song." It was genuinely the only time that I could actually hear them sing above us. The noise just never stopped throughout the game and even the equaliser knocked it out of us a little bit but not much.'

While De Gea was being an annoyance, the Hammers fans were really tired of seeing Martial. His only other brace in a United shirt had been in his second game for the Red Devils, a 3-2 win over Southampton in which he was gifted one of his goals. It felt typical that the forward would get one on this special night.

He had also been a pain for West Ham at other points in the season. The 0-0 league draw at Old Trafford was the only time he didn't get a goal contribution against the Hammers that term. It was the Frenchman who had knocked the ball in at the far post to force the FA Cup quarter-final into a second leg. He had then gone on to assist both of the goals that knocked West Ham out of the competition. All in all, he was far from the most popular person in this part of east London.

Then there was Rashford, who officially recorded the assist for Martial's second of the night. The attacker had only made his United debut in February but was already a key part of Van Gaal's squad just a few months later. He had burst on to the scene with a brace in his first appearance for the club, a 5-1 win in the Europa League against FC Midtjylland, following that up with two goals and an assist against Arsenal.

By the end of the campaign, the teenager had eight goals in all senior competitions. This tally and his performances had even got Rashford in the conversation regarding England selections. He actually made his England debut 17 days after the final game at Upton Park, scoring three minutes into a 2-1 friendly win against Australia. Since then, Rashford has gone from strength to strength for both club and country, having recorded well over 250 appearances for United and England combined by the age of 23.

As well as becoming an incredibly talented footballer, Rashford also showed that he is an exceptional person in

2020. After the coronavirus pandemic began, he went about ensuring children in the UK were fed by directly influencing government policy through his campaigning. Considering how big a name Rashford has become both in and outside the game, it is strange to think of him as the fresh-faced youngster still in his first season as a senior player, being among those attempting to taint the Boleyn's farewell. At this point, Rashford and Martial were doing a pretty good job of just that.

72:46

As the whistle blew to restart the action, there was a very clear difference from the rest of the game. With plenty of Hammers fans left shell-shocked by the goal, for the first time all night it was the visiting supporters who could be heard the loudest. Martin Tyler said on commentary, 'Those missed chances from West Ham are biting them badly here and this talented 20-year-old Frenchman, Anthony Martial, is writing his name all over the final match at Upton Park.' While it took the fans a few moments to recover from this heavy blow, the players got straight back into their stride.

James Jones remembers the feeling of dread that followed Martial's and United's second of the game, 'That was when I got worried because the clock is ticking and I just really felt that at 2-1 we've now got a job on our hands. Losing wasn't an option, but when you're 2-1 down at that point, suddenly it comes into the back of your head that we could lose this game. It will forever be in our history that we lost on the final day at Upton Park. Even though that's not an option, it could be a reality. When you're completely powerless in the stands, that is the worst feeling in the world in a game like that. It's bad enough when you're losing in a cup final, but when you're losing the last-ever game at Upton Park with less than 20 minutes left, that's a completely different worry. I was just thinking, "Don't fuck this up, West Ham. Do not, of all days, of all games, of all occasions, mess it up now."'

On the opposite end of the scale, Joseph Fordham was among the supporters who remained confident. 'I just kept saying to my mate, "This is gonna be fine. It's absolutely fine. I've got no doubts here." I've never felt less stressed out about being behind at home, which is crazy to think because the clock is ticking down and there's only so many minutes left of the last game, but I felt completely at ease with the result.' The Hammers looking just as authoritative as ever will have helped that.

Cresswell was the outfielder closest to the jubilant away section, but he didn't allow that to impact him. 'You don't want to get too caught up with everything emotionally and let that get the better of you, because that's when things can change really quick. So, I was just trying to stay focused on the game.'

The ball was passed around the back following kick-off until it reached Cresswell, who picked Carroll out with a lofted ball forward. Carroll managed to get his head on it and knocked it down, but the ball just evaded Sakho before bouncing through to De Gea. The Spaniard was lucky there wasn't more power on the header as his thigh control was far from convincing, but there wasn't enough pace on the ball for it to go out of play. The 25-year-old had taken his chance to run a couple of seconds off the clock, but decided to hit a long pass once he finally had the ball in his hands. Reid got up above Martial to head clear, but the ball went straight back into United's possession, with Rooney's off-touch going to Herrera.

The men in white knocked their passes about until they found Blind, who decided it was time to make something happen. The Dutchman split the Hammers men ahead of him, playing the ball up to Herrera's feet, with the midfielder having roamed into the West Ham half. Herrera and Rojo both played first-time passes which released Martial, who was running in behind the claret and blue defence in a wide area. Considering what the Frenchman had just done, there was a sense of relief for many in the Boleyn Ground as the whistle blew due to the attacker straying offside.

West Ham took the chance to get up the pitch, sweeping the ball to the left, and after a few headers from each side Cresswell was able to get it down and pass into Carroll's feet. The striker popped it off to Lanzini, who just managed to keep hold of possession despite an unconvincing touch, getting in ahead of Rooney to pass to Noble. The pair tried a one-two, but Herrera dangled out a leg and caught the captain, giving away a free kick in the process. Having had his patience tested enough, Dean gave Herrera a yellow card, explaining to the Spaniard that this was for an accumulation of fouls, rather than for the one challenge.

Once again, Upton Park looked to Payet in the hope that his wand of a right foot could create yet another special Boleyn Ground moment. Despite the fact he had failed to deliver his best so far, this was the same sort of distance from which the talisman had scored at Old Trafford in the FA Cup. He couldn't do it against De Gea again, could he? Ogbonna made a nuisance of himself in the wall and Sakho hindered the goalkeeper's vision of the ball with his positioning. However, it was down to the Frenchman to make the most of the opportunity, even if it was a tough one.

Payet smashed the ball into the jumping wall's midriff, hitting it so hard that he had to run back and retrieve it. There was a collective groan of disappointment from large parts of the ground, but this scenario ultimately gave Payet extra space to manoeuvre in. Cresswell pointed to go back, before running around the number 27, giving Payet another option and Carrick a dilemma about who to cover. The United midfielder stopped for a second to decide, but Payet was always going to trust his own ability enough to put the ball in himself, and he did just that.

This was a floated effort that drifted slowly through the Upton Park air, but there wasn't anything aimless about the pass. There were so many bodies in and around the United box. Despite all of that hustle and bustle in such a tight space, Antonio was able to find himself unmarked just outside the six-yard box. It was as if a pathway had been set out specifically for the ball to reach Antonio, and if anyone was going to find him it was Payet. As the delivery approached Antonio, he leapt into the air and threw his head at the ball, sending it flying into the top corner, way out of De Gea's reach.

There were no groans from the Hammers fans anymore, as we all went completely wild. Antonio made a second attempt at the celebration he had done for his disallowed goal, but Carroll was having none of it, pulling the man playing at right-back, signalling to get back into position to go again and win the game. There was nobody telling the fans to calm down, though, and if they had done, it wouldn't have made the slightest difference anyway.

Even James Datson, who was commentating for the visually impaired in the stadium, couldn't maintain complete control. 'I remember there was a moment where I lost it a bit as soon as Antonio equalised. I was still commentating, but anyone listening at that stage would've known I'm a West Ham fan, no matter where they were tuning in from.'

The one feeling that crops up when looking back at this moment, as well as the elation of the goal, is the relief

A young West Ham fan was carried through the packed crowd on Green Street pre-game.

The Manchester United bus struggled to make its way through the crowds.

The teams came out to be met with a rendition of 'Bubbles' and a mosaic reading '1904 – 2016'.

Somewhere under this pile of Hammers, Diafra Sakho was celebrating the opener.

West Ham players looked on in disbelief as Anthony Martial celebrated his second of the game.

Michail Antonio emphatically headed home West Ham's equaliser.

Every West Ham fan went wild when Antonio equalised, including Mark Noble.

Winston Reid and his team-mates celebrate West Ham's winning goal.

Slaven Bilić orchestrated the team for the whole 90 minutes, showing the passion fans came to love him for.

Noble and the rest of the West Ham squad wave to supporters after the game.

Mabel Arnold is one of the Hammers fans who received thoroughly deserved recognition during the ceremony.

We were all incredibly lucky to have Martin Peters with us for the ceremony.

Paolo Di Canio waves to supporters from the spot in which he scored his outrageous volley against Wimbledon.

Sir Trevor Brooking takes in the adulation of fans from where he scored his iconic goal against Eintracht Frankfurt.

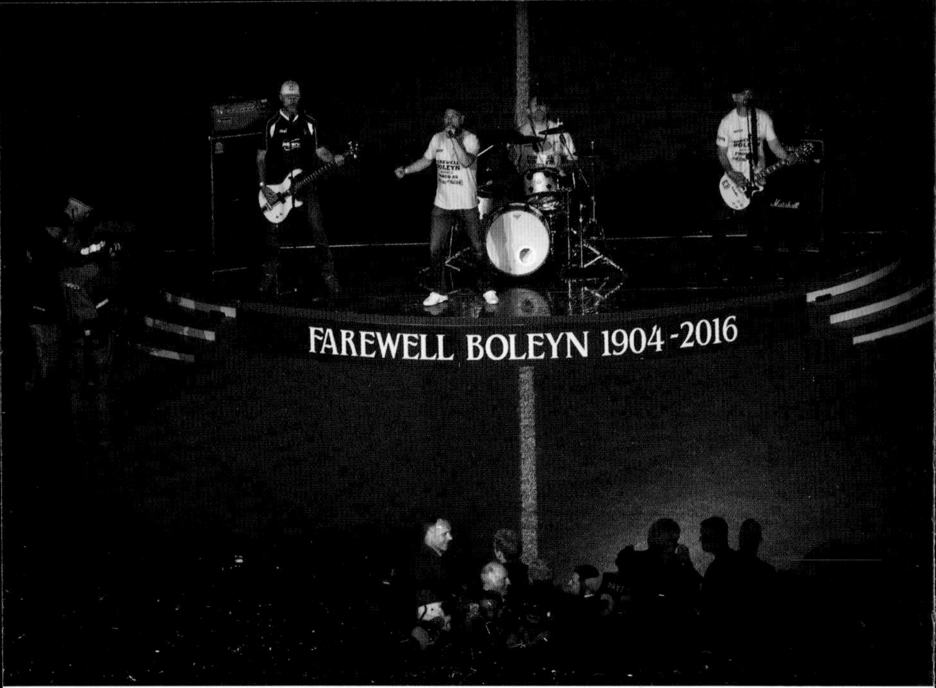

The Cockney Rejects performed their version of 'Bubbles', which Jeff Geggus says 'meant more than anything'.

Everybody watched on as Bobby Moore turned out the Upton Park lights, bringing the night to a poignant end.

attached to it. As Joseph Fordham says, 'People put their lives on that kind of thing. They go to the football to get away from their week, however bad it's been, and the last thing people needed was to walk out of Upton Park for the last time having been beaten.'

'We'd scored another goal, we've been given the opportunity to celebrate another goal at this ground,' James Jones enthuses. 'Everyone's hugging each other and there's smiles on people's faces, just sheer joy. I've never seen that in any sporting event, even when West Ham have won and we've won in play-off semi-finals and play-off finals and got to FA Cup Finals in my lifetime and stuff like that. I've still never seen joy like I saw on people's faces with every goal that night.'

Daniel Hurley was probably the last Hammer in the ground to celebrate it. 'I thought it was offside. At the time I panicked, looked at the linesman and saw him running away. I had three people jump on me and I'm still trying to see if he was offside, because I thought we're all going to look really stupid if we were all going like this and he was off. I just thought, "Thank God."'

It may have felt as though some sort of divine intervention had been in play, pulling the ball past De Gea and into the net, but it shouldn't have been too much of a surprise that Antonio popped up at the vital moment. The 26-year-old had opened the scoring with a bullet header after just ten minutes against Liverpool, he curled the ball into the net against Sunderland for the only goal of the game, as well as heading in the Hammers' first against Everton as the team came from 2-0 down to win 3-2.

However, the goal from that season – aside from the equaliser against United – that will be most fondly remembered came against Spurs. Every West Ham fan will have been desperate to beat the club's rivals in the final match against them at Upton Park. Thanks to Antonio, that hope became a reality. He nudged Nacer Chadli out of the way before getting so much power on his header that Hugo Lloris couldn't keep it out despite getting both hands on to it.

These all contributed to Antonio's tally of 11 goals and five assists for West Ham that term, which is remarkable considering he spent a fair amount of it at right-back, mainly due to injuries to Carl Jenkinson and Sam Byram. He had joined the Hammers from Nottingham Forest at the beginning of the 2015/16 campaign for a fee that was reported to be around £7m. Stepping up from the Championship to the Premier League was a big enough achievement in itself, but that was nothing compared to where Antonio had started out.

At 17 years old, the winger was playing for Tooting & Mitcham United in the Isthmian League, in the seventh tier of English football, while going to sixth form college and working as a lifeguard. He wasn't there for long, though, playing just six games, as he was snapped up by Championship side Reading. Antonio then went back on loan to Tooting & Mitcham, before heading off for spells at Cheltenham Town, Southampton, Colchester United and Sheffield Wednesday. Having helped the Owls get promoted from League One during an emergency loan, Antonio signed for them permanently, staying there for two years before that move to Forest – his final stop before joining West Ham.

The versatile star didn't look out of place on the big stage at all, though, as Dan Lawless recalls, 'Antonio was exceptional that whole season, he was a player who could take players on. On that night, he really brought his A game. He just added that energy that we needed and I think that's been the case from the moment we signed him.' Joseph Fordham adds, 'I was so happy it was him; he had a fantastic season. It was just like, "It's him again, good on him."'

When the man himself discussed his goal as part of the My Favourite Match feature in West Ham's official programme, he said, 'Dimi could put in amazing balls and it was just a case of getting on the end of them. I had to jump a bit for this one, but it worked out perfectly as my header gave David De Gea no chance. There was only one place that header was going! I've always been confident with my heading, and I've always believed I can do it. It was a sick, sick night.'

The mixture of scoring goals and displaying versatility is something Antonio has continued throughout his time at West Ham. Since the Boleyn's swansong, Antonio has played in his originally more recognised place on the wing, along with filling in at right-back on various occasions and also acting as the main striker. In addition, he scored the first Premier League goal at London Stadium and the first away goal at Tottenham's new stadium, bringing out more of his much-loved celebrations – without interruption most of the time.

Antonio was a regular on the scoresheet at the end of the 2019/20 campaign, recording eight goals and an assist in six games to help keep the Hammers up – and win the Premier League Player of the Month award for July 2020 in the coronavirus-extended season. This included scoring the equaliser and assisting the winner in a dramatic 3-2 win over Chelsea, an incredible four-goal haul against Norwich City and the opener in the 3-1 victory against Watford that secured safety.

Considering Antonio signed from Championship side Nottingham Forest for a fee that was below £10m, having originally risen up from non-league, it is remarkable how well he has done in a claret and blue shirt. The Londoner has given West Ham fans so many superb moments, but the equaliser on such a historic night has to be among the best of the lot. For many, it may even be one of the greatest moments any West Ham player has ever given them.

76:11

There had been just two minutes and 57 seconds between play restarting after Martial's goal and Antonio's header hitting the back of the net. As the whistle blew once again a few moments later, there was a very different mood around the Boleyn Ground. As play resumed, Bilić could be seen on the sideline frantically waving his arms about and shouting in order to organise his players. Meanwhile, the fans were still on a high, with random shouts of support ringing out around the stadium, before everyone got their heads together enough to start shouting, 'come on, you Irons' in unison. The noise emanating from the supporters was almost deafening, as everybody willed the team on to go and score a winner. At the time, it felt as if all of our lives depended on it and nobody was afraid to show it.

David Blackmore, who filmed parts of the day and night from a fan's view for BBC Radio 5 Live, recalls, 'I remember doing my video on it and almost being out of breath because people had been celebrating that hard that I was being pulled all over the place. I was sitting in quite nice seats, so I wasn't really expecting to be pulled around by these quite well-off men. Everyone's just pulling themselves to one another, people with kids, so that in itself was a special moment and that's when we realised we were very much back in the contest.'

The stands weren't the only places where there had been a change in attitude. Joseph Fordham remembers seeing a difference in the United players, 'For me, that goal signified a shift in momentum, and I was just wondering when the next one was then. They didn't fancy it, Rooney was walking around spitting on the pitch, but not just spitting on the pitch like a footballer does. He was doing it and gesturing as if to say, "This is a shithole," and he was aggressively spitting on the floor. I thought, "They've lost it, their heads have gone, they're not bothered about this anymore, they don't fancy it." It showed, I think, that our players were up for it, the crowd were up for it. As soon as it went to 2-2, I think the Man United players just thought, "Fuck this, let's get out of here." That's the impression I got anyway.'

The West Ham players definitely fancied it. The away side got a throw shortly after kick-off, from which Noble won the header. Sakho flicked the ball on and it was soon Cresswell who sprang into action, getting his head on to a Smalling punt up the field to clear it away from danger. Lanzini was unable to take the ball under his spell though, allowing it to get away to Carrick. A few passes later, Mata almost allowed the ball to run out of play but reacted just in time to keep it in before finding Valencia. The Ecuadorian tried to flick it past Cresswell and messed up his attempt. Cresswell wasn't about to make the same error in judgement and put his right foot straight through the ball, getting it up to the halfway line.

There was no respite for West Ham though, as Smalling sent a big header back towards the Sir Trevor Brooking Stand. It was Ogbonna's turn to deal with it now, which he did, although his header only went as far as Carrick near the centre circle. An image of calm among all the restlessness and anticipation in the stadium, the former Hammer brought the ball under control and passed it to Rooney, who sent it out wide to Martial.

The Frenchman tried to hit a pass into the area but could only find Cresswell, who was still showing plenty of energy as he collected the ball and sprinted up the pitch from inside his own box. As he got close to the halfway line and was shut down by Valencia, the left-back tried a through ball to Payet, but Smalling was across to deal with it easily, passing back to the goalkeeper.

By this point, with all of the energy coming from the stands and the very air within the stadium feeling like pure electricity, there was no time for possession football. West Ham were on the front foot and had to make the most of it – not only to win this match, but to give the Boleyn Ground the magnificent send-off this magical place deserved. Daniel Hurley hadn't been able to take his son due to a SATs exam the next day but remembers, 'The guy who sat next to me, he brought his daughter to every game. His daughter was maybe a year older than my son and when she started going, she was really timid and quiet. I think he was kind of trying to get her into it rather than taking her because she was into it. I remember at one point near the end, it was 2-2 and we were on the attack. I looked and she was screaming and I thought, "That's what it does to you once you start going."

'It's the same with my son, really. He was into it and I started taking him, and he says to me about that night, "You can't remember my SATs exam, we all remember that, we should have gone." He still brings it up. This guy's daughter, who I didn't even really think liked it at the start, was an absolute lunatic wanting us to win. That's the sort of experience I think going to the football gives you that you can't get watching on telly. I've always thought that. I just smiled. I don't even know if the girl or her dad will remember it, but that just felt like a funny moment to me.'

De Gea probably would have taken time on the ball if he could, but he had Carroll charging towards him, so looked to pick out a team-mate with a first-time pass. Ogbonna came rushing across the halfway line, leaping above Herrera to get his head on the ball after it had bounced off the ground. West Ham were winning all of the 50-50s at this point, as Noble got above Rooney to flick the ball towards Sakho, who did enough to stop Blind reaching it. Antonio attempted the pass forward, but it went adrift. The Hammers were let off though, as a swing of Rojo's left boot sent the ball spinning off the pitch and into Bilić's arms.

Almost anything was being seen as reason for encouragement – even something as little as the defender's minor error – and cheers rang around Upton Park as the scorer of West Ham's second got the ball back into play. Once again, it was worked to Cresswell who swiftly got it forward to Carroll. Carroll got up well above Blind, who didn't even bother to jump as the Geordie flicked a pass behind him in Sakho's direction.

The ball soared over the head of both the striker and Rojo, setting up a foot race between the pair with the Argentine holding the advantage. Sakho rushed him into a poor clearance which went to Antonio, but the Hammer messed up his own attempt at a first-time pass and the ball rolled harmlessly to Herrera.

Finally, United had the chance to catch their breath. They played a few passes around the midfield and – offering an indication of just how manic the previous minutes had been – this was enough to earn them boos from the West Ham faithful.

Perhaps due to how little time he had been given throughout pretty much the whole game, Rooney got a bit too relaxed, took his eye off the ball and allowed it to roll under his foot, giving Sakho the opportunity to come in and steal it away.

A couple of passes later, the ball was heading back to the Senegalese striker but Blind came in from behind – while Hammers fans thought this warranted a free kick, Dean didn't. Carrick was able to turn away from Kouyaté and offloaded to Mata, who quickly got it to Herrera. West Ham could have been in big trouble as the Spaniard fronted up Ogbonna, with Reid the only man covering him at all, but the United midfielder stumbled while trying to jink past Ogbonna and the defender was able to come away with the ball.

It was now with Cresswell who roamed up the pitch, before putting another wonderfully shaped ball into the box. Showing the determination that had been there all night, Smalling managed to get his head on to it, conceding another throw. The throw went to Ogbonna, who played it slightly behind him to Reid. If the few seconds of thought involved in this had anyone linked to United thinking they were getting a break, they were very much wrong. Reid played a sweeping pass out wide to Cresswell, who was still pretty much in line with the United box. He nudged the ball past Valencia who tried to take the ball but just ended up getting the left-back's legs. West Ham had another free kick in a dangerous area. The West Ham faithful were cheering and applauding every little thing that could give the tiniest hint of encouragement: a good ball into the box that was cleared, a nice pass, winning a throw. This was certainly something to get excited about.

Payet had trudged over to the ball and was now teeing it up ready to put in another one of his impeccable deliveries – just a matter of minutes after he had set up Antonio. There were so many different songs ringing out around the stadium, dedicated to Carroll, Payet and just about anybody who might have a chance of getting that ball into the back of the net. There wasn't one collective chant coming from all corners of the ground, there was far too much emotion for conformity – so many in the stands did whatever came naturally to them.

David Blackmore encapsulates what was running through the head of many a West Ham fan at the time, 'With Payet, you always knew you were going to get a good delivery. But it needed to be an excellent delivery, it needed to be extraordinary, completely on the money, and you've just got to hope that the West Ham players wanted it more than theirs.'

On commentary, Martin Tyler declared, 'They were 2-1 down, it's now 2-2 and here comes Payet again.' The referee blew his whistle, Payet raised his hand and West Ham roared, willing for this to end in a goal. Carrick was waving his arms and shouting at his team-mates to get their line higher, but it was futile as his team-mates couldn't hear the midfielder over the wall of noise they were being hit by. Carroll juked around the box, with Smalling desperately trying to stick with him. Sakho and Ogbonna held their ground near the back post as United men tried to push them around. Noble and Lanzini stood near the edge of the box watching everything unfurl in the penalty area, ready to strike any ball that came out towards them.

Neither of them were needed, however. Payet swung that sweet right boot of his and sent the ball flying through the air, away from all of the United defenders. Reid managed to get in ahead of Blind and flung himself forward, arms everywhere, legs in the air and head powering through the ball. For a second it looked like De Gea had made the save as the Spaniard got a strong hand to the ball. His efforts were futile, though, as fate, physics, the fans willing it in or whatever powers are out there meant this was destined to cross the line. It felt as if this was all playing out in slow motion. After De Gea's initial contact with his left hand had made the ball pop up, he clawed at the air as he attempted to keep it out of the goal with his right. He couldn't reach far enough at the second attempt, though, and when the ball eventually bounced on the floor, it had made its way well over the line.

As the disbelief subsided and the realisation hit that Reid had put West Ham in front, pure pandemonium broke out. The hero sprinted off towards the corner, jumping into the air just like he had done moments before and threw a jubilant fist up. His team-mates weren't far behind as they all piled in on top of him, shouting towards the supporters in the Bobby Moore Stand. Being one of those in the upper tier, I had completely missed the iconic celebration until the players were almost parting ways, as vision and any sense of anything at all melted away in the presence of such extreme and unbridled emotion.

'I wasn't sure at first. Was it in? I was standing right there, I could see it,' says David Blackmore. 'I can remember just looking and seeing the Bobby Moore Lower erupting. It was pure ecstasy, it was everyone looking around, and everyone couldn't believe it, they were shocked, it was all the emotions that I think people were feeling all at once and you see grown men crying in the stands and you could see how much that goal meant to everyone. If there was ever a goal that was likely to rip the roof off Upton Park, I think it was definitely that one.'

Daniel Hurley was also overcome with emotion. 'Me and my brother just grabbed each other and I half burst into tears. There were people behind us, in front of us jumping on each other. I'm 35 and I've been going since I was seven, and I can't even think of a goal that comes near it in terms of how much it meant.'

'My mate Will is huge and he's a quiet bloke, known him for years. He put me in a headlock, arm around, I'm sure there was a kiss on the head,' Joseph Fordham recalls. 'There was definitely an outpouring of emotions and I think it wasn't even just a case of, "Oh look, we're winning the game now, it's just given us one more thing to cheer about." I'm sure he hugged the person next to him and I don't even know who that was. It was one of them where you just feel hands on you, the row behind have gone a bit too far so you've got someone's hand on your back so they don't fall over and you don't mind.' Matt Datson adds, 'I remember I jumped up and I had people all around me, round my shoulders, people were going crazy, absolutely crazy.'

Joseph continues, 'I guess it's one of the few times – because you don't really think about anyone else when you're at the football – but you're just happy for everyone. Everyone was getting something to go home with, everyone was leaving happy. Watch any other week you don't really care, you just think you'll take the win. I just genuinely felt happy for other people. That's not like me, so it must have been the emotions getting the better of me, because usually I don't care about people in the nicest possible way. I was even happy for the ones that sat around me that wound me up.'

While a lot of people in the stadium may have lost control, many of them will have been able to stay in their seat. Not James Jones, as he confesses, 'I'm pretty sure I ended up a couple of rows ahead on the floor somewhere and it was a surreal moment.'

De Gea may have been regretting turning towards the supporters after Martial's goals at this point, as Joseph remembers, 'His life must have been terrible because he was getting absolutely battered by the first few rows of the Bobby Moore Lower.' There was even a fan who ran on to the pitch to say something to the stopper but was quickly dragged away by the security in the stadium.

Joseph continues, 'De Gea should have really saved that and he fucked it. And that cheered me up because of what he'd been doing before. But I couldn't have been happier for Reid. I've always been a big fan of him.' Rob Pritchard, who knew the goalscorer more personally, felt the same, 'Reidy's a fantastic guy, it could not have happened to a nicer bloke.'

Cresswell also has a lot of appreciation for his defensive partner, 'I was delighted for him. Around that time, Reidy didn't get enough credit in my opinion. I think he was one of the best centre-halves. He was so strong, so powerful but also good with the ball. Then he was unfortunate with the injuries he's had over the years. What a fantastic lad and I was delighted for him to get the last-ever goal at the ground.'

Focusing on the goalkeeper, James adds, 'Part of me thought that maybe De Gea deliberately let it in just to give us that moment because the more I watch it, the more I think, "How has he not saved that?"'

There may have been some focus around De Gea at the time, but the man going in the history books and earning eternal glory was Winston Reid. The New Zealand international could be so understated in his play at times, doing exactly what is needed of him at the back with no frills. Maybe this makes him the perfect man to have scored the final goal at the Boleyn Ground.

As is to be expected from a centre-back, Reid didn't hit the back of the net that often, scoring ten goals in over 200 appearances for the Hammers. However, he had shown an ability to grab goals of incredible magnitude before setting foot in east London. Going into the 2010 World Cup, New

Zealand had only ever appeared in one previous tournament, in 1982, coming out of it without a single point to their name. Therefore, there wasn't too much expectation on the shoulders of the All Whites ahead of the tournament.

It had seemed as though they would remain pointless in the World Cup during their opening game against Slovakia, when they went 1-0 down to a goal from Róbert Vittek. However, as he would go on to do against United, Reid popped up at the vital moment. With 93 minutes on the clock, the man wearing his usual number two got his head on to a cross from Shane Smeltz, directing it into the back of the net off the base of the post. Despite not reaching the knockout rounds, New Zealand managed to catch the world's attention, being the only side not to lose in the tournament, holding both Italy and Paraguay to draws – with Reid playing an integral role in each of those games.

It wasn't long after this triumph that a 22-year-old Reid made his move from FC Midtjylland to West Ham. As was to be expected for a relatively young defender taking a massive step up, Reid had an anticlimactic start in the Premier League, playing a total of 403 minutes across seven appearances as the Hammers finished rock bottom under Avram Grant.

Reid came into his own in the Championship, playing a key role in the side that got promoted at the first time of asking – through the play-offs. Keeping with the trend of his goals being massive ones, Reid scored what is one of the most memorable of that campaign. In an atmosphere teeming with hatred, the Hammers were drawing 1-1 against Millwall with Reid having provided an unorthodox assist for Carlton Cole to score the opener. Just three minutes after Millwall had equalised, Joey O'Brien had sent a long, looping ball into the box that was punched away by David Forde under pressure from Julien Faubert. As the goalkeeper fell over the Frenchman on to the floor, the ball bounced towards Reid who made no mistake, smashing it past the desperate defenders trying to block it and into the back of the net.

The centre-back may have been endured a tough time during his first season in claret and blue, but that man was nothing more than a distant memory when Reid got his second crack at the top tier. In the two seasons preceding the final one at Upton Park, Reid made 36 and 30 Premier League appearances respectively.

The New Zealander had impressed so much that Manchester United, Liverpool, Arsenal and Tottenham were all trying to sign him before the 2015/16 campaign. However, Reid snubbed any advances that came his way in favour of signing a six-year contract to stay at West Ham. While the defender had to contend with three injuries, Reid continued to be an integral part of Bilić's team, playing 24 times. He had become a truly reliable performer since those early days at Upton Park, being seen as somebody who would put his body on the line for the cause, while there was real quality in Reid's defending. This goal scored during Upton Park's final game is what Reid will be remembered for, but he still had to fulfil his defensive duties in that match. He did just that, as his four clearances were the most of any West Ham player, while only Antonio bettered his five interceptions.

There were plenty of immediate changes at West Ham following the move to London Stadium, but one thing that continued in the early stages was Reid's importance for the team. That is until the 27th minute in a 4-1 loss against Swansea in 2018 when he tore his anterior cruciate ligament. It was two years, five months and 19 days until he stepped on to the pitch for a competitive first-team match again. It wasn't in claret and blue though, as he went out on loan to

MLS side Sporting Kansas City, with his return coming in a 2-1 win over Minnesota United on 22 August 2020.

Reid didn't play a part in the MLS is Back tournament that kicked things off in the States, but once the season resumed, Reid was an important part of the team. After the long wait he had endured to get back on the pitch, he was rewarded with a brilliant campaign, in which Sporting Kansas City topped the Western Conference. He even got a moment in the spotlight again, scoring the only goal in a 1-0 victory over Chicago Fire.

The biggest opportunity for eternal glory comes through the play-offs, which Kansas got into due to their strong position in the league. Reid and his team-mates got through their first match by beating San Jose Earthquakes on penalties. There wasn't to be a grand finale for them, however, as they were defeated 3-0 by Minnesota in the quarter-finals. Still, the loan spell offered Reid the opportunity to show that he was still able to perform – one that he took, just as he had done when his opportunity came to score against the Red Devils.

When Reid looks back on Upton Park's final goal, he does with great sincerity, 'It meant a lot for the club, for the fans, for the players. We had a good year that year, probably didn't finish as well as we wanted to. But, for the fans, for the people that have been supporting the club for 30 or 40 years and going with their fathers and grandfathers, that was the game for them because they've been there and supporting the club through good times and rough times – there's been a lot of rough times with West Ham. So, hopefully that gave them a smile. That's probably the thing I'll take away from the game.' He also goes on to discuss one part of the match that he is proud of, 'One thing about the fans that I've always appreciated is they always appreciated people that worked hard and I think that year, that game, man, the players were definitely willing to work hard and do their best to represent the club.'

All the players in claret and blue that day will hold a special place in West Ham fans' hearts for what they gave everyone. Reid is among those who will be held in especially high esteem for their contribution, as James Jones declares, 'Winston Reid, for me, is an absolute god now for what he did.' You're far from alone on that one, James.

81:00

The Boleyn's stands were filled with joy following Reid's goal, but there were some issues as the stadium's gates opened – as they always did ten minutes from the end. Jacqueline Lange, who was the chief steward for the Lower West, recalls, 'There's one exit gate steward on each gate and they're on their own, unless you go down and help them. Unfortunately, there were a lot of drunk people, or people on drugs, wearing a West Ham shirt, saying they've been fans for years and they're gonna make sure they're gonna get in and see it. It's like, you can't, you haven't got a ticket and how dare you assume you're just gonna come in. So I did have to find some police to help me and walk them on and put a barrier up, so that it was safe. If you've got a ticket then fine, come in, but you've not, you're people off the street that think you can just come in and I'm not having that because that's not fair.'

Back inside the stadium, if Joseph Fordham thought United's players looked annoyed after the Hammers' equaliser, Martin Goldeman indicates how that turned into helplessness after Reid's header, 'There was this look of disbelief on the Manchester United defenders when they showed it again.' Joseph looks back on a moment filled with contentment, 'Every time we scored, I would just hang back from sitting down, so that I could see my brother who sat slightly away from us. He'd look back over his shoulder and we'd give each other a thumbs-up. We couldn't see each other when we stand up because he's shorter than me. Then you've got all these people between us, so we would both just hang back a little bit and then have a little moment together. They were special, those three little thumbs-up.'

So many of those in the Boleyn Ground will have had their own little rituals they did when Reid's goal went in, knowing it was probably the last time they would ever get the chance to. There was still time to be played, though, meaning the Hammers had to focus once again to ensure the three points and an incredibly historic win would be confirmed. Most of the people in the stadium probably didn't even hear the whistle that marked the continuation of play as home fans continued the celebrations. But it did go off and United tried to get the ball forward quickly, smashing it up the pitch, although Ogbonna headed it away convincingly. Sakho was unable to get the ball under control and Mata nipped in to hit a first-time pass towards Martial. The Frenchman did a few kick-ups to get control of it, but in this atmosphere, with this level of intensity, there was no time for that and Antonio stole the ball away from him.

James Datson remembers how the emotion inevitably took over his commentary at this point, 'Once Reid scored, I felt I was commentating as a fan and just for the West Ham fans. I was counting down the clock, like, "That's another minute gone, there's only this left. Surely this is gonna have to ensure the win." Slaven Bilić, for me, is one of the best managers to watch while you commentate; he's like a conductor. He takes in every emotion, he kneels down, he jumps up, you can tell that he's really passionate about what he was doing and even towards the end, I was trying to get that into the commentary as well, letting the listeners know it's not just about what's going on down on the pitch.'

The ball was with Noble, who was faced by Rooney and tried to get it to Antonio, but the United captain was able to step in. He played a one-two with Carrick and then passed back to Smalling. The United number ten wasn't playing the ball backwards to take his time and take the heat out of the situation anymore – not that he could have done with the atmosphere – as there was far more urgency about the away side's play. They tried to work enough space to make a cutting pass and Carrick was the man who eventually found it, fizzing the ball towards Martial, who touched it off to Rooney. The United skipper swung a long ball towards the byline where Valencia, chased by Payet, managed to keep the ball in, directing it towards Rashford. Reid slid in and just managed to get a block on the teenager's effort in the box.

The ball dropped temptingly for a second, just waiting for somebody to strike it. To the relief of plenty around the ground, Antonio got rid of the danger by smashing his clearance up the pitch. United tried to conjure up another immediate wave of pressure, as Blind and Carrick headed the ball forward, but the latter could only find Noble, who nodded it down to Sakho.

West Ham might have already had the lead, but it wasn't a case of merely sitting back and protecting what they had. Suddenly the men in claret and blue were on the attack as Sakho got the ball to Kouyaté who then passed it on to Carroll, setting up a superb counter-attacking opportunity. There was an initial groan of disappointment when Carroll was forced to turn back, but excitement was soon reinstated as he swept the ball forward and wide to Payet who took it down masterfully.

Sakho was waving his arms in the air as he screamed in desperation for the ball to be passed across the box, where he was completely unmarked. Lanzini made a run of his own, darting off Blind's shoulder and behind the defence. However, Payet was convinced that he was going on his own, looking to mark the historic occasion with a goal to go with his two assists. That wasn't to be, though, as Smalling, Valencia and Carrick teamed up to dispossess him, before Blind came in and touched the ball away. United came forward and were soon starting an attack of their own as Rojo played the ball deep into the Hammers' half. Martial, who had already caused so many problems, ran off the defender's shoulder and called for the ball, but by the time Rojo gave it to him he was offside and Dean's whistle went.

Both teams took the break in play as an opportunity to make changes. Jesse Lingard was brought on for Herrera, while Lanzini was replaced by Pedro Obiang. Given his role in the game, including the assist for the evening's opener, the Argentine received a deserved standing ovation. The number 28 also got appreciative high-fives from Noble and Reid as he walked off the pitch. Obiang looked like a man on a mission as he entered the field of play, immediately relaying instructions to midfield partners Noble and Kouyaté.

Like some of the others in the team, Obiang joined West Ham in the summer of 2015. The 24-year-old, who represented Spain up to Under-21 level, had joined from Sampdoria. He showed himself to be a reliable performer when called upon, taking part in 30 games across all competitions during his first term in east London. The man who would go on to become an Equatorial Guinea international in 2018 was never the first name on the team sheet at West Ham. He did conduct himself well, though, and his absolute cannon of a strike at Wembley to draw with Spurs will live long in the West Ham memory. Obiang eventually headed to Sassuolo in 2019, and remains a popular figure among supporters, as can be seen through his social media interactions at times.

It was then announced that James Tomkins was coming on to replace Sakho, the man who had got the evening off to such an emphatic start. As the Senegal international exited, 'He scores when he wants, he scorers when he wants, Diafra Sakho, he scores when he wants' was all that could be heard around the stadium. Tomkins's introduction meant that Antonio would be able to get up and play on the right wing, with the Academy of Football graduate going in at right-back. It may not have seemed it at the time, but Tomkins's arrival was monumental. Not only was he on the pitch to help secure the historic win, but there was a lot that his time on the pitch represented. Up to this point, Noble had been the only academy graduate to set foot on the pitch for the Hammers – with Carrick doing so for the opposition.

George Parris, a fellow product of the Hammers' famed Academy of Football, was pleased to see Tomkins get some involvement in the action. 'It was quite fitting that he was on there. It was great that Tomkins was on the pitch because he had quite a long career at West Ham, so I would imagine he and Noble would have a better understanding of what was riding on the game than some of their other team-mates. I'm sure he'll look back on his career with pride when he played for us.'

That recognition of his West Ham career is definitely deserved, as the defender made a great contribution during his time at Upton Park with 243 appearances in total. His debut came in 2008 when he played the full 90 minutes in a 1-1 draw against Everton in the league. Following on from that, he played in some massive games for the club, including every minute of the 2012 play-off campaign that saw West Ham beat Blackpool 2-1 in the final to get promoted.

Tomkins wasn't always Bilić's first choice in 2015/16, but he was still able to play an important role and provide big moments. He scored twice in the failed Europa League qualifying campaign, with one of those helping to avoid a complete embarrassment against Birkirkara. While it didn't completely turn the result around, he also gave the Hammers hope in the FA Cup tie with Manchester United, when his brave header in the second leg brought the score back to 2-1. His contributions weren't all in the cups, though, as he started 23 league games, going between centre-back and right-back depending on where the manager felt he was needed most at the time.

The 27-year-old did feature in the season-ending loss against Stoke City but didn't go on to play at London Stadium in claret and blue, signing for Crystal Palace in the summer. That made this historic night his last home appearance for the Hammers. As Tony Cottee says, 'It's a special game for your last game, that's for sure.' However, this definitely wasn't a testimonial or anything of the sort, as Tomkins had a clear job to do upon entering the action. The concentration this inspired was written across his face as he took the short jog to his position.

84:20

Randolph's clearance up the pitch made its way right to the edge of the United box, but Smalling was able to reach it ahead of Carroll to get the ball away. Obiang got involved straight away as he latched on to the loose ball, lost it to Mata and then immediately intercepted the Spaniard's attempted pass. Obiang then had the composure to get his foot on the ball and pass it off to Kouyaté.

Possession ended up with Noble, who gave Tomkins his first touch of the game, which was used to play the ball up to Kouyaté. While the defender found his target, the West Ham number eight's attempt to chest down to Antonio failed to make its way past Blind. Having got hold of the ball, United worked it to Carrick after a few passes. Uncharacteristically, the away side's number 16 showed a lack of awareness as after being put under pressure by Obiang, he played a pass to a space where there were absolutely no men in white anywhere to be seen.

Rather than letting the loose ball roll out of play, Payet chased it down and passed it to Cresswell, who roamed forward a little and rolled it back to the Frenchman. Payet managed to split two United players with a pass for Noble near the centre circle, but the West Ham skipper was taken out by Lingard after beginning to roam forward with the ball. It wasn't necessarily in the most dangerous of areas, but winning the foul was enough to give the already jubilant Hammers fans an even bigger lift as everyone began singing, 'We all follow the West Ham over land and sea, we all follow the West Ham on to victory'.

It felt like the stadium was shaking as the fans applauded and sang, waiting on Payet to put another delivery into the box. As expected, it was another quality ball in and Kouyaté was able to get the jump on Carrick to reach it. The attempt was awkward for the Senegalese midfielder, though, as he tried to flick it towards goal with the back of his head. He did just that but the ball wouldn't drop in time for him, hitting the roof of the net.

De Gea, who was public enemy number one until Martial's brace, got himself an ironic cheer as he smashed his goal kick straight out of play. This allowed Van Gaal to have one last throw of the dice in an effort to get United back into the game by bringing Adnan Januzaj on for Valencia.

Although with 86 minutes already gone the winger wasn't exactly being given much time to make an impact.

Despite the lack of time on the pitch, this will have been seen as an opportunity for the 20-year-old to show what he could do. He had first made his mark in the Red Devils first-team in 2013, announcing himself as a fresh-faced teenager with a brace to secure a 2-1 win over Sunderland – the second goal being a brilliantly taken volley.

While many expected him to kick on, Januzaj would only regress in a United shirt, to the point where he was loaned out to Borussia Dortmund for the first half of the 2015/16 campaign. The youngster, who would go on to represent Belgium, managed just 161 minutes in half a season with Dortmund, which saw his return to Old Trafford. He was Van Gaal's final solution at Upton Park, but it was the youngster's first taste of first-team football since February – although an injury had played a part in some of that absence.

86:26

Tomkins launched the ball forward and Carroll was able to bring it down, but as he tried to turn, Rojo came in with a tackle that allowed Rooney to run away with possession. The game might have been nearing its culmination, but the West Ham players weren't wavering at all, as Carroll and Obiang set off in pursuit – United were able to shift the ball around quickly enough to marginally evade the pair.

After it was eventually worked back to Rooney, the United skipper looked for yet another one of his big switches, picking out Lingard on the right wing. Rooney raced over to the other side of the pitch to get it back and, again, tried to switch the point of attack. Tomkins read his intentions and managed to cut the attempted pass out by clearing up the pitch in a no-nonsense fashion.

Noble had been absolutely everywhere throughout the game, so it wasn't much of a surprise to see him sprinting forward to compete with Blind in the air. Mr West Ham won the header and reclaimed possession from Carrick with some help from his team-mates, before being tripped by Martial. It was this dedication that earned Noble plenty of appreciation from Hammers fans, who got up off their feet to applaud the man temporarily lying face down on the turf to catch his breath. Meanwhile, Martial looked just as frustrated as he had made everyone associated with West Ham feel a quarter of an hour earlier.

From the free kick, the ball was switched out to the left flank where Payet was waiting to take it down, looking forward immediately. Despite being in too deep a position to be crossing for most, the Hammers talisman didn't bother to run forward as he had spotted Antonio at the back post. Antonio raced in to try and reach the cross, but Rojo stood strong and headed clear. Mata touched the ball down for Carrick, who then passed it out wide to Januazaj.

The substitute, who hadn't seen much of the ball since coming on, was immediately put under pressure by Cresswell, then Payet. However, the 21-year-old was able to spin away from both of them after initially being pushed back and clipped the ball behind the defence to Lingard. The United academy product had no chance of maintaining possession, though, as Kouyaté was in hot pursuit and held Lingard off to retrieve the ball. Not only that, he then had the composure to nutmeg the United midfielder and pass to Cresswell, who cleared up the pitch and out of play.

For the Senegal international to do this so late into the game verges on the superhuman, but it won't have been surprising for many Hammers fans. Kouyaté had the sort of engine that is reserved for the finest of cars, but not only that, he knew how to use it. Due to this, United's was far from the first midfield to be largely stifled by the reliable midfielder.

He had signed from Anderlecht in the summer of 2014 and slotted straight into Sam Allardyce's side. That didn't change at all under Bilić, as the Croatian played him 42 times in all competitions during the final season at Upton Park. It is easy to see why considering the start he made to the campaign. The number eight scored the Hammers' first goal of the season when he got on the end of Payet's free kick delivery into the Arsenal box ahead of the onrushing Petr Ćech. Having done the hard work to get there, he was making no mistake and headed the ball into the gaping net.

That was immediately followed by a goal and assist in losses against Leicester City and Bournemouth. While the goal contributions dried up slightly, as he ended the season with five goals and four assists, the midfielder's influence certainly didn't. As was highlighted by that challenge on Lingard, he had the physical capabilities to get across the pitch and the intelligence to ensure he was filling the correct spaces while doing so. It was this that made his partnership with Noble work so well, as well as the passing ability of both.

While Kouyaté put in the same level of intensity pretty much every week at this time, George Parris suggests his performance during the final game at Upton Park was one of the best he had seen from the Senegal international. The West Ham academy graduate, who was a respected midfielder himself, adds, 'He was here, there and everywhere.'

Kouyaté's intelligence and technique, on top of his physicality, made the 26-year-old's performance so impressive. There was also precision in the midfielder's defensive work as all four of the tackles he attempted throughout the 90 minutes were successful. It was a truly supreme showing.

Aside from being an integral part of the team on the pitch, Kouyaté was also a big character off it. One of Martin Godleman's stories from after the game shows this. 'The club chaplain was there celebrating at the end. The funniest thing is Cheikhou Kouyaté, who's six foot two inches and Alan the chaplain is about five four, and Kouyaté – because he's quite a religious guy – took him in this great big hug and Alan's head is in his chest. That was at the end of that game, that was so funny.'

There was a moment that pretty much anyone familiar with the internet will have seen as well, which saw Kouyaté bringing smiles to everyone's faces – apart from Sakho. At the end-of-season awards in 2016, the midfielder was filmed laughing and grinning as he sang, 'We've Got Payet'. While Sakho tried telling him to be quiet, the midfielder just carried on singing yet again. It's pretty much impossible to watch that video without laughing.

The Senegal international was sold to Crystal Palace in 2018, but there will be plenty of Hammers fans who are able to appreciate what he offered our club when at his best, both in terms of his displays and ability to warm hearts. The final game at Upton Park highlights the qualities he brought to the side better than any other.

When he looked back on the game as part of the My Favourite Match feature in West Ham's official matchday programme, Kouyaté said, 'What a night it was at the Boleyn Ground that night! It was unbelievable. Even now, when I think back about that game, I cannot believe it. We stuck together, we worked together, we scored our goals and we got the victory. My team-mates did everything to get the win. It was the perfect way to finish our time in Upton Park, for sure. The atmosphere was amazing, the fans never stopped singing and we wanted to win the game for them. Even when

I think back now, that night was so special. I will never forget it.'

88:02

The ball was quickly thrown into play and Mata turned and fed Rooney – the veteran was seemingly their go-to man to break down West Ham's defence at this point. He shifted the ball to Rojo on the left, leaving the Argentine in a good position to cross into a box that was full of bustling United players. However, Antonio was able to deflect the attempted delivery, making it spin high into the air, allowing Randolph to come out and pluck it out of the sky. It was actually Reid who was closest to getting his head to the ball over the Irishman. The New Zealander ended up colliding with his goalkeeper, who winced slightly while holding his ribs. Most importantly, Randolph still had a hold on the ball.

He got a thankful pat on the chest from Noble before kicking it long. That contribution won't have got quite as much appreciation as it went nowhere near any of the men in claret and blue, rolling through to De Gea. This gave the away side the opportunity to build yet another attack as the ball was thrown out to Blind. West Ham fans showed nothing but support, though, cheering on the team with a chant of 'come on, you Irons'.

Considering we were now approaching the game's dying moments, it may have been expected that the losing team would look to speed things up as much as possible in a desperate attempt to get something. It seemed even more obvious than usual due to their Champions League aspirations being on the line. That wasn't the case, though, as the Red Devils knocked the ball around near the halfway line, waiting for space to open up. There wasn't anywhere to exploit, though, as every Hammer was behind the ball, showing the team's discipline and determination.

Four passes were played to find Blind in pretty much the exact same position he had been in when he played the first. In the end, the Dutchman attempted an intricate looped pass forward, but Tomkins was able to get his head on to it. Noble initially lost out to Rooney in reaching the loose ball, although the captain wasn't giving anybody a second to think. He slid in and managed to push the ball back slightly. United passed it around again, but they still couldn't find the route they so desperately needed to get behind the West Ham back line. This time, Carrick urged Rashford to show for the ball before spraying it towards the teenager, but Reid rushed in to ensure he got to the attempted pass first. It shouldn't be any surprise that Noble was on hand to toe the ball away from Mata.

However, Blind got on to it and evaded Antonio's sliding tackle to push forward. He got the ball out to Martial, who was able to get Noble in a one-on-one situation – with Antonio temporarily completely out of the game. The Frenchman managed to get his cross in, but Cresswell leapt across the box to head it back out wide, before Tomkins raced over to clear the danger via a deflection off Martial's outstretched boot.

While the defensive work was impressive, it wasn't the only reason us Hammers fans in the Boleyn were on our feet applauding and singing a few moments later. That came with the announcement that Payet was coming off the pitch to be replaced by Enner Valencia. We immediately started chanting about the talisman as he trudged off the pitch. He also got a high-five and a hug from Bilić.

In all honesty, this wasn't the Frenchman's best performance in a West Ham shirt. Some good chances that he usually would have converted were squandered, while there were a few moments in which he was a bit too indulgent on the ball. It says a lot about the pure talent he possesses that the 29-year-old still managed to play an integral part in both of the Hammers' last two goals.

As Daniel Hurley mentions, the expectations around Payet were unnaturally high due to his consistent performances, 'Payet was good every game, but at that point we were almost taking it for granted how good he was, because he had been like it week in, week out.' After all, he played eight key passes during the Boleyn Ground's final game – five more than anybody else on the pitch.

In addition, the deliveries he put in to set up Reid's and Antonio's headers were superb – they were the sort of deliveries supporters had come to expect from him. There wasn't always this extreme level of anticipation around the Frenchman, though. When he signed from Olympique de Marseille at the beginning of the season, for a fee that was over £10m, he was described as 'a world-class player' by David Sullivan. While there was mild excitement from a lot of Hammers fans, nobody could have predicted just how big a star Payet would become at the Boleyn Ground.

The winger scored 12 goals and assisted a further 15 in all competitions during the 2015/16 campaign. However, it wasn't purely the volume of goals Payet contributed that made him such a hero in east London, it was the magnificent way in which he did so. Payet had the rare talent and arrogance that allowed him to make things look nonchalant yet emphatic simultaneously. The most obvious example of this came at Old Trafford in the FA Cup. No matter what the end result was, that tie will always be remembered for the moment West Ham's star stepped up and sent the ball flying off the post and into De Gea's net from at least 30 yards out. The best part of it all was the magician had been so confident that he ran off celebrating before the goal had even gone in.

He stayed calm for that, but Hammers fans didn't, as Joseph Fordham recalls, 'I was in line with the post where Payet's free kick went in. When he scored it, my chest felt like it was about to explode. I can't remember ever having that kind of feeling before; it was like an out-of-body experience. I was at Old Trafford for the first time in my life, somewhere that I'd grown up watching on TV and on European nights – for me, it's an iconic ground. Then Payet from 30 yards, off the post as if it was nothing. It's like how dare you, but the atmosphere that day was incredible. I felt like my lungs were going to pop.'

It is this sort of capability to pull off the unfathomable that has given so many West Ham fans their own special moments with Payet at the centre. For me, it is the free kick against Crystal Palace that defied science by looping up into the air before somehow ending up in the top corner. I had said, 'Well, he's messed that one up,' when it was at its peak, only to have a chuckle with those sitting around me after the ball dipped far more than logic should allow and soared past Wayne Hennessey, looking like a bit of a fool for doubting his genius for even a second.

There were so many other magical moments from the Frenchman that season: the free kick to set up Kouyaté on his Premier League debut win against Arsenal; sitting Hennessey down before dinking the ball over him; his incredible free kick delivery to assist Ogbonna's winner in the dying moments against Liverpool in the cup; his two magnificent goals against Blackburn Rovers; his corner to set Antonio up against Tottenham; the goal and assist against Everton. There could be various other brilliant moments included here, but the list is getting pretty long already.

For many games during 2015/16, it felt as though we were turning up wondering what Payet was going to conjure up this time. We were expecting to be entertained by our talisman and he very rarely disappointed. Rob Pritchard goes as far as to say, 'Dimi was the best player in the league and was just untouchable, he was unstoppable.' It is this that earned him the adoration of so many West Ham fans. The fact he was able to produce two superb assists on the Boleyn Ground's final night, despite not being at his best, only came to strengthen that.

Following his incredible first campaign in east London, Payet even got into the France squad that reached the final of the 2016 European Championships. There was an immense sense of pride from plenty involved with West Ham in different capacities when we got to see him perform on such a massive stage. That only intensified when he became the hero in a team that included the likes of Paul Pogba, who was about to move from Juventus back to Manchester United, and Atlético de Madrid star Antoine Griezmann. Payet scored an 89th-minute winner in the tournament opener against Romania. I distinctly remember being in the pub as Payet took a touch out of his feet near the edge of the box and smashed the ball into the top corner, having already assisted Olivier Giroud's opener. I had found true joy in seeing everyone else marvelling at our talisman's genius without club allegiances getting in the way. Payet also added goals against Albania and Iceland during the tournament.

Six months later and Hammers fans had a completely different set of emotions around Payet. He left acrimoniously in January 2017, having refused to play at the end of his time with the club as he forced through a move back to Marseille. The midfielder still had his moments in that season, notably the incredible run for his goal against Middlesbrough.

There was rage from top to bottom when that transfer did eventually go through. Fans burned shirts with his name on the back and there was a viral video of one being used as a doormat at London Stadium.

That fury was matched by Sullivan, as was made clear in the club's official statement upon Payet's departure, 'I would like to make it clear that we have no financial need to sell our best players and that the decision to allow Payet to leave was in accordance with the wishes of the manager and the interests of squad unity. To be frank, my board and I would have preferred for him to have stayed in order to make an example of him, as no player is bigger than the club.'

However, that anger has subsided for many as time has gone on, paving the way for admiration to return. While there will always be memories of how disappointing it was to see such a heroic figure leave in a severely unsettling way, there are so many positive memories that Payet gave us all to treasure. The final game at the Boleyn Ground, and the two assists he provided to help secure the win, undoubtedly rank among the very best of them.

90:35

Valencia's time on the pitch was to be short-lived, a little bit like his time in east London. The Ecuador international had arrived from Mexican side CF Pachuca in 2014. The attacker never managed to perform consistently in claret and blue, but he did have some great moments in a West Ham shirt. There was a brilliant strike against Hull City, his unstoppable free kick against Bournemouth and a brace against Manchester City to secure a 2-2 draw. He was loaned out to Everton the summer after the Boleyn's farewell, before returning to play in Mexico by joining Tigres UANL in 2017.

Once Valencia was on the pitch, Tomkins launched the ball forward again, but Rojo and Smalling teamed up to stop Carroll reaching it, with the Argentine stretching so much he was only able to flick it backwards. Antonio came agonisingly close to stealing it away with the defence gaping behind him, but Carrick stepped in to stop the danger by stabbing the loose ball back to De Gea.

After United bided their time in their own half, Carrick eventually had the ball again and roamed forward, picking out Rashford, who wasn't too far outside the West Ham box. The youngster was quickly dispossessed as Obiang hassled him, leaving Noble to steal the ball and look to get his team up the pitch. The West Ham captain shifted the ball out of Carrick's reach and passed it out wide to Valencia. It ended up with Kouyaté who was taken down by Rashford, winning a throw. While the midfielder was left on the floor for a moment, it gave the home side respite and a chance to take a breath, getting ever closer to the final whistle.

While the majority of supporters were completely gripped, willing our team to hold on to the historic win, some were pre-occupied. Joseph Fordham remembers, 'There was a guy in front of me, he used to really wind me up. He used to turn up 15 minutes late hammered, leave 15 minutes early to go back down to the bar for half-time and come back for the second half late. He was barely in his seat and he was always turning around looking for his mates, I'd think, "Can he just turn around?" But that day, he pulled a drill out of his coat pocket. The whistle hadn't even blown yet, everyone was standing up and he just started undoing his seat. I couldn't believe it, it was hilarious. It just cracked if you tried to kick it. He was passing the drill around like it was a bottle of whisky, it must have been at least 15 to 20 people that were taking that drill off of him and undoing their seats.'

Cresswell had initially put the ball on the floor, thinking Kouyaté had won a free kick before Dean signalled otherwise. The Hammers weren't able to maintain possession once the ball was back in play and Obiang ended up clearing after it was headed clear, though his attempt went straight to Rooney's feet. Yet again, the United number ten tried to play a long pass wide, but all he got himself this time was an ironic cheer from the Hammers fans as his effort soared out of play, going nowhere near Martial.

It was at this point that Martin Godleman announced that Mark Noble had been named man of the match, news that was met by a massive cheer of appreciation from the stands. That was then followed by lengthy applause and more chants of 'too good for England'. There hadn't been quite as much enthusiasm from the fans moments before when Martin had announced that there would be four minutes of added time. He recalls, 'The thing they're saying to me in my earpiece is "it's four, it's four" – they tell me on about 89 minutes. So, I say, "The fourth official has just indicated there will be a minimum of four minutes." When you say that everyone goes, "ahhh", because it was unlikely we were going to lose the game, but to draw it after fighting back would have been devastating.'

The team in claret and blue was putting everything into getting the result, and so was its manager. As Tomkins walked over to take another throw, Bilić was waving his arms frantically to organise his players. Even when it came to the defender getting the ball back into play, the Croatian was in his ear instructing him, pointing up the pitch and clenching his fists as he willed on success. It paid off, because despite having Smalling and Rojo all over him, Carroll was able to bring the ball down and win another free kick.

Hammers fans could sense that the final whistle was approaching, as we all clapped our hands in unison and shouted 'West Ham'. Meanwhile, the captain clocked that Antonio was in acres of space and rolled the ball out to him. After being shut down by Rooney, Antonio shielded the ball and won yet another throw, right in the corner this time.

Looking increasingly frustrated, Rooney eventually won possession back after a couple of attempts, before Mata cleared up the pitch. Ogbonna stepped in but a heavy touch allowed Rojo to clear United's lines again. Reid swung a foot at the loose ball but completely messed up his attempt as it spun behind him. Luckily, Obiang was available on the cover, smashing clear to get the ball up to the edge of United's box.

Blind chested it down and – while Hammers fans called for a handball – got the ball moving forward. The home faithful were now whistling to signal that the game should be over, but that made no difference on the pitch as Lingard was pushed back by Valencia, with Carrick ending up on the ball in the middle of West Ham's half. The United midfielder passed out wide to Rojo, who managed to evade Tomkins with his low delivery into the box, but Reid was on hand to clear it, getting himself another massive cheer from the stands.

With 94 minutes gone, United were finally in a state of desperation and Blind looked to get the ball immediately into the box from a deep position. However, the Boleyn Ground's swansong felt as important a footballing motivation as any imaginable, which Carroll showed when he sprinted back and flung himself at the ball to head it clear.

The ball flew towards Noble, who hooked it forward and suddenly Antonio was able to get in behind the United defence. Picking up possession on the halfway line, he sprinted towards the edge of De Gea's box. With Smalling and Blind for company, there was likely a temptation to run into the corner, but Antonio split the pair of them, making a break for a goalscoring opportunity. The United duo were just able to hold him up long enough for Carrick to recover and steal the ball away, guiding it back to his goalkeeper. There was an initial groan from the stands but that died down almost immediately. When De Gea passed the ball to Blind, the referee put his whistle to his lips and blew for full time, leaving relief and jubilation to fill the Boleyn Ground.

Final whistle

As the whistle blew and any tension around maintaining the result was lifted, it was clear to see how much the players cared. Reid, the match-winner, put his arms in the air while wearing a grin on his face for a second, looking as though he was trying to take in everything that had just happened. Well, Winston, you had just made yourself the last goalscorer at the Boleyn Ground and helped your team to win the final match at its spiritual home. The whistle confirmed that fact and allowed it to be placed in the history books. There were delighted hugs and high-fives to be had between the players, which were thoroughly deserved.

Looking back, Reid offers an indication of this moment's importance, 'It meant a lot to the fans, the players, coaches, chairmen, everyone associated with the club, especially as it's the last game. To be a part of it was amazing, and something I'll always remember. It meant a lot to the players as well.'

Bilić hugged his coaching team in celebration while pretty much everyone linked with West Ham rejoiced. After 112 years of history, the club was saying goodbye to the Boleyn Ground with one of the most spectacular wins this stadium had ever seen. As the fans sung 'Bubbles' once more, Bilić took an emotion-filled moment to himself, putting his fingers over his eyes for a second to compose himself, before looking on and holding back the tears. 'I think you only need to look at Slaven Bilić's emotions at that full-time whistle to really sum up how everyone was feeling,' is what David Blackmore says about this touching moment.

Perhaps some of that emotion had come from the dilemma he had faced internally regarding the stadium move. When interviewed days before the game, as part of the *Iron Men* documentary, the manager said, 'I'm having two heads for that and I have two opinions, and both of them are very strong. The first one, okay it's amazing and it's shivering to even think about going there, it's going to be brilliant. On the other hand, if I'm talking as a football manager, we are talking about a bit of positive, hostile, old fashioned atmosphere – it's Upton Park. There's no way that we're gonna get that, no matter that you're gonna have more than 20,000 extra fans, but you aren't gonna get that atmosphere at the Olympic Stadium. You hear the same that it's not only a football game, the family can spend the whole day there, you have restaurants, you have the shopping centre, the kids can play, but what about home? What about the football game? For me, if you still want a proper football game, then it's the Boleyn Ground.'

Upton Park had been filled with so much emotion throughout the entire season, and Bilić had done an incredible job of harnessing it. Using emotion in the right way was always going to be very important during this particular season. As Rob Pritchard puts it, 'Slaven's character was unique, even the way he managed, the way he spoke, the way his team played.'

Having come in at the beginning of the campaign, after leaving Beşiktaş, Bilić had shown a completely different character to his predecessor Sam Allardyce. While the former Bolton Wanderers manager had always been capable of getting results, he wasn't the most personable. He even called West Ham fans deluded and other similar terms throughout his tenure. The final season at Upton Park was about so much more than merely getting results. More than ever, it was imperative that supporters felt as close to every aspect of the club as possible. Bilić's relationship with the supporters allowed us to feel that, following his time as a player in claret and blue.

He had, for a period, been the most expensive signing in the club's history, joining from Karlsruher in January 1996 for £1.3m. Playing at centre-back, the Croatian became a popular figure during his time with the club. He even gained further respect upon departing east London. Bilić went to Everton but six months later than he could have done. The offer was there in January 1997, but the defender refused to leave, feeling a sense of responsibility to help ensure West Ham stayed in the Premier League. That was achieved as the Hammers finished two points above the drop zone before Bilić headed off to Goodison Park.

Martin Godleman has a memory of Bilić and Julian Dicks, who would become his assistant in management, from their playing days. 'When we had an in-house commentator in the 90s, I used to sit up on the other side of the ground. When you think of Upton Park, I used to have to get up on a ladder. We had finished the game – I don't know what the score was – but as the cameras were being taken down I said, "Hang on a minute, have you got the camera? Just go over to the South Bank." There at the back, Julian Dicks and Slaven Bilić were both having a cigarette; they were chatting away to each other, both in their West Ham kit, they hadn't changed.'

A passage from Bilić's programme notes reads, 'As manager and as a former player of our fantastic club, I know how much our ground means to everyone associated with West Ham United, and I will of course miss it hugely. There are so many fantastic memories and stories that we all have to tell about the Boleyn Ground – including those which we have created this season.'

There is no doubt that the former Croatia national team manager played a major part in this happening. It's brilliant to think that he and Dicks had gone from two fan-favourites in their playing days to being the masterminds behind one of West Ham's most historic victories. For everything he had done, Bilić was absolutely adored by the majority of supporters. So, if there was anyone who deserved that little moment to themselves on the sideline, it was most certainly him.

The manager wasn't the only person in the stadium feeling emotional, though, as there was a true mixture of feelings among many of the fans in the stands. On the one hand, there was palpable relief that the final whistle had been blown. Pretty much every West Ham supporter will have seen a lead squandered in the final moments more times than they care to remember. That happening on the most historic of Upton Park nights was simply not an option. As Dan Lawless puts it, 'We did it, we got through it, there's not going to be the equaliser that I was just waiting to happen, they can't burst our bubble.' While Daniel Hurley adds, 'I was so pleased we had done what we should have done: played well, won the game – won the game so dramatically as well. It really felt like if there was to be a last game it was the perfect way to do it, it was like a film but within a match.'

However, the final whistle also brought another part of the Boleyn Ground's goodbye to an end. In my mind, there had been a series of mini events that formed the big one: getting to the ground, soaking up the atmosphere on Green

Street, taking in the stadium one last time before kick-off and the game itself had all now been ticked off the list. The ceremony and leaving the ground were now the only things left, which was gut-wrenching in itself. Nigel Kahn admits, 'I got a bit emotional at the final whistle because that is it then, the game seemed to go quickly. Far too quick for what I ever wanted.' Brian Holmes says, 'It was the end of an era. I remember going there with my paper-round wages, buying a ticket, paying cash on the door. So, it's quite a few years gone, I ended up working there which is a dream job. I don't even see it as a job.'

There were some fans who couldn't think straight, completely caught up in the emotion of this specific moment. James Jones was one of them, as he remembers, 'It took a while for things to set in. Singing "Bubbles" at full time was more emotional than at the beginning. I don't think I did actually sing it. I had my arms up in the air, I was opening my mouth, but I don't think the words were coming out. Again, tears were streaming down my face. I think even then, because of what we just witnessed in that 90 minutes and particularly towards the end, I don't think it really registered that that was it: we won't see them on the pitch at Upton Park again. It was sheer emotion. When you watch a game like that with so much at stake you do lose your thought process a little bit. You forget why you're there and what's going on around you. It took about ten to 15 minutes to really grasp the whole experience and the situation.'

I vividly remember that for large periods of the match, it had felt as though there were tears packed in behind my eyes. They never broke to the surface, but the evening's emotion was impossible to ignore and that near-constant feeling acted as a reminder of how much this meant. There was some respite once the final whistle blew, but there was still an awful lot to process. It is perhaps inevitable that such extreme emotions will take their toll, and Joseph Fordham admits, 'I felt tired because it's a lot to take in and it was a long day and I think there was a feeling of exhaustion, maybe you don't know how stressed out and anxious you are watching a game of football. Even though I was quietly confident, it was like, "That's done now, we've won and we can all relax, we've given it a send-off that's good."'

'The first thing for me was that I'm glad I was here to watch it. I think that was the most important thing for me: that I was there to see it and it's stuff that I can tell my kids, my grandkids, my great-grandkids,' David Blackmore says, giving a sign of how the emotion also led to some people thinking deeply. 'There was that long delay and I didn't really know what to do, because normally for the other times you go to Upton Park you have your same post-game ritual and you're looking forward to leaving and going to various pubs or wherever you go normally or if you're going to get food. Nobody moved, everyone was still there, nobody was leaving.'

He was largely correct about people staying put, but there were some who felt the need to get home. Joseph Fordham tells a story that offers a brilliant insight into the beauty of being a season ticket holder at Upton Park, 'It was so sweet, but at the end of the game, final whistle blew, big roar goes up, the elderly lady next to me touched me on the arm and said, "Cheerio," and just left. That was it, I never saw her again. I didn't even know if she had any intention of going to London Stadium or whether she was going to call it a day. It was a really sweet full stop on five years spent sat next to someone that I barely spoke to, maybe we'd offer each other the odd crisp or bit of chocolate or something like that and say hello. But it was just a really sweet moment with a stranger. It ended it perfectly for me, it was such a nice way for her to bow out. I think of that often, actually. It's one of the things I think about most from the game, because I just wonder what she's up to now. I don't even know her name.'

This was the sort of moment that didn't need many words. In all honesty, there won't have been many people who could articulate how special that time was in the moment. That's why even James Datson didn't speak much, allowing the occasion to breathe. 'I remember when the final whistle went, there was no need for words at that time. For at least a good 30 seconds to a minute there was no need for words. Whoever was in that stadium at that time, and even the people outside the stadium would have known what happened once that final whistle went. It was like a burst of relief, but then the excitement of what they had achieved, what the players had achieved, what the club had achieved. Then, I think, the real reality of what's happened set in.' Though he did eventually say to a friend, 'That's it then, that's it, the final game. What a rollercoaster we've been on, what a game it was, we've had ups and downs, that delayed kick-off, we've had this, we've had that, but they've managed to get the win and what a way to end.'

Everybody will have had their own emotions and thought processes when Mike Dean blew the final whistle and put an end to that game. What will be the same for most people in the stadium is that their senses were heightened to the extreme, as they attempted to soak in the evening's atmosphere, digested the incredible match we had just witnessed, while also coming to terms with everything the evening represented. There will have also been plenty more attempting to prepare themselves for the extra emotion that was to come during the ceremony.

There was a break between the game and the celebration that followed it. Martin Godleman took this as his opportunity to take a rest. 'For me, my strongest memory of the game is the 30 or 40 minutes after the final whistle. Everybody and his wife was down the tunnel, and it was fantastic. I was just sitting there, I was exhausted. There are loads of pictures that people have taken of me just sitting there. It's like you've done a marathon or something like that, and I'm only sitting there reading stuff on the microphone, but I haven't made a mistake, I didn't get anyone's name wrong, which I shouldn't anyway, but you still worry that you will.'

Despite the tiredness, Martin was still able to enjoy the buzz around the tunnel, as he says, 'Everyone was really excited because there was this release that we won and we came from behind. It's so like West Ham to do that. What was really nice was the Manchester United players – who must have been a bit gutted – were part of it as well. They were still around. They didn't go straight off, some of them did, probably the ones who were wondering how they were going to get back if they'd smashed the coach up.'

There was still work to be done by Rob Pritchard, who says, 'We had all the post-match stuff to do like interviews and stuff for the website. Then you had the lap of honour and the ceremony, but I remember going down to the tunnel after the game and seeing Dimitri Payet there with his daughter and getting a couple of lines from him about the game. You think he was literally the best player in Europe that season, arguably, and I shared moments like that with someone who, at that time, was arguably the highest-profile player in the country.'

It wasn't too long after the lap of honour came to its conclusion that the proceedings moved on and West Ham were back pulling at the fanbase's heart strings.

8

The Ceremony

DUE TO the delays that preceded the game, there had been some worries that fans wouldn't stick around for the final ceremony. Martin Godleman recalls how the club used him as the mouthpiece to ensure that wasn't the case. 'I had to give an announcement to say, "Just to let you know, we will be finishing in time for you to get home, there'll be plenty of time, don't worry." People had to be reassured because they said to keep all the fans comfortable.' He did get to have some fun with the fans, though. 'I was shouting, and everyone was cheering. It is lovely. It must be like that when you're playing a live gig at Madison Square Garden or something. It was absolutely packed; you couldn't see a space anywhere. I felt like I had them in the palm of my hand, but I knew I could have said something like apples and oranges and people would have shouted back.'

There were always going to be some who didn't wait around, even if there hadn't been delays, but the announcements seemed to have worked – that and the fact that so many Hammers fans had forgotten their everyday lives. For that night, the Boleyn Ground and West Ham

United was all that mattered. This meant that there were plenty who stayed.

The ceremony turned out to be a grand affair, but Rob Pritchard recalls that it came from humble beginnings. 'Essentially, a few members of staff brainstormed the ceremony. Obviously, it was with the assistance of people who were experts in fireworks and putting on events and stuff in terms of putting the stages up and getting the taxis and all that sort of stuff, but a lot of the ideas for what actually happened came from us.' After a long wait, the ceremony began with 'Twist and Shout' by The Beatles blaring out, while fireworks were let off and flames filled the air. Judging by the cheers once the opening rendition was over, it seemed as though plenty of Hammers fans felt this had got proceedings off to a good start.

It also provided a brief moment for chief steward for the Lower West, Jacqueline Lange, to relax, as she says, 'For the ceremony, I made sure my staff were all in their correct positions before I went out front on to the pitch side, because the more stewards on pitch side, when asked, the better in case anyone tried to run on. But everyone respected the ceremony, they stayed in their seats. So, I managed to sit down where the tunnel was, enjoy the fireworks and enjoy the interviews. But then I knew I had to go again to carry out my duties, so I got to experience some of it but not all of it – that wasn't a problem because I understand that's part my job.'

Next up was a light show, accompanied by Russ Budden's choice of 'Blind Faith' by Chase and Status, featuring Liam Bailey. The stadium DJ had made a very particular choice with the songs he opted to play. 'I kept it traditional with the playlist. At the end of the season we used to do a little lap of appreciation. I remember that was always my time to shine, so I played half a dozen tracks. I remember, although I tried to keep a few of them the same, I definitely tried to play as many songs with a West Ham connection as possible. I played a David Essex song, a Chesney Hawkes song, played some Rifles, some Chase and Status because one of them is a West Ham fan, and that type of thing. So, it wasn't totally different from the others, but just a little hint here and there, just to get some West Ham stuff in there, rather than just playing generic stadium rock.'

Russ, who is a West Ham fan as well as the club's stadium DJ, discusses how much his role means to him, 'I love being part of West Ham, I love doing my job. It's opened up a lot of doors to me but also, for that last game, it was a privilege. I felt really lucky to be part of it. Whether it's been at Upton Park or London Stadium, it's always been a privilege to work at West Ham. So often in modern football it's all run by marketing departments and stuff like that. Here there's a West Ham person, who, when someone says, "We're gonna play this song," I can say, "No, I don't think so, we need to play this one." It's a small cog, but at least they know that cog is claret and blue rather than just generic.'

Russ wasn't actually the one playing the music at that time, though, as he continues, 'Literally as soon as the game had finished, we had the changeover while they were setting up and from then on, they took over. So, I could sit there and literally watched it from almost like a director's box view, which was amazing. It was nice just to sit back and watch it, so I could appreciate that closing ceremony, rather than thinking, "Oh god, I've got to turn that up or down," or getting people in my ears, which was lovely.'

There had been countless renditions of 'Bubbles' before and during the game, and there were bound to be more afterwards. As the lights ranged across the Boleyn Ground, bringing the introduction to its culmination, that song rang out from the stands yet again. That is until the lights fell on Ben Shephard, one of the two presenters for the ceremony.

Martin Godleman recalls, 'When Ben Shephard went up to do the actual thing, his microphone didn't work. He's a famous guy in his own right doing the stuff he does, and I have to say a very nice guy. He was very good, he was professional. He didn't panic and they got the mic working in the end, but I thought isn't that typical? I have to say, it was one of the very few things that went wrong on the night, because there were so many things that could have gone wrong, with the fire, the dancers, the music and the brilliant bit at the end.'

As the presenter was met with applause, he bellowed out, 'Good evening, Upton Park! Good evening, one and all at the Boleyn, what an extraordinary night. We can never make it easy, can we? What a way to sign off this fabulous old stadium of ours – by beating Manchester United 3-2. Come on, you Irons! That's how you write a Hollywood script; 1-0 up, 2-1 down, but the boys came back. Three-two to the mighty Irons. Well played to our team, what a sensational night, ladies and gentlemen.'

After taking in the crowd's applause, he continued, 'It's just the way of being a West Ham fan, isn't it? They keep you on the edge of your seats, but you keep wanting to come back for more. Tonight, that's exactly why we're here, so together we can make history and give this fabulous place of ours, the old Boleyn, the send-off it deserves – a final knees-up for the famous Boleyn Ground. Tonight, we're going to celebrate the legends, the magical moments, and, of course, you, the fans that have made this ground what it is. Tonight, we celebrate the place that we've called home for 112 years.'

With Frank Sinatra's 'My Way' playing in the background, a video began playing on the big screen that depicted the history of West Ham and the Boleyn Ground. There were shots of the stadium before the rebuilds, iconic matches, West Ham's heroes and the fans who had idolised this ground and the players who had graced it for generations. All of that was finished off with the three goals scored on the night – which all, of course, got cheers from the crowd – and Bilić's emotional moment at the final whistle.

As the video came to its climax, Hammers fans started chanting 'Irons' repeatedly, as Ben said, 'What incredible memories, ladies and gentlemen, fitting to put the goals in at the end. We've had a message from David De Gea to the Bobby Moore, he wants his ball back.' As was always going to be the case, this gag got an instant cheer and chuckle from the home faithful.

There were to be more cheers in a moment, as he introduced the former players, over 150 of them, 'some young and some not so young' as Ben put it, who were in the Betway Stand. He crossed over to Bianca Westwood by declaring, 'Bianca, I'd imagine being surrounded by all those West Ham players, you must be in your element.'

It turns out he was right, as she replied, 'Oh Ben, it's just a dream come true for me to be here tonight surrounded by our history. The West Ham family have reunited for one final hoorah to say goodbye to our beautiful Boleyn. We're all a bit emotional up here.'

There were players and representatives from across the world who had travelled from places such as Canada and South Africa. In addition, there were plenty more local lads, while the academy players who had just won the Under-21 Premier League Cup the week before were also in attendance.

Once Bianca had announced who was there, she was soon interrupted as plenty of the fans filling the stands began singing, 'Carlton Cole, always believe in your soul, you've got the power to know, you're indestructible, always believe in Carlton Cole.'

The man himself was pretty reserved, as when asked why he's so popular with the fans, the former striker responded, 'I'm not sure, maybe Twitter. I've just got a nice rapport with the fans, I've got great memories here and I'm really, really going to miss the place, I already do.'

He also struggled to identify one memory of being at West Ham, and said, 'I just enjoyed every minute of it, from the training ground, to the fans, to the people that work around the ground, to the supporters. Every time I went on that field, I gave 100 per cent. Maybe it weren't good enough sometimes, but I did try. That's how life goes.'

Next up to speak was Anton Ferdinand, who was asked about what makes the Boleyn Ground such a special place, to which he replied, 'The history here is unbelievable, but the fans are just amazing. I tweeted it this morning, there's no better place to play under the lights than here at Upton Park. It's a pleasure to play here, being here as a player and a fan, it's been unbelievable.' This was before he went on to call the fans the '12th men' on the night and referenced that 'nothing ever surprises me here'.

Marlon Harewood was the last of the former players in the stands to speak, discussing his two favourite moments at the stadium: his hat-trick on his debut and coming off the bench to score in a win against Arsenal. The conversation soon turned to why the Boleyn Ground was so special, to which he said, 'We are going to miss it because the fans made West Ham, it's unreal. As a player coming out to play on the pitch, you just want to give 110 per cent. Like tonight, it's been unreal. I just want to go out there and try to play but obviously now I can't. It's indescribable as a player because when you're out there, they give you that drive to go on and do well – and obviously as a striker to score goals.'

The former players were thanked by Bianca and the fans filling the stadium, and attention turned back to Ben on the pitch, who moved on to a new subject. 'It's the fans that make this place what it is, the 12th man for the team. Through thick and thin, your support has never, ever wavered. We want to salute the supporters from our roots in the Thames Ironworks, the pals who went to the Great War together, those that roared us to victory at Wembley, those that never ever miss a game, those who have handed down the cast-iron loyalty from generation to generation. Tonight, we're celebrating on behalf of each and every one of you. There are a few people in particular we'd like to pick out that represent everything that this club embodies.

'A very special young lady over in the East Stand, just behind me over here. She knows all about loyalty. She came here for her first game at the Boleyn in 1934, there she is 82 years on. She celebrated her 100th birthday, where else but at the Boleyn, she's even danced with the late great Bobby Moore. She is our centurion, the wonderful Mabel Arnold.' The applause for Mabel had started long before Ben had finished introducing her. As the spotlight fell on her, Mabel could be seen thanking everyone for the love and support she was receiving from all around, with most people on their feet by this point.

There were more shoutouts to be had, as a nod was given to the Belgian Irons, who had 58 season tickets in the Bobby Moore Lower. Following the applause they had received, there were momentarily boos as one person ran on to the pitch, to which Ben responded, 'Bless him, it's a night out for him, it's a night off for his family.'

The pitch invader was quickly dealt with and Ben swiftly switched the attention again, saying, 'There's one more young man that we think it's important we acknowledge tonight. A young man who has gone way above and beyond – perhaps no one has more than this young lad. He represents everything that we hold dear as a club: endeavour, support, ambition, loyalty and family. He's raised over a quarter of a million pounds for the Bobby Moore Fund, he would walk to the end of the earth in memory of his nan and Bobby. The youngest recipient of an award in the 2016 Honours List, we're very proud to have you as one of our own and it's Jonjo Heuerman BEM.' He didn't have the title at the time, but Jonjo would go on to add BCyA to his name. What he did have in that moment was a clear appreciation for the recognition, as the youngster waved and pointed towards the sky, wearing his England 1966 shirt.

With a tight schedule – especially after the delay – Ben moved the focus again, 'Over the past six decades we have come together as a club to crown our Hammer of the Year. Ask any player and they'll tell you that this is the accolade they all love, it's the one that means the most because it's voted for by us, the fans. So, ladies and gentlemen, in addition to the four winners in our current squad, we're delighted that so many past winners of the award are able to join us here this evening. To take the applause from you lot in the Boleyn Ground for one final time, they're on their way on to the pitch now. So, without further ado, here are your Hammers of the Year!'

While balls of fire were hurled into the air by the sidelines, this was the point where West Ham-themed taxis made their way on to the pitch, with 25 of the 38 award-winners in attendance. The taxis were clad in claret and blue, with a West Ham badge on the front and 1904–2016 on the side.

If you were wondering what the ex-players were doing before the cabs came out, Tony Cottee is able to provide some insight. 'As soon as the whistle went, within a minute I had to disappear down the stairs to the main reception. They then took me out the back and stuck me in a taxi. They said, "When they call your name out, you get out and you wave to the fans," which was great. We must have been sitting out in the taxi for about half an hour just talking and the taxis eventually pulled in. I don't know who came up with the idea of a London cab, but we were just sitting in the cab.'

The use of taxis to get the ex-players on to the pitch did get mixed reviews from fans. Freddie Bonfantini wasn't too impressed, stating, 'It was all strange, but at that point I was really wasted to be honest, but I thought that was a bit too cheesy, they could have done something that was a bit more subtle than that.'

No matter what people thought of the transport on to the pitch, there will be few who weren't happy to see the former players there. That point is only accentuated by the details Ben provided upon their arrival, 'We have Hammers of the Year representing our club all the way back to the 1960s right up to the present day. In 1957 we founded the West Ham United Supporters' Club and we've had a total of 38 different winners of this prestigious prize. They hail from ten different countries, our 38 includes three World Cup legends, including the three-time winners Geoff Hurst and Bobby Moore and the 1965 winner Martin Peters, and no fewer than ten FA Cup winners as well. Despite the fact we haven't got some of the Hammers of the Year we'd like to be with us, we do have 25 of our 38 here.'

Work and different commitments had meant some players weren't able to attend, while issues surrounding the build-up outside the stadium before the game stopped others. There were also those who had passed away, including Andy Malcolm, the very first recipient of the accolade, and winger Andy Musgrove, the winner in 1960. Those who were at the Boleyn Ground on the night had 7,057 appearances and 711 goals between them.

It was brilliant to see all of these former stars. If anything, it would have been nice to have even more, as Tony Gale argues, 'I think they should have had every ex-player on the pitch. I didn't agree with just having the guys that won the Hammer of the Year. There were a lot of players in the stands that the fans would have loved to see. I didn't mind because I was with my friends anyway and I'm on the TV quite a lot, so people see me. I was just sad for a lot of the ex-players who came into the country. They should have been on that pitch; they should have just introduced different eras of players on the pitch.'

Ben was the one who announced the first set of players and representatives to get out of taxis and walk over to the stage in the middle of the pitch, as he said, 'So please welcome to the Boleyn for one last time, in taxi number one, from the 60s, FA Cup winner and Hammer of the Year in 1967 and England international, the late Johnny Byrne who's represented by his daughter Karen Hunt. The bright Scot Laurie Leslie, represented by his son Grant Leslie. And also, a man we know very well indeed, a World Cup winner, he made 364 appearances, scored 100 goals, Hammer of the Year in 1965, the legend that is Mr Martin Peters.'

Seeing Peters standing and waving to the supporters, while having an umbrella held up to shield him from the rain, felt like a truly special moment for plenty of people who were in attendance. Peters, who had scored in the 1966 World

Cup Final, died in 2019, which only accentuates how lucky everybody was to have him there for this historic evening. Especially as he had been diagnosed with Alzheimer's earlier in the year.

Phil Parkes recalls a memory of the great man from that night, 'He got off the stage and started to wander off across the pitch because he had got the start of the dementia, and he didn't really understand what he was doing. His daughter, Leanne, was with him and then all of a sudden, she looked around and panicked because he had disappeared and I said to her, "He's gone, look, you better get after him." And he was going across the pitch, but she got hold of him and brought him back again. That would be the last thing that happened, Martin Peters gets lost at Upton Park.'

Bianca announced the next group of Hammers of the Year, 'In taxi two, we have Hammer of the Year in 1979, an FA Cup winner the following season, a wizard of a footballer – I used to love watching him – one of the boys of '86, the one and only Alan Devonshire. We also have the world's most expensive goalkeeper, Hammer of the Year in '81, gentle giant Phil Parkes. Then the youngest player to appear in an FA Cup final, made his debut at 17 and won Hammer of the Year in '85, Paul Allen.'

All of the players gave the fans a wave when they walked on to the stage, but Parkes had seemingly got extra enjoyment out of his moment, initially throwing his arms up into the air. It is clear how special it still is to him when he looks back, 'It was amazing, I've still got videos of that. I remember it was raining as well, which put a little bit of a dampener on it. But it was just brilliant, it was probably very apt for the whole occasion.'

Ben continued with the announcements, 'Taxi number three, his goals fired West Ham to third in '86, he was voted

Hammer of the Year in the same spell that special season, he scored 146 goals in two spells, it's the one and only Tony Cottee. Emerging from the taxi with TC, signed by the great John Lyall in January 1987, it took him just 18 months to win the acclaim of the fans in '88, it is Stewart Robson. And finally, from taxi number three, an absolute legend between the sticks, Hammer of the Year in '91, he comes from near Moscow, need I say more? Ludo!'

There was plenty of appreciation for the stopper, as chants of 'Ludo' rang out around the stadium when he stepped forward to applaud them back. Like Parkes and plenty others, Cottee was visibly pleased to be involved, with his grin growing especially wide when his goal tally was mentioned – it's something he is rightly proud of. The reaction he got from the supporters is also something he looks back on fondly, 'I got a lovely reception, it was a nice way to say goodbye.'

It was back to Bianca, 'In taxi four, he made over 500 appearances during a career spanning the best part of two decades at the Boleyn. Former captain, winner in '93 and '95, Steve Potts. He top-scored in West Ham's promotion winning seasons of '91 and '93, 70 goals for the club, Hammer of the Year in '94, Trevor Morley. And winner in 2002, he made the trip from Luxembourg to be here with us tonight, you'll remember him as a flying full-back, Sébastien Schemmel.'

Ben wrapped it up, 'Last but by no means least, in our fifth and final taxi, voted Hammer of the Year in his first season here in 2004, he scored one of my favourite goals ever scored here at the Boleyn – a belter in that classic against Ipswich – it is Matty Etherington. Alongside Matty, Hammer of the Year in the 2005 promotion back to the big time, a genius in front of the goal, the one and only super Teddy Sheringham. Last but by no means least, he loved a penalty save, just ask Jermain Defoe, he spent six seasons here, your 2008 Hammer of the Year, Robert Green.'

Everybody in the stands will have had their own personal memories attached to certain players who came out of those taxis that nobody else had – both bitter and sweet. Mine was that I had missed a penalty and then watched Sheringham do exactly the same thing later that day. It's a silly thing to remember, but the fact so many would have something like this is why bringing out the Hammers of the Year was such a special thing to do.

Dan Lawless recalls how much of an impact the ceremony's emotive nature had on him, 'I remember tears started coming out of my eyes. I was sitting there and it was really dawning on me that this is it, after all these years that I've been coming here. When you know you cannot do something again, no matter what, you can never come back here again, the emotion really dawned on me. For me, more so than what they were doing on the pitch, it was more, "This is it, now we're wrapping things up."'

Bianca remarked, 'Well, this isn't a bad squad, is it?' And there was a real sense of pride in seeing so many players gathered together who had been idolised by the fans at some point. It was also a real representation of the Boleyn Ground's history, with some of the elder statesmen lining up alongside the younger former professionals. There was also something quite poignant about some of the Hammer of the Year winners having to be represented by family members. There were some others who hadn't been revealed yet, as after making a joke about the rain and what it was doing to her and Parkes's hair, Bianca added, 'We always have room for more truly wonderful players and we've got a couple of very special ones coming up.'

Attention turned to the screen, as between them, Kris Convill, Billy Evans, Miller Evans, Mark Rushman, Steve Blowers, Karl Smith and Sue Scanlan gave their recollections of Paolo Di Canio's wonderful volley against Wimbledon in 2000, arguably the best goal ever seen at Upton Park.

'I can remember the emotion and just how green the grass was, and just everybody all together chanting, singing, the warm-up. It was fantastic. We loved him, he was the man, Di Canio, he had the swagger and the suave and he was a great player, he was my favourite West Ham player by a mile. He was a crackpot weren't he, having a sulk on the pitch because he wouldn't get a free kick, but he played with his heart on his sleeve and every West Ham fan loves a player who does that. He loved his time here and we loved him.

'I was behind Sinclair as he passed the ball, I could see the sightline of the ball. You just never could have imagined, ever, that there was going to be a goal coming from that. Then the shot, nobody could actually believe that they'd seen what he'd actually done. And you look back now and you think that's a great pass from Sinclair, but actually you thought it was, at the time, sort of a lucky hoof. As soon as he left the floor, because it was an impossible volley, you knew something special was going to happen. One of the security guards came running in and said, "I've just seen the best goal I've ever seen at the Boleyn Ground." It was only him who could probably hit that volley how he hit it. A framed moment in the history of the stadium, that was something very, very special.'

There had been snippets of that day and moment running throughout the video up until this point, but once the final words were spoken, the full clip of the goal was played. Marc-Vivien Foé switched the ball out to Trevor Sinclair who touched it down, saw Di Canio running off the full-back's shoulder and swept the ball towards him. The masterful Italian leapt into the air and us mere mortals don't have a clue how he managed it, but he volleyed it in mid-air, sending the ball soaring past the goalkeeper who had absolutely no chance, before wagging his finger to say that there was nothing more he could do.

It was at this point that the lights in the Boleyn Ground focused in on him, standing in the very spot where that absolute beauty of a volley had been struck all that time before. Of course, his name was chanted by the fans still in the stadium. The ultimate talisman looked around with pride, blew kisses and waved to his adoring fans before patting his chest. As would be expected of such a man, Di Canio was dressed to impress, and of all the things associated with his inclusion, it is this that sticks out in James Datson's mind, as it was 'typical of Di Canio'.

When Bianca asked Di Canio how it felt to be back, the Italian replied, 'It's an emotional moment. It's difficult to explain what I'm feeling now but I can say only one thing: every time I come into this place, I feel something special, of course. For me, it means heart, love, passion, loyalty and claret and blue family.'

He got a massive cheer at the end of that answer, and his name was chanted further as Bianca asked why the fans and this place are so special, to which he responded, 'Because there are no better fans than West Ham fans. They are unique, they are special and what I want to say is we're never going to forget this place and we're never going to forget these people that are magic and fantastic, and they are the only fans in the world.'

The attention was passed on to the next great man, as Bianca continued, 'It was an absolutely wonderful goal, Paolo, from a wonderful player. But he's not the only wonderful player we've got here tonight. Here's another very, very special chap.' The collective attention was on the screens again as a video came on in which Paul Cramer recalled West Ham's European Cup Winners' Cup semi-final second leg against Eintracht Frankfurt in 1976, and Sir Trevor Brooking's everlasting goal.

'My friends and I, not only did we come to West Ham together, we all played for the same football team. We were 13 at the time, so we weren't that tall – and it was all terraces then. On the night itself, the game had absolutely everything: it was midweek, it was under the lights, it was raining, the pitch was wet. Billy Bonds was in his element doing his 20-yard sliding tackles and something clicked that night in terms of the crowd. I've never heard them sing "Bubbles" in that way before. It was as if there was one voice and it was just fantastic, absolutely fantastic.

'Considering the conditions on that night, soaking wet ground, mud everywhere, for him to gracefully hold his balance and switch the ball from his left foot to his right and then – with everyone so tense – just to coolly curl the ball into the bottom corner. You couldn't make this up, stuff that dreams are made of.'

After Paul had described that moment so eloquently, it came up on the screen, on a pitch that would likely be outdone by Hackney Marshes in the current day – let alone the standards in the Premier League. Despite that, as had been described, Brooking ghosted through the middle of the pitch, cut across the defender and slotted the ball into the net, helping the Hammers get on the way to a historic 3-1 win. That was actually his second goal of the game, as he had opened the scoring with a header that went right into the top corner.

The legend was given a big cheer by the supporters as the light fell on him, standing in the same spot from which he had scored his momentous goal – as Di Canio had done with his. No introduction was needed, because, as Daniel Hurley put it, 'For fans of our club he's pretty much the man.' Bianca gave him one anyway, 'Standing in front of the very stand that bears his name – as it will in our new home – our only five-time Hammer of the Year, FA Cup final hero, he's West Ham royalty, he's a knight of the realm: Sir Trevor Brooking.'

She remarked that 'the pitch looks a little bit better here tonight', to which he replied, 'Similar weather isn't it, but there was nothing better than a wet night at Upton Park. I mean tonight as well, the script was fantastic, awesome for the last game and night games have always been special here at Upton Park and tonight was nothing different.'

He then went on to chat more about the historic night he had played a part in, 'Eintracht Frankfurt, we'd lost 2-1 out there, Graham Paddon got a 25-yard goal so we got an away goal. It was the sort of night where the place was rocking. We got 3-1 up, I'll always remember Tommy Taylor kicking off the line in the last minute because, obviously, if they'd scored a second goal we were out. So, it was a great night, pretty scary that it was 40 years ago now, but here we are tonight and another great night. So, it's great to see all of the familiar faces here.'

There was a slight applause as he concluded that answer, and he was asked whether the emotions of the night had kicked in for him yet. Brooking's response was, 'I think, when it's time to go and leave, you suddenly realise it's the last time but anyone who's been here the last couple of years, 35,000 and can see the progression of 54,000 at Stratford. It'll create its own history. More than anything, it's a fantastic reflection on everyone here that we can go from 35,000 to 54,000 in the space of a couple of months, so I look forward to seeing everyone there in a few months' time.'

There was yet another star to be recognised, as Bianca continued, 'This is a legend, we've got another one for you. As legends go, they don't get much bigger or better than this.' As the video started, Billy Bonds could be seen smashing the ball into the top corner, as Brian Williams gave his thoughts about the man and player, 'Just a very classy individual and he gave everything for the club. He was a leader in every sense of the word. He never hid, he had a personal integrity and decency about him, when you think he was actually voted Hammer of the Year when he turned 40, it's just inconceivable that anything like that could happen now. The greatest of them all is Billy Bonds, who, for me, embodies everything that this club is all about. He is West Ham in my eyes, really.'

That was followed up by Miller Evans and Brian speaking about the 2-0 victory over Cambridge United in 1993, which got West Ham back into the top tier, with Bonds as the manager, 'It was a baking hot day, the streets were packed, we had to queue up for about an hour and a half just to get into the ground. Probably because of the emotion of it was the last South Bank, it was a nice sunny day and we were up against it. We needed two goals to get promoted and get back up with the big time again. We got in the ground at ten past one and you couldn't move; it was bang to the rafters with people.

'It was back in the days of transistor radios and listening into scores from other games and the rumours were going around the terraces as to what was happening elsewhere. The South Bank was bouncing up and down for 90 minutes cheering the team on and the atmosphere was just electric.'

While this was happening, David Speedie could be seen volleying in the game's opener, before Clive Allen tapped in the second – and final – goal. For the last effort, hordes of people could be seen standing inches away from the lines marking out the pitch, ready to burst on when the ball hit the back of the net. Finally, Bonds was shown standing with all of his players and celebrating the massive victory by swinging his arms in the air, while receiving the plaudits and thanks of adoring Hammers fans.

As Brian wrote in his book, *Home From Home*, as he sat in the East Stand Upper watching this unfold, he received a series of surprised looks from those sitting around him. His son had also been sent various texts asking if he knew his dad was on the TV. Within his book's pages, Brian, who Bianca Westwood helped arrange the interview with, disclosed what the experience was like. 'The interview with West Ham TV was held in a broom cupboard. I'm serious. On agreeing to speak to the two young men who were keen to film me, I was ushered into a tiny, unlit closet and warned not to trip over the vacuum cleaner on the way to my seat.' It wasn't quite the glamorous experience many may have expected. It also turned out that the interviewers hadn't told Brian that this would be played on the big screens during the final game, so when his voice bellowed out of the speakers and his face appeared for everyone to see, he was just as surprised as all those sitting around him.

Ben, who was now with Bianca and the other Hammers of the Year on the stage in the middle of the pitch, continued to illustrate why Bonds is such an important man for the club. 'The only West Ham captain to lift the FA Cup twice, a four-time Hammer of the Year and all-time record appearance holder, six foot two, eyes of blue, Billy Bonds is coming for you. The legend that is Billy Bonds, ladies and gentlemen.' The great man couldn't be in the stadium on the night but sent his regards to the fans. This didn't stop him from getting a big round of applause from his fellow former players, as well as the supporters he had given so much to.

Looking back, Rob Pritchard is able to say why Bonds wasn't there and what would have happened if the Hammers hero had been in attendance. 'There would have been the spotlight on Billy Bonds in the directors' box, where he was when he won promotion after the famous footage of him waving to the fans from there. Unfortunately, the sheer weight of traffic meant Billy couldn't get to the ground that night, which was a real shame. To have the three iconic moments in living memory at Upton Park be recreated and then the players to appear in that area was my idea, which I'm proud of.' It was certainly an idea that was appreciated by plenty of the fans in attendance.

Ben kept the ceremony moving along, 'There are, of course, a great many other legends who can't be with us tonight, some who sadly can't make the journey to our pastures new. In particular, our thoughts turn to two of our greatest managers, Ron Greenwood and John Lyall.' The very mention of these two men, who are so respected among the Hammers fanbase for all they have done, brought about long and heartfelt applause from the stands. 'Ten years after their passing, we are delighted that we have been joined once again by representatives of their family – thank you so much for coming,' Ben added after a pause.

Throughout much of the celebration, there will have been one man plenty of West Ham fans were waiting to see remembered. That time came, as Ben went on to say, 'But, of all the legends we have lost down the years, there is one who will always be first in our thoughts and forever in our hearts.' Just before the video kicked in, one fan could faintly be heard shouting, 'Go on, Bobby', a tiny, but lovely reminder of how close supporters still felt to our hero.

Between them Ray Fuller, Donald Adams, Bill Smith, Jack Hess, Rob Robinson and Mabel Arnold described why the World Cup winning captain still holds such an important place in West Ham hearts, 'The 60s, they were good years, good years. It's been the Boleyn Ground all my life coming here since 1958, Malcolm Allison was our captain then. The traditions of the club, the great players that West Ham have had over the years. We won the cup in '64 and the Cup Winners' Cup in '65, a brilliant game, absolutely fantastic game it was.

'He was just another youth player at the time, he didn't mean too much to me. He was always in the right place at the right time, he was a unique footballer. As an English player, he was the best. You couldn't help but love him, could you? He said, "I'd love you to show me a few steps, Mabel, I've got two left feet." "Move your feet ordinary like you do at football." He said, "I kick a ball at football, I can't." We obviously knew he was a very good player and he stood out, what he went on to achieve, you know, obviously '65 and '66 and the legend that he became meant that much to you because he was our player and our captain.'

As the testimonials came to an end, one of his finest West Ham goals, scored against Queens Park Rangers in 1968, was shown for all to see. The man who wore the number six – as nobody else will ever do for West Ham again – received the ball in the centre circle. Moore strode forward with true authority, as the men in blue and white hoops stayed off him. In no time, he was just outside the box and despite three QPR men doing their best to get in front of the shot, he fired it past all of them and the goalkeeper, managing to keep the effort just below the crossbar. The greatest of West Ham icons was so greatly respected, which could even be seen in the way his team-mates congratulated him.

When the video came to its end, applause rang out through the stadium as Ben declared, 'Heroes come and go but legends never die. Ladies and gentlemen, our greatest son, Bobby Moore, represented this evening on the pitch by his grandchildren Ava, Freddie and Poppy and his daughter Roberta.' There was a clear sense of pride emanating from the family members who were representing Moore, standing in front of the stand that had taken on his name. Roberta clapped while looking around at the fans who were all chanting 'Bobby Moore'.

'I felt very connected to my father, and felt a bit of a rush of emotion, because it just brought everything back,' Roberta says. 'It felt really quite spiritual. I felt that whole evening was very moving, I felt very proud.'

Having looked back on the greats who had graced Upton Park in years gone by, attention turned back to those in the present day. Bianca went on to say, 'What an absolutely amazing season it's been. We did okay away from home as well, didn't we?' There was a big cheer every time she announced, 'We beat Arsenal, we beat Liverpool, we beat Manchester City. No problem. We had some great moments here at the Boleyn as well: Andy Carroll's winner against Chelsea. Ogbonna's last-minute winner against Liverpool in the cup. We've absolutely loved it. I think we need to now introduce the guys that made it happen this season. It's been one of the best seasons I've enjoyed for a very, very long time. So, I'd like to welcome to the stage Slaven Bilić, captain Mark Noble and the West Ham United squad 2016.'

'Bubbles' played out once again, smoke machines went into action and flames rose into the air, as had happened at the beginning of the ceremony. While this took place, the squad could be seen walking back on to the pitch with 'THANK YOU FOR YOUR SUPPORT' printed on the back of their shirts to a massive round of applause. Most of the players just looked around the stadium and took in the atmosphere, but Sakho was filming himself as Lanzini had his arm around him and Antonio nearly caught Cresswell in the face while mucking about with an umbrella.

Once they had all joined the former Hammers of the Year on the stage, Noble was called over to talk to Ben and the West Ham fans. The presenter remarked, 'You can never make it easy, can you?' As the chant 'too good for England' rang out from every corner of the ground, Mr West Ham was stopped in his tracks and wore a smile full of pride as he took in the adoration he was receiving.

Ben moved on, 'Mark, talk us through how you're feeling right now. I know it must be emotional, you're a West Ham boy through and through, you were a ball boy, you played through the academy, you've come all the way up, you've just captained West Ham to one of the most memorable wins in our last-ever game here. How are you feeling?'

It was written all over Noble's face how much this meant to him, as he replied, 'Emotional, blown away, that is the best atmosphere I've ever played in in my life by far. Firstly, I want to say, can everyone give every member of staff in this place a round of applause please?' The Hammers faithful obliged, and he continued, 'I've said it before, this is a family, this ain't a football club. When you come to this football club, you get embraced and that's how a lot of players have felt this year, who's come and signed for us. You've embraced them and we've given you something back tonight that you'll never forget and we're proud of that.'

He certainly wasn't wrong about that, as this match is seen by many people as the best one they have witnessed in their entire life. Nigel Kahn reflects that feeling, as he says, 'If I look back now on 40 years of watching West Ham over there, I was there the night we beat Bury 10-0, I was there when we beat Newcastle 8-1. Yet I look back and think the best night I had at that ground was that last night. To beat Man United the way we did, the build-up to the game, I can't say I expected that many people to be outside. I don't think it could have gone better.'

Ben continued, 'If you just want to make a nod to the board. There's been an extraordinary turnaround in fortunes for our club over the last six years. They're sitting up there watching now tonight, what have you made of it from the players' side and what do you want to say?'

Noble responded, 'Well, firstly, I'd like to say because I've been at this club so long and I've played here and I've witnessed what's gone on, we've got a board that believe in the team, believe in the manager and have put their money where their mouth is. Everyone's talking about this club moving to the next level and if we're gonna do that we're going to have to sign good players and that costs money. So, this club ain't run like a circus anymore, it's run like a proper football club and we thank them for that.'

A lot of Noble's answers to these questions have been completely forgotten. His comments about David Gold, David Sullivan and Karren Brady – especially the part about the club not being run like a circus – have endured. As Mark Gevaux says, '"This club's not run like a circus anymore," that's all I can ever remember from the ceremony. My god, but we believed him. Well, not everyone, but for those of us who did it feels like you've been part of a massive con, like something's been taken out of your bank account.'

The feelings of many have changed now, but Noble took a pause due to the level of applause he was receiving at one point, while there was more clapping at the end of the answer. Looking back at what Noble said, James Jones is able to encapsulate both how it felt in the moment and with hindsight, 'At the time, I think many people believed what he said about the club not being run like a circus anymore. There was a genuine feeling that something's happening at the football club. We've got Dimitri Payet, Diafra Sakho's scoring goals for fun, we bought Michail Antonio for pretty much nothing and he's great. Mark Noble's still bossing the midfield and Lanzini was brilliant. We really felt that something's happening, we've got a great manager in charge in Slaven Bilić and narrowly missed out on the Champions League – which is unheard of at West Ham – and we've just said goodbye to Upton Park in the best possible way and we're moving into this 60,000-seat stadium.

'Maybe something is gonna happen, maybe Noble's right. I don't think anyone scoffed at what he said on the night. I don't think anyone heard him say that on that night and went, "He's just talking rubbish." Obviously, what happens six months later and then beyond, you look back now and you laugh at what he said, and he probably looks back now and cringes and thinks, "I shouldn't have said that." But in the moment, you do say those things because you genuinely believe them and it's a shame that what's happened since this has happened because it taints and tarnishes that speech from Mark Noble, because he did make a great speech as captain of the club and as a fan. It's just a shame it's now an infamous speech rather than a famous one.'

The final part of Noble's speech was a message to the fans. The captain puffed out his cheeks as he was hit with emotion and after supportive applause from the stands, he continued, 'As I said, I've got my family here, a lot of my family up in the corner: my children, my wife. And when I say my family, that's what I mean, every West Ham fan out there is my family. Thank you and we'll see you next season.'

As Noble finished up and Ben acknowledged him and his team-mates, the players took a step back as another song about the skipper was sung, with Hammers fans chanting, 'He's coming after you, he's West Ham through and through, Mark Noble, woah, Mark Noble, woah.'

There was a wry smile on Ben's face as he said, 'Bianca, that's it.' To which she replied, while looking slightly tense, 'It's nearly time to say goodbye for the final time at the Boleyn, but to do that we need a proper send-off.' Ben continued, 'We absolutely do, now it's been an absolute privilege for Bianca and I to host this farewell party, an absolute privilege to be here and represent each and every one of you. We have loved being here at the Boleyn, we're very excited about our new adventures at the new stadium. But for one last time, from us, goodnight. But to play us out with their very own unique rendition of a West Ham classic, please welcome the Cockney Rejects, goodnight!'

Looking back on the ceremony, particularly the part centred around the players, Parkes says, 'It actually went very quickly because once everybody came out, there wasn't a long break between people getting out of the taxi and on to the stage. It was all very quick and then all too soon it was over. I just took the whole thing in, looking around at the stadium and the fans, trying to remember it and say, "This is it. We won't be back here again." I've never been back there at all. I know a few of the lads have gone back to have a look at what happened to it, but I've never been back.'

The light came down on the Cockney Rejects and their stage, but due to the delay caused by the Manchester United bus incident, there was a chance their performance wouldn't have happened at all. Their lead singer Jeff Geggus explains, 'It was the time frame because Newham Council wanted everything shut down by a certain time: for people coming out of the stadium, there can't be any noise for residents and stuff like that. So, it was in the balance for a little while, but we got the all-clear with about half an hour to go during the match that everything would be okay but beforehand it was anybody's guess. It was all pretty chaotic, but that's West Ham for you, looking back now that added to the greatness of the night.'

Punk is often characterised by rebellion and while it was nothing massive, Jeff had his own little moment, as he recalls, 'There was a little step and I remember the groundsman or whatever said, "When we start filming, don't jump on to the grass from this little stage." I said, "Well why the fuck not? You've just had 22 geezers running all over it and it's never gonna be used again, so what are you telling me that for?" So, I just decided to jump down and give it large, why not? It's just a natural thing, it's a typical West Ham thing, yeah stay off the grass.'

The Cockney Rejects clearly put everything into their performance of 'Bubbles' – and got a lot of enjoyment from it – with many of the claret and blue army singing back to them. Jeff was able put into words just how special this was for him, 'We're used to playing all around the world in front of thousands of people and we play "Bubbles" wherever we go. We've played from Australia to Chile to Brazil to Moscow, all over the place. It doesn't matter, you could give me any gig or festival around the world. That's it, just that one-off performance, that one song, to be at your spiritual home, live around the world as well. That meant more than anything because that's close to the heart.

'That's where it all began, the idea of being in a punk band and all that. It was born on the terraces at West Ham and that was our message as a band. A lot of the punk ethic, Sex Pistols and all that was pretty anarchistic and The Clash political, we were boys from the terraces and that was our take on punk, and we'd come home. Playing that is the peak of your career, there's not really anywhere to go after that.'

Once the song was over, Jeff shouted towards the crowd, 'Upton Park, you've got your own band, the Cockney Rejects, we love you, we'll never forget, goodnight the Boleyn.' As the band walked off the pitch, Jeff started a chant of 'Irons', which the fans relayed back to him. It was something that fans had done so many times when leaving and the lead singer states that it wasn't something he planned to do and that 'it just came naturally'.

However, it wasn't long until most of the lights went down and the sound of a piano slowly playing 'Bubbles' filled the Upton Park air. Then, the name that was cherished most by Hammers fans was uttered by a commentator, 'Now, Bobby Moore, they've got to go for Moore soon, a shot, goal.'

If it wasn't for that piano, you could have heard a pin drop in the stadium. Everybody in the Boleyn looked up at the screen in awe of the man who was standing with a ball under his arm, looking over his kingdom one last time. After his iconic goal against QPR was shown, Moore could be seen walking down the tunnel, hitting the ball with his fist in a way that had become so synonymous with the West Ham legend.

As focus was drawn in on the Hammers badge and the number six he had made his own, Moore slowly approached a light switch, as the piano continued in the background. His hand could be seen closing around the switch and with one movement of his wrist, all of the main lights in the stadium were turned off, leaving just some spotlights, applause and an incredibly emotional set of West Ham fans.

This fitting end to the evening had a profound effect on those in the stadium, as it encapsulated so much of what the evening had been about, all in the space of 30 seconds. David Blackmore remembers, 'There were definitely tears around me, there were definitely tears in my eyes, that was the most emotional point for me.'

James Jones adds, 'I remember one of my mates going, "I didn't need to hurt any more than I already do, that's just tipped me over the edge." It was a difficult scene to digest as a fan, because that was it then. You knew then and it made it reality, when no one really wanted it to be a reality after what we'd just experienced.'

Even though Roberta Moore will have seen the video plenty of times, she couldn't help but be swept away by the emotion of it, as she recalls, 'I remember glancing up at the seats I used to sit in as a little girl, because we used to sit in the same three seats every match. And I remember looking over there and thinking, "Oh, that was the Chicken Run over there, and I used to sweep these." I used to sweep the terraces when I was there on Christmas Day, helping the groundsmen because I was bored. And it's all those kinds of things that you think about, and you kind of think, "That's it now. That's it." So, it felt very final and that gave it its power, I suppose.'

It was at that point that it felt to some as though West Ham was coming to an end, rather than the club's time at Upton Park. In the world of some people, it actually was, as they had made the decision not to make the move to London Stadium. James Datson was able to look at that moment and see how it could play a part in the club's future, as he reflects and says, 'When the light went off, Bobby Moore did it, West Ham's most famous player of all time, a lot of people's West Ham player of all time. The most important thing in my life as a West Ham fan, commentating and working in a school, is honouring people and respecting them. We turn a light off, but we don't forget, we never forget the history. Despite the fact you're only moving a few miles down the road, you never forget your history. The light was turned off, but it's up to us to make sure it's not actually faded, like our dreams they fade and die.'

'It was a really nice touch and I think there was a suddenness to it then, it pulled on the heart strings a little bit, but then once that blacked out, it was almost like, "Oh, that's it." It was a nice full stop to the night,' Joseph Fordham adds.

After the video's hard-hitting nature, there was soon to be a lighter moment in the stadium. When the applause had begun to die down, Martin Godleman's voice rang around the ground, saying, 'Mr Moon has now left the stadium.' The applause was quickly replaced by chuckles and cheers, and Daniel Hurley laughs, 'It was such a great in-joke just for West Ham fans, nobody else would get that, but I love that they did that.' Looking back specifically at that moment, Martin also remembers, 'There was the reaction and then you're alone with your thoughts, really, because we're in the dark. Suddenly, everyone was in the black.'

Martin had relayed that message countless times, as it was used to give the all-clear after a fire alarm had been set off. There was special significance behind the words this time, though, as they were the last to be said to a packed-out crowd at the Boleyn Ground. This wasn't lost on Martin or those he knew, as he remembers, 'My friend Steve Blowers texted me on 14 May 2016 at 10.38am. "Morning MG. We were talking last night and you probably realise this already, but you go down in Boleyn Ground history as quite literally having the last word ever. Mr Moon has now left the stadium. Legend MG. Legend." I confess that, especially after Steve wrote that text, I started thinking about it and thinking, "Wow, that's pretty big."'

'Bubbles' had been sung so many times throughout the evening. When the lights came on and a sign that read 'Farewell Boleyn 1904–2016' was revealed, it was sung once again. There was just as much passion being shown as any other time that evening, with the pent-up emotion of the match and ceremony being released.

There was a strange silence at the end of that final rendition, tinged with confusion. Throughout the celebrations in the street during the day, delays caused by the bus incident, the pure spectacle of the match itself and the emotion surrounding the ceremony, it had felt incomprehensible that everything around the game could ever come to an end. It had been so all-encompassing that it was almost impossible to think of anything outside of Upton Park. But here we were, it had finished, and it was now time for all of us to leave our spiritual home for the last time.

9

It's All Over

Leaving the ground

Hope made some people think there may have been something else to come, as David Blackmore likens it to 'when you go to the cinema, and you wait until the end of the credits because there might be some bonus material at the end'. However, there was no more entertainment to be had and it was time for people to leave the Boleyn Ground.

I and many others felt an incredibly heavy weight when standing up due to the extreme emotional impact of the act. There were the older blokes behind me who I had come to deeply respect, a man who I would celebrate with who was two seats to my left and the bloke my dad always chatted to on our right. Speaking to these people had become an integral part of going to games, so it was very strange to think that we would probably never see any of them again after walking away.

I had spoken to a girl who was a similar age to me after pretty much every game for years, and while I had her on social media, I knew I would never see her again in person. That was exactly the same for the family I always walked past on my own way out. Then, as I got to the aisle, there was a man in the front row I would always briefly analyse the game with. Sometimes it was something as simple as, 'Well, that was shit, wasn't it?', but I had always enjoyed our chats no matter how short they were. Things were different this time. There was a wry smile as we discussed what had happened that night, knowing full well that it was the last time we would ever do it.

The little things like this are what I knew I would remember and miss whenever I looked back at the Boleyn Ground. Winding one fan up with the Carlton Cole song, the man behind me accusing opposition players of having 'a twisted sock' and the bloke next to me who always bet on us winning 2-1. Upton Park was filled with special people, so there will be plenty of fans who had pretty much the exact same experience getting up out of their seats one last time, with questions like 'Are you going to the new stadium?' ringing out, and a sceptical 'Maybe I'll see you there' often accompanying them.

Dan Lawless remembers one relationship built with a fan that came to an end. 'This guy and his kid were next to us all season and he's a really good bloke. We'd often chat and it was crazy because we knew we weren't going to be sitting together next season. I've bumped into them a couple of times since then. We really were a bit sad because we really got on well.'

One thing that differed between many Hammers fans was when they decided to leave the stadium. There were some who exited as soon as the action was over, whether that was due to worries around getting home or the emotional turmoil of staying behind with nothing to distract them from spending the rest of their lives without this stadium. Meanwhile, there were others who wanted to stay behind as long as they could. 'If they could have switched the lights off, they would have done. I think everyone wanted to stay and switch the lights off, just to say, "I was one of the last to leave,"' is what steward Brian Holmes says. Inevitably, there were some fans who eventually had to be ushered out by stewards, as Jacqueline Lange, the chief steward for the Lower West, recalls, 'I didn't want to because people were in tears, but we also have a home to go to and we've got control saying, "Get people out."'

James Jones's experience sums up the two sides of fans' dilemmas. 'I sat in my seat for a while. One of my mates was like "I can't deal with this" and just had to leave the ground, otherwise he said he'd never leave. I sat there for a little bit and had a couple of pictures – I took a picture of my seat number. I was just trying to take in every last detail of that football ground for one last time, just for my own memories. Eventually, a steward came up to us and said that unfortunately we've got to leave because they had to close the doors. It's mad how you get emotional about literally bricks and mortar but it's more than that.'

For Nigel Kahn, it was absolutely imperative that he was the last person to leave the Sir Trevor Brooking Stand. 'As a kid, I'd been going since my uncle got my first season ticket when I was seven. I've been going virtually regularly ever since. But at the age of 13 we used to sit in the West Stand and he said I was old enough to go on my own now. My mates were in the North Bank and generally, from then, I've always been at the north end of the ground so that's where I felt more attached to. I sat in the stand the day it opened, I was on the North Bank for the last game it was called that, then when they reopened it on Boxing Day as the Centenary Stand, we got tickets to go behind the goal that day. It was the longest ever place I sat, for that last ten years or so. So, I thought that was my part of the ground, meaning the only thing I could do that night was for me and my mate to be the last people to walk out of it.'

He had definitely gone out of his way to ensure that was the case, as he says, 'There were three people in the middle who were just sitting there, I think they wanted to be the last to leave. So, me and my mate hid out of sight, the stewards cleared them off, then we went out and had some photographs in the stand and then we left.'

As tough as it was, everyone had to make that walk up or down the stairs, into the concourse and out of the stadium eventually. There were those who made a point of thanking the stewards they would likely never see again, which meant a lot to Jacqueline. 'I was quite overwhelmed by how many people actually respected me and my job and what I did for them. You can get some jobs where once the jacket is on, they can be rude to people, but these people I've known for all that time. I know the families, children, grandpas and a lot of people came up to me to say, "Thank you for everything you've done, thanks for sorting out my ticket that time years ago, thanks for checking my little girl was in the toilet, making sure they could get out." You didn't think people would appreciate silly little things like that, but they come and tell you that they do. You know you've done a good job when that happens.'

When I walked out, I found myself touching everything I possibly could, whether it was a handrail, the seats, the walls or doors. Dan did the same and adds, 'That was the worst part because I just wanted to stay there, I didn't want to leave. I physically had to drag myself back into the concourse. I went as slowly as I could and tried to take everything in, trying to imprint everything into my memory as much as I could.'

I had wanted to see everything in its place one final time, but there were many fans who wanted to keep a piece of Upton Park to be their own. Freddie Bonfantini remembers, 'Somebody I knew was nicking the seat at the end of the game, it was brilliant. There was the whole thing where they were like, "We'll sell you the seat at the end of the season if you want it." So, a lot of the people I hang out with, the old school old boys, said, "Fuck that," and took out the seat at the end.'

Some people thought smaller by picking the sticker showing their seat number to keep, while there were others who thought bigger. The concourse had been home to a plethora of signs for years, guiding people to the toilets, the different sections of stands and concourse areas. Well, some fans decided they wanted to keep the signs and plucked them from where they had hung.

The stewards had no chance of stopping everyone who wanted to have their own memento, as Jacqueline says, 'What can you do? You can't be chasing people for that when you've got other things to be looking out for.' It was inevitable that plenty of supporters would want to take a piece of their spiritual home to have as their own – even if it was something like a toilet sign.

Everyone had their own walks they had to undertake, with the majority experiencing their very last moments in the Boleyn Ground. This eventually led to the moment they had to walk through the big doors and leave forever. Daniel Hurley recalls, 'I was in favour of the move at the time, I thought it made sense. I didn't really appreciate how much I'd miss it. I remember getting ready to leave and thanking a few of the stewards on the way out – I didn't know them, but they work there and you knew you wouldn't see them again. It was a real wrench walking out of the big doors at the bottom of the Centenary. It was genuinely quite upsetting to leave. There was this big weight as I walked out as I thought, "That's it, now I can't go back in there."'

The only thing more final than people having to walk out of the big doors after West Ham's last match at Upton Park is those very doors being locked up behind them. 'I always supervised locking up the gates once everyone had gone. We all had to do our checks to make sure the ground is completely cleared out and then, once you get the go-ahead over the radio, you lock it up,' Jacqueline says. 'That was really sad because that's the last time I'm ever going to lock that door, make sure all the turnstiles are locked up, the count numbers are taken. The last checks altogether were sad, sad times.'

She says in passing that the stewards had to make sure nobody was locked inside the Boleyn Ground on its final night. The way so many supporters were feeling as they dragged themselves into the concourse and through those doors, there will have been some people who probably would have loved nothing more.

Staying behind

Working on the final day at Upton Park will have been a very divided experience for any West Ham fan. There was a real sense of responsibility and duty for those who played their part in the evening and how it would be remembered. Even with the importance of their roles, it was only human nature for some to want to soak up the evening during a time that was so steeped in emotion. However, some of the people working that night had an opportunity that many Hammers supporters were absolutely longing for: they could stay in the Boleyn Ground for a little bit longer than everyone else.

It wasn't necessarily a glamorous point for Jacqueline Lange, but once all of the fans had left, she continued her duties, as she explains, 'We had to count the numbers and carry on our checks and security and get everything locked up, put the radios away, lock the gates up, doing our sweep for lost property and damaged seats. We still had to get that on the go, so you sort of flow into your roles and responsibilities.'

Jacqueline and her colleagues would definitely have been busy considering the number of people who took their seats with them. There are many people who might have thought they wouldn't have bothered, but she recalls, 'We all had a section to check before a game, then you do it again after. If anything is damaged, then you take down the seat number and the row and you give that to control. I write it down and usually ground staff correct it for the next game, but obviously there weren't going to be any more games. The ground was still used after for charity games and the filming of *Final Score*, so we still had to do our checks. There were internal telephones on the wall that were red or white, some people tore them off the wall and took them home, posters about West Ham, all the toilet signs were taken off, little things like that.'

Matchday programme manager Geoff Martin must have been one of the last people in the ground that night, as he explains, 'So much has to be deposited to West Ham at the end of a fixture. Then, anything over and above that, I used to have to go and pay into a bank on Monday. Can you imagine for that Man U one the amount of cash I had? We stayed there until three in the morning sorting all of the cash out. Another side to that as well, you're only allowed to pay so much money into a bank. It took me multiple trips, so I hardly left the house – there's always a chance of being burgled and it's someone else's money.'

It wasn't all work for everybody, though, as some fans-turned-employees were able to have their own moments of personal glory that they could hold on to for a lifetime. Rob Pritchard was one of those. 'I remember us walking back to the office, which was in the Bobby Moore Stand, and we're walking on the side of the pitch and it's all covered in the ticker tape and I thought, "Let's just have a run around on the pitch." I didn't have a ball or anything but just did a little doggie in the corner, just to say I had a run around on the pitch one last time.'

Darren Randolph also had his own special moments to himself after most people had left, as he says, 'I went back out on to the pitch and sat in the dugout, sat in the changing room for ages, had a walk upstairs, went back to the pitch and sat there for a while. I was there for three or four hours after the game, easy, just taking it all in because it would be the last time I was going back there. I went to the car park and there were still fans out there.'

Suri Krishnamma even had the opportunity to go into the changing rooms with the victorious players and manager. Looking back on it, he says, 'We were in there right up until there were only two or three players left and we went into Slav's managerial office, which was a smoky den. I think he's one of the only people in Britain that gets away with being able to smoke inside a building in a public space. So, you had a really smoke-filled room and beers and they were partying. We got to see that going on and I wanted to stay in the stadium as long as possible, so we were pretty much the last people out.'

There was one member of Suri's crew who wasn't quite as enthusiastic as their peers at the end of the night, though. 'After we won, we're all celebrating and I'm just being really enthusiastic about it, "Let's get this shot, let's get that shot."

The cameraman is really enthusiastic, and I see the sound recorder is going, "What time are we finishing tonight?" I suddenly looked at him and he was the Man United man, and he couldn't wait to get out of the stadium.'

As much as this night was about the match and giving the supporters an experience to remember for a lifetime, there was also plenty done to ensure the former players who attended had the best possible time. That included allowing them to all meet up for a drink after the proceedings had come to an end. 'We went down into the Ironworks Bar in the reception. It was quite packed out with all of the old ex-players,' Phil Parkes recalls. 'So, I saw a lot of the players who didn't go out on the pitch. They invited pretty much everyone who's alive who played for West Ham. There were quite a few there – some that I hadn't seen for a long time.'

Tony Cottee didn't stick around for the longest time, but he enjoyed the hospitality. 'I had my wife there and I was flitting in between the boxes and the lounges and I was genuinely doing my best to get around and see people that I haven't seen for ages. I think Ian Bishop was over from America, Trevor Morley was over from Norway, there were players coming from around the world, I think Ray Stewart came down from Scotland. There were players from everywhere. I remember seeing the great Martin Peters there on the night, there were a lot of ex-players there.

'I went down and had a couple of drinks, but you don't want to get into a drinking session with Ian Bishop anyway, trust me on this one. I went down, said hello, and went back up to the box, I'd had enough anyways. It was great to see all the old faces and I think everyone turned up with the same intentions and the same feelings as me: to celebrate what was 112 years of fantastic history. For a lot of the players, it was just as a player, but for me it was a little bit more special because I'm a fan first and foremost.'

It can only be imagined how incredible it must have felt to be one of the men in that room at the end of such a historic evening, who had grown up as a Hammers supporter, surrounded by all of those fellow players who had become heroes in claret and blue.

Roberta Moore is also among those who stayed behind for longer than most, as she explains, 'We couldn't leave because there were so many people, so we left really late. I remember actually talking to some of the Man U players. It felt sad leaving for the last time, but I also felt on such a high from the evening. It was so emotional, it was such an amazing, moving and uplifting evening that even though you felt sad, you're kind of running on adrenaline so it carries you along. There was a lot to take away from that evening, it was overwhelming. But you can't stop it happening, so you've got to just go with it, make the very best of it, and there's no point coming away in tears. I just felt incredibly proud and very touched, very moved. There was a lot to take away from it and what I took away stays with me and even the kids.'

Even the current players and staff, ex-players and anyone who had been given that extra time in the Boleyn Ground had to leave eventually. Looking back on his departing moment, Suri says, 'It became a little bit depressing towards the end because you did have that kind of feeling of coming down from an amazing event and then realising that's it, it's over. There were people crying and there were supporters hanging around the gates and tying their scarves. I tied my scarf that I've had for about 20 years. I just wrote my name on it and tied it to the gates outside the stadium. I don't know what happened to it. You're just leaving your most personal stuff, just to sort of say goodbye and say thanks.'

Phil Parkes had similar emotions when leaving but didn't stick around for long once he was outside the stadium's walls. 'Unfortunately it was pinging down with rain by that time, so you couldn't hang around outside and savour the moment and look around. You just had to get out and get to the car park, in the car and come home. But to actually leave the ground at that time and knowing that you're never going to go back, it was sad.'

Tony Gale adds, 'It was really sad. There have been times where I've been back but it felt kind of like the club had died at the ground. Our West Ham had gone, it was kind of a new West Ham. It'll always be West Ham to all of us, don't get me wrong, but a chunk of us passed away when that ground was closed. I still wish we were in it. I was one of the ones who was against the move to the new stadium. As nice as it may be, it'll never ever be Upton Park and it'll never be a football ground in its current format.'

No matter when people associated with the club had left, that very same feeling of resignation to the fact they would never return was inescapable, even if it was delayed for those lucky enough to stay in the stadium for extra time.

Walking away

Leaving the ground was hard enough for so many, but walking away from it will have been even harder in many cases. For those who hadn't been able to get into the stadium, leaving Upton Park only compounded that fact. 'I felt quite annoyed that I didn't get a ticket. I'd started to hear stories that people were taking their seats with them and trying to take a little part of the stadium with them home,' Georgina Hunt recalls. 'I remember feeling a bit gutted that I wasn't part of that, but especially because we won and there was this whole ceremony after with fireworks and I was pretty gutted that I didn't feel like I got the full experience of our last game at the stadium. It felt like I kind of got the cheap tickets version of it, which is a bit of a shame. I was still happy to be there, and at least I know that I got to go there for the last game.'

Joe England felt even more downtrodden after missing out on the experience of being in the stadium due to the ballot. 'I left during the fireworks. There were no West Ham fans there, they were all back outside the ground or inside the ground. Waiting for the tube at Upton Park, there were just regular people going about their business. To me it had a symbolism. It's the last game, we've won 3-2 and here I am alone. I could be anybody, just going home after a day's work to see the family.

'It took something out of my being that night, as a West Ham fan. I think I must have been one of the first to leave, if not the first to leave outside the gates. The fireworks went on for ages because I could still hear them at Upton Park station, but I looked and I just thought, "I'm going home," and I got to where Ken's Cafe was and I looked back and thought, "I'm never going to come back here again and it's never going to be the same again."'

Giving the stadium a last look was something plenty of Hammers fans, including myself, did. It was such a natural thing to do, as it would be the last opportunity for so many of us. James Jones says, 'I don't think I looked back until I got to Green Street and I just gave it one last glance, but leaving the ground I didn't look back, I couldn't.' While many supporters will have felt a similar way, with one glance being all they could take emotionally, I had carried on looking over my shoulder as many times as I could possibly manage without bumping into something, before making my way to Canning Town station. I would never forget the stadium and the feeling of being there, but this felt like an attempt to imprint the image of the Boleyn Ground on one of its greatest-ever nights into my brain as much as possible.

Another natural reaction when looking back at the ground is to have thoughts of both the past events that made it so loved and the future that will unfold without our spiritual home. 'It was strange. It was one of them where you have to think of what it would be like going forward, with the fact you're never going to do that journey again – whether as a player or as a supporter. So, I just walked away with fond memories of playing there,' George Parris says.

Martin Godleman is another who thought of his past experiences, as he says, 'The number of times, as an 11-year-old, I saved all of my pocket money, which I had a newspaper round for, so I could always pay for my own tickets. I went in the North Bank later, but when I was 11 and 12 my dad didn't like me going in the crowd, he wanted me to get a seat because he didn't want me to go with the "bother boys" as they used to call them. That was what I was thinking when I was walking back to the station. You suddenly realise you can have that walk back from Upton Park to the station for the last time, that walk down Green Street, the number of times I had the smell of those foetid burgers and onions.'

There was one thing that was clear for Martin though, 'It's probably my best West Ham day. I hope maybe there's one to come, maybe we win the league one day. I still think even that wouldn't beat this. This was wonderful. And if you think about it, it didn't actually mean anything in the end in terms of the season, but in terms of the ground and in terms of it being our spiritual home it meant so much. There are special moments in your life that you remember and I would say that's up there with the best ever. I would have felt it as a fan, but I always think when I do my job, even now, it's unbelievable.'

The pouring rain of that night had previously been seen as something that would never dampen the spirits of the evening and everyone who was enjoying it. Although, at this point, it felt fairly fitting – almost like pathetic fallacy for some. Matt Datson remembers his sombre emotions, 'It was very, very sad because it was somewhere that I loved going because of my love of West Ham and to know that I've done that for so many years. Anybody that knows me, if they knew West Ham were playing, they would know where to find me and I was actually quite emotional walking out of the gates. I was quite upset by it really.'

Daniel Hurley adds, 'I knew I'd never go to that area again. So, I met with my dad, who was there but sat in a different bit to me. I think we got in his car and I was like, "Well, that's that then." Although we knew we'd be going to West Ham again the following year, it did almost feel like you weren't at that point. It was like the chapter had ended.'

If there is anyone who would feel the evening's emotions after the game, it is probably Dan Lawless and the West Ham Fan TV team, who were outside the stadium doing fan-cam pieces. 'For the most part, people were emotional, people were overwhelmed and talking about how great the game was. Some people were unhappy and didn't want the move to happen. If that was any other game, you'd come out with no mixed feelings at all. You'd come out completely over the moon, buzzing, going to the pub talking to your mates and you wouldn't be able to sleep that night for the happiness,' Dan says. 'But because of the fact that everyone knew they can't go there again, there were these real intense mixed emotions. I think that's how it was for everyone. To know that we've won in the most spectacular way on the night that you want to win like that, but we can't come here again and it's all going to be knocked down, that created a real conflict, I think, in a lot of people.'

This is West Ham, though. Even at times where things can seem too hard to take, there is often something that can cheer us up – even just a bit. James Jones found that in his fellow supporters. 'We spent the journey home on the train reminiscing but also laughing at fans walking along with random memorabilia that they'd nabbed, like the toilet sign and signs off the walls and people were walking down the road with it all over their shoulders one by one, which was good fun.'

Russ Budden wishes he had taken a memento of his own. 'I didn't nick anything and thinking about it we still had a tape deck that no one used, but I could have put that away. They sold the score boards and stuff like that and it's one of those big regrets. I came out thinking, "I wish I could have nicked something." I'm just too honest for my own good.'

Everyone had their own plans of what they would do after the game. Some wanted to go to the pub but found that it was too late by the time they had got away from the ground; some managed to find somewhere to have some drinks, others stayed with relatives to save long commutes due to how late the game was, while others headed straight home.

Following the emotions of the evening, there was nothing that was going to keep Jeff Geggus from having a drink. 'Once my performance was done and I got off of that pitch, I wanted to get out of there because I knew it was locked down. I wanted to get into the pub and down as many pints as I could to celebrate the night and celebrate all of those years, because I was lucky enough to support a great team like West Ham and be over there. There's the family and all the ups and downs, it's been a great roller-coaster. I never managed to speak to anybody after my performance, I just headed out of the ground and walked my way to the boozer.'

David Blackmore also went to the pub, but he was standing across the road from the Victoria Tavern speaking to the BBC, as he recalls, 'I was trying to think how to sum up my emotions and try to talk about the processes I was going through and trying to work through all that in my head before I spoke to them. I haven't got a copy of that interview but if I did, I probably just sounded like gibberish, I think.'

Having missed the final trains back to where he lived, David had looked at getting buses but realised it would have taken ages and thought of getting a taxi before coming to the conclusion that it would cost an extortionate amount. So, he did what many others will have done that evening and turned to a family member. 'I went to my sister's and just buzzed on her flat until she eventually answered. It felt like a lifetime before she answered. I slept on her sofa that night.'

Unlike David, I didn't have a back-up when I realised there weren't any more trains running. I had already managed to reach Waterloo, but had missed the last train back to Bournemouth by ten minutes. This meant I had no way of getting back unless I wanted to get into a taxi and pay out about half of my student loan – even getting back to my mum's place in London would have cost a lot. So, having been turned away by various hotels and being told I wasn't allowed to wait inside the station, I ended up sat on the steps of Waterloo station armed with a bag of McDonalds until I was allowed back in at 5.30am.

There had been so many points throughout the day and night that I'd been concerned the whole experience would come to an end too early for me to accept. Well, if nothing else, my time on those steps certainly ensured that wasn't the case. People came and went, but after I had taken a walk around and seen the London Eye, there were three of us who stuck it out until the station doors re-opened. An elderly man joined me who had also been at the game, before a gypsy traveller came along who had lost his mates on a night out and couldn't have cared less about football. This sounds like something my extremely tired mind might have conjured up after 24 hours that were full of extremes, but I can assure you it's true. It was also very surreal, making it a strangely fitting way to end what had been one of the most memorable days and nights of my life.

There were plenty who found their own beds, though, and Martin Godleman remembers the joy he felt before hitting the hay, 'It was that feeling when you have one of those days in your life where everything goes right and when you finally go to bed, it's the first time it suddenly hits you what just happened.'

Aaron Cresswell felt just as content, as he recalls, 'I had my dad down, my little brother, my dad's mate and by the time we got home we were absolutely knackered. I remember we got home and we were all speaking about the game. It was the stuff dreams are made of in terms of the pressures of the game, the way the game went, to see all the old legends there. I remember looking into the crowd and seeing 50-year-old and 60-year-old men crying their eyes out. It was special and it'll live with me for the rest of my life.'

No matter whether people were in their own bed, staying with someone else or making do like I had to, one thing we all will have had in common is that we were reliving everything we'd witnessed throughout the day, trying to process it all.

The morning after the night before

It was 6.30am by the time I finally got the train back to Bournemouth, and 9.30am until I was back in my room in student halls to get some much-needed shut eye – luckily, I didn't have any lectures until five in the afternoon. By the time I had even re-started my journey back, David Blackmore was up and out of bed to make television appearances, as he recalls, 'I had to get up at six, because I was speaking on the Vanessa Feltz show off the back of the violence that there'd been the night before. Then I was on my way back after being on the show and I remember I had to miss two or three tubes at West Ham to go back heading towards Waterloo because I was still waiting to be put on hold to Vanessa. I remember having a blazing row with her over West Ham and the fans. She was saying a lot of things I didn't think were particularly fair about our fans, and especially not fair given some of the facts – especially that West Ham had said to Man United to be early because it's going to get busy and how they ignored all of that.'

It didn't stop there for him, though. 'Then when I got back all the way, I'd literally just got out of the shower, the Victoria Derbyshire show had rung me and said, "Can you come into the studio like now?" So, I got in a car with them to get to their studio and the traffic just wasn't moving near where I was staying at the time. So, I had to hop out and get on the train and I just made it on time to then defend West Ham fans again.'

The club had just witnessed one of its greatest-ever matches, but the Manchester United bus incident from before the game was what widely dominated the headlines. Looking at the articles published across the mainstream press the morning after, the *Guardian* reported how 'West Ham party turns sour' and the *Telegraph* stated that the celebration was 'overshadowed' by the incident. Meanwhile, Eamonn Holmes was left to apologise on Twitter after telling Sky News, 'This is going back to the 70s and 80s and everything you were seeing that was bad about Hillsborough, for instance.'

There are often two completely polarising opinions of West Ham's fanbase from those who look at the club from the outside in. There will be those who see the Hammers as their second team, feeling that those supporters who adorn claret and blue week in week out are part of a family club. 'The West Ham Way' and a desire to play entertaining football that's easy on the eye can also contribute to that.

Then there are those who still link the Inter City Firm and hooliganism to West Ham. The ICF were mainly active in the 1970s, 1980s and early 1990s, with Cass Pennant among the most famous of the firm's members. However, there has still been an attachment to that side of fandom when it comes to West Ham, as I have memories of Bristol City's away supporters chanting, 'Where's your famous ICF?' on Green Street after a game in an attempt to intimidate Hammers supporters leaving the Boleyn Ground. This comes after the calling cards that read, 'Congratulations, you've just met the famous ICF'. Popular culture has also helped to keep this link alive, with films like *The Firm* and the *Green Street* trilogy having become well-known representations of West Ham supporters as hooligans.

It seemed as though the incident that had occurred outside the ground transported the media straight back to that time, with Hammers fans being branded as troublemakers and thugs by many. 'We are aware that there were some supporters outside the Boleyn Ground who didn't act in an appropriate way,' a club statement from West Ham read. 'It was an extraordinary night full of extraordinary moments in front of extraordinary fans, 99 per cent of whom behaved impeccably and were a credit to the club. We have already had thousands of tweets and e-mails from fans to say how proud they were to be a part of such a special evening in West Ham's history.'

However, the club said the behaviour of some fans was 'not acceptable' and stated that it 'will work with the police to identify those responsible and ban them for life'.

Karren Brady took to Twitter to have her say. 'The events in the stadium last night were incredible and it would be a shame if the actions of a mindless few outside overshadowed them. Their behaviour was unacceptable and won't be stood for. But my overriding memory will not be of them but of a fitting farewell to the Boleyn.'

While many Hammers fans have grown to have a disdain for Brady, plenty of us held the same sentiment as the vice-chairman. The bus incident was undoubtedly something that had to be dealt with and addressed, but it wasn't the only thing that happened that night. As I walked around university the day after, I had wanted to do nothing more than to tell everybody I knew about just how incredible the final night at Upton Park was and re-live it as much as possible. Of course, that was after watching the highlights again pretty much as soon as I got up.

I was far from alone in watching the game back, as Martin Godleman re-lived it without the pressures of being the announcer. 'I remember watching the whole thing the following day – luckily, I wasn't going to work. I was sitting on the sofa watching it from beginning to end. I just sat there, didn't say anything, just got to watch it and it was almost like I hadn't been there, like I'd missed the game and I was on catch up.'

Russ Budden did exactly the same thing. 'The whole game was just a blur to be honest. It was a surreal day and it's one of those games – I don't do it often if at all – where I got home and then watched it all over again. I also watched it the next day as well, again, not really taking it in. It was very strange.'

There was simply so much for the senses to take in during that 90-minute period and the hours that came either side of it. That made it almost impossible to digest everything that was happening in one go. It was a completely overwhelming experience for so many that there was almost a hangover in getting to grips with the smaller details. As Joseph Fordham mentions, 'I think what came was hard to process throughout the day. It's something quite monumental in your life as a fan and I think it was probably something I was only going to get a real grasp of in hindsight, rather than being aware of it in the moment.'

Phil Parkes says one thing was clear, though, 'There were a lot of people, obviously the likes of Bobby Moore, John Lyall and Ron Greenwood who would have made it extra special if they were there. They were sorely missed, but it was a good evening. I think they did the old ground proud, gave her a good send-off. It's just a shame that West Ham aren't still playing there, I think.'

For some, they may have felt as though they were dreaming the day after, with the Boleyn Ground's incredible final night infiltrating their normal life. Daniel Hurley recalls his strange moment, 'I remember going back home the following day, going through Canary Wharf to get back to Waterloo and one of the cabs that they used in claret and blue was parked picking people up. It was just there, they obviously took people's cabs and painted them up. It was legitimately the exact same design that they'd been going around the pitch with and he was just picking people up – I would have got in it if I had anywhere else to go. I genuinely couldn't believe my eyes because I didn't think they were real cabs at the time, I thought they'd just done them. They've clearly just paid a few West Ham fans to change their cabs.'

Seeing things pop up on social media and speaking about the game would have been more than enough to keep the game at the forefront of the minds of many Hammers fans, let alone encountering something that played a massive part in the ceremony. Then there was the t-shirt and bracelet that had been handed out for free at the game, the match programme on the table and ticket still in people's wallets or purses. There were constant reminders of the once-in-a-lifetime experience that we, as fans, had all just been a part of. Even without these physical reminders, it would have been impossible to forget where we had all been. In fact, due to the nature of what had gone on, there would have been small fragments of information that had been lost among the complete and utter madness of the event popping up in the minds of many as the day went on.

Even when I've been conducting interviews for this book over four years later, phrases such as 'I'd forgotten about that until now' have not been completely uncommon. Throughout that following day, each time something new came into my head I felt the immense sense of joy or the wave of emotion attached to it all over again, and I'm sure there are many who had the exact same experience.

Going back

The longer time has gone on, the more I have longed for an opportunity to go back into the Boleyn Ground. Go through the turnstiles. Walk up and down the concourse.

See that pitch. Sit in my seat. Look around at the banners and everything else. Maybe even sneak down to take a look at the places behind the scenes. I'm far from alone in this, as there are so many out there who desperately miss the great stadium. While not even the most privileged of people could magically make that happen now, there were some who went back before it was knocked down.

There will have been various reasons for this, including work, the filming for *Final Score* and the auctions that were held at the stadium. Joseph Fordham is one of those who returned, and he recalls his emotions on doing so, 'I've been a couple of times, me and Will walked around, through the stands, opened up store cupboards, went in the changing rooms. The security guard let us in and we had a really good walk around, found some burned lamb chops in the players' lounge. We heard a fridge whirring in the lower stand of the Chicken Run, we thought we'd see if there was a drink in it because we were thirsty, opened it up and there was just a square of cheese in the bottom.

'As I knew I'd be going back, it didn't register that it was the end during the game, for many people it was the end, but I essentially still had work to do. One of the times, a film crew was there because there was that Pierce Brosnan movie, so some of the rooms were blocked off for crew, but in the lounges at the front there were just so many glasses everywhere. We were just going in everywhere, looking in storerooms, there was so much stuff everywhere. I got my brother's seat for him, asked the security guard if he could get it for me, he said, "Ask the window cleaner and he'll be able to help you." He had some tools, so he dismantled the chair for me, even the steel poles, and my brother has reconstructed the whole thing. So, I walked down Green Street with the chair and some dirty, greasy poles in my hand.

'Leaving knowing I was coming back didn't really hit me. It hit me when I was in there, though, I started to look up at where we used to sit, then I started thinking about where I first used to sit with my dad back in the 1993/94 season. I didn't start going over there until I was about ten because I couldn't afford it really. My brother started working, so he could pay for his own ticket so I could go. It started coming back and I started to feel quite melancholic because you begin to think how that's where it started. I started to remember my first game, what the pitch looked like, where was the pitch in comparison to where it is now because it moved a little bit … just to remember those things. What really hit me is I remember looking at the pitch, and it was all overgrown, the lines have started to fade out already – this is in July, so it's been about six weeks since the game and it hasn't been touched since.

'I was looking at where I used to sit and started thinking about those early games with my dad and the fact that it was getting knocked down felt like another link to him was going. He's not around anymore, he died in 2001 and I think the fact that I could just go there and have that access to those memories was subconsciously quite comforting. I remember thinking this is going to be gone, that's essentially a part of us, a part of him that was going, which is not the case really because I can still remember those things. The memories don't go, but it's nice when you've got somewhere to remember those things, but now that place isn't there anymore. There will have been a lot of people leaving the ground on 10 May thinking the same thing. It was just a bit of a delayed reaction for me I guess, knowing it was the last time.'

It would be almost impossible not to think about memories that had developed at Upton Park when in the stadium for the last time, especially without the distraction of all the other fans and a scintillating match. Tony Cottee also took his chance to reminisce further, 'I was involved in a charity football day about a week after the game. I went with my friend and when the football day was finished, we walked around the pitch together. We took pictures of me standing on the six-yard line where I scored against Spurs on my debut, then pictures of me in front of the Bobby Moore Stand, in front of the Chicken Run, in front of the West Stand, standing on the North Bank where I was stood as a seven-year-old and all the things that were special to me. It was only me and him in the ground because the football event had finished. We just walked around the empty stadium and took all the photos which I've got on my phone. They're just memories for me really and memories for him as well – where he stood and what he'd done as a fan. So that was really nice to do.

'Then the last time I went to the ground was when I did the filming for *Final Score* and I had to go there – they blew the stand up and all that sort of thing. That was the last time I went to the Boleyn and that was different because it was sort of working behind the scenes. So, I had some quality time where I obviously had the match itself, I had the week later and then I had the filming, so it was nice in my own way to sit and think of it.'

There were also three auctions held with a plethora of items on offer, including goalposts, stadium signs that hadn't been taken, a bubble machine, the manager's dugout seat, a small turnstile, a fax machine and a bath tub from the home dressing room. As is perhaps expected when money is involved, there wasn't the same emotion when Nigel Kahn attended one of the auctions at the stadium. There were plenty of others bidding online, but Nigel says there were a couple of hundred in the room and admits 'it had no real atmosphere at all'. He adds, 'The prices paid were beyond silly for me. I went with £500 and didn't buy anything but managed to get some items at another online sale.'

It wasn't always possible for people to get into the stadium, but there are those who made sure they looked at it again while they still could. After all, once it was gone, photographs and memories would be all we had left. Mark Gevaux recalls, 'I went back once every few weeks to go and have a look. Then when you see that first board go up and half the stand is coming down, that was the worst part, to see it actually come down. Leaving the stadium was quite sad, but to watch them rip it down, that was hard. That felt like losing a member of the family then. That's how it was, everything's gone forever.'

10

The Aftermath

FOR MANY who went to Upton Park on 10 May 2016, nothing else in the world mattered. Time had paused, purely for West Ham United and this club's spiritual home. It didn't feel like it at the time, but there was a point where the world – footballing and otherwise – was going to carry on, leaving this historic night a memory. People had to go to work or study and West Ham kept playing football. It's safe to say that the aftermath of the Boleyn Ground's farewell was eventful.

All of the emotion of that night must have been physically and mentally draining for the players. With this in mind, perhaps it was inevitable that they would be unable to reach that same level of performance for the final game of the season, having travelled up to the Britannia Stadium.

After scoring the equaliser against United, Michail Antonio got a brilliant opener against Stoke City. Manuel Lanzini's corner was headed back into the danger area by Winston Reid, who found Antonio's chest. Antonio brought the ball down and swivelled marvellously to find some space before smashing his shot into the net – with a Stoke defender's efforts to clear off the line proving futile. It wasn't to be the Hammers' day, though, as Giannelli Imbula and Mame Biram Diouf scored a goal each to hand the Potters a 2-1 victory.

After everything the players had given us a few days before, and throughout the rest of the season, it was difficult to hold too much of a grudge over this result. However, losing did mean that the Hammers came seventh in the league, so they entered the Europa League qualifiers for 2016/17. Victory at Stoke would have taken them past Southampton and straight into the group stages.

As much as a friendly against Juventus was marketed as London Stadium's big opening, the first Hammers game played at the arena was actually the Europa League third qualifying round second leg against NK Domžale. It was a competitive fixture by name, but in reality, this felt just as much of an exhibition as the friendly that would follow it. Singing 'Bubbles' felt a bit underwhelming to me compared to Upton Park. It was also a pretty easy night for the players on the pitch, as Kouyaté bagged a brace and summer signing Sofiane Feghouli scored his first goal for the club, securing a 3-0 win.

Matt Datson may not have been able to see the stadium, but he was able to feel the difference to Upton Park. 'I was surprised by how vast and massive the London stadium is to what it was like at Upton Park. I couldn't understand the severity of the size. My brother and Tony had both done their best to describe the London Stadium to me and I've got my own picture now of what that is.'

The move had been touted as West Ham making progress so many times, but fans being able to judge the stadium for the first time was the most important thing. There had been plenty of promises, with the club having the largest digital screen in Europe often being mentioned, while there was plenty of talk about the stands being brought much closer to the pitch. That's before moving to 'the next level' was constantly mentioned. In reality, this meant putting up temporary stands over the other ones, with the scaffolding still on show for quite some time.

Freddie Bonfantini described his first experiences of being in the stadium, 'I admit I was sold on the idea that you're leaving, you're changing your personality, you're not gonna be that crappy, rough east London football club anymore. We're gonna move on and we're going to become something else. For me, it was the first match, the second match, the third match, when I saw the reality of it, I was so devastated. I absolutely hate going there. I hate the walk from Stratford, I hate the pubs in the area, I hate that we're on an island, I hate that we're in an athletics ground. Every year, I go through the whole season ticket renewal, but I don't want to be there. I just don't think it's ever going to happen. There's nothing about that place that I like, not one thing.'

The stadium wasn't the only outward-facing part of West Ham that had changed. The club's badge had as well. The castle that had adorned the crest – linking to the Boleyn Ground – was removed. In addition to that, the word London was added to the bottom of it, with West Ham's official website stating that the change was 'in reference to both the club's move to the Olympic Stadium on Queen Elizabeth Olympic Park and its growing global standing'. This seemed to further annoy plenty of Hammers fans, playing into the idea that this was becoming more of a club for tourists than the hardcore supporter. One very nice touch was that the hammers, which had always been prominent, were now inscribed with TIW for Thames Ironworks.

The walk from Stratford station to London Stadium is something that many West Ham fans came to dislike. At

Upton Park, there was always a sea of claret and blue as fans sang while walking down Green Street, looking forward to another game – even if there were plenty of times where they were let down on the pitch. Fans would be able to buy some bits from stalls, pick up a fanzine and get their pre-match food from cheap and cheerful shops or vans. There's hardly any of that now. There have also been other annoyances over the years, such as the time it takes to get out of the stadium, as well as the fact West Ham have been unable to play at home on Boxing Day.

Mark Gevaux, commonly known as the Rib Man, is one of the very few who has made a successful move from Upton Park to London Stadium. When speaking to him, it's easy to see why many others didn't make it. 'I fought for three years to get in there. From the very first moment we knew we were going to be leaving, I started looking into getting in there. The hurdles and the high jumps they put in front of you are incredible. It's like they didn't even want any of us there and that's how it felt.

'You had David Gold in *Iron Men* telling the sweets guy, "We'll do everything we can to get you outside"; this, that and the other. They've got no control over it, none at all. The only reason I got there was because apparently when they did the contracts and they said about moving people to the stadium, my name was in that. They said, "We've got to move people like the Rib Man," and yet it seemed like I was the only one from that place who came. All the burger vans from Upton Park wouldn't go because they've got their own burger vans at the stadium, they've got their own contract. It's difficult to break into it. They won't even have the flag-sellers and the badge-sellers. They said they were going to make the bridge like Green Street, but they didn't do anything for us.'

Despite his struggles, there is still the sense that it's been worthwhile for Mark, who adds, 'I feel proud and I felt like I earned my place to be in there. I fought for three years. I went to so many meetings and the amount of visits I had from their health people to come and check it out. It's crazy, the hoops you have to jump through just to get in, but I did it and I'm glad. For me, that was another step to being the Rib Man of West Ham, you can't be the Rib Man of West Ham if you're not outside the stadium, can you?'

When you walk out of the station, there are signs to show where Westfield shoppers should go and others directing West Ham fans. At times it feels like the area wants the status of having the club but doesn't want the supporters interacting with anyone else. Joe England had felt ostracised by David Gold, David Sullivan and Karren Brady before this, largely because of the ballot that had robbed him of the chance to watch the Boleyn's swansong. This sense only worsened, as he explains, 'I was already cynical about London Stadium because of what had happened. It's about a bond of trust. They said this is a world-class stadium, well, you've already broken my bond of trust with you. When I got there and saw what the stadium was like, I despised them even more.'

Mark initially felt differently to Joe, but now shares a similar view. 'I kind of bought into the dream that we were sold. I was behind it and thought this could be the making of West Ham, this could turn us into a top club. Obviously, as things have transpired since, we all know what's happened. We all know how we feel now. We feel like we've been lied to, it just doesn't feel good at the moment at West Ham. Something's got to change, we can't carry on like this.

'It could've been done so differently. If they did it the way they said they were going to, we would have been a lot happier. Maybe some of the people who didn't want it would have turned around, but I think all it's done since is turn the people like myself who was behind it back around. We can't go back, but I do feel like we were lied to. Not being able to have games on Boxing Day and that kind of thing, it's a bitter pill to swallow.'

There were also plenty of aspects about the stadium that annoyed many Hammers fans once they got inside, especially at the beginning. A lot of them were deemed to detract from the West Ham identity. Some supporters bemoaned the selling of popcorn, with remarks like 'I didn't realise I was going to the cinema' often being heard. People were turning up to games in the shirts of other clubs. Fans had been told not to stand up during games, which led to retaliatory chants of 'stand up if you love West Ham'. This could often cause arguments between supporters as there were no designated standing sections. There were full-on fights between West Ham followers during a 4-2 loss against Watford, while there were also clashes with Chelsea supporters and incidents in some other matches.

There were also various complaints about the stewarding. Brian Holmes, a steward who moved over from the Boleyn Ground, says it was 'hell' working at London Stadium in the early days, as he states, 'Upton Park was family, but London Stadium is hard work, it's just abuse now. "That's not my job" is all you used to hear from other stewards, "That's nothing to do with me, that's to do with them." No one was pulling in the right direction and that's what the fans were picking up on. They initially brought in non-footballing stewards and that was the problem.' He does indicate that things have got much better as time has gone on.

While it wasn't enough to make the move completely seamless, Russ Budden points out that it wasn't all change, 'Obviously, some of the people that worked there don't anymore. Fortunately, the people I work with, they brought them all across to the London Stadium, so my floor manager and my sound guy and Martin, the announcer. I'm very fortunate that we still work together, so it wasn't like a goodbye.' There were small switches to be made, as James Datson recalls, 'It took me a while to get used to not saying, "Welcome to Upton Park, the Boleyn Ground," when I'm saying the London Stadium.'

Looking specifically at stewarding, it is easy to see why even the honest ones struggled when Brian speaks about the early stages, 'There was no organisation because we were just told to turn up on the matchday, find your way around and work it out because they didn't get the keys until late. It was just learning on your feet, trying to work your way around the stadium. It took us about three or four games to work out all the shortcuts. Upton Park was so nice because you knew all of the rat runs and how to get around the stadium, but you go to a new stadium and it's like an away game. They're going, "Right, quick, learn how to get around, learn where the lifts are, where all the first aid is, where the toilets are," because these are the questions you get asked. We had maps, there was nothing to start us off with.'

There were also promises broken in terms of the club's transfer policy as West Ham were linked with big-name strikers throughout the summer window, with one of those being Olympique Lyonnais striker Alexandre Lacazette, who eventually joined Arsenal. Meanwhile, the Hammers got Simone Zaza – best known for an embarrassing penalty miss in Euro 2016 – and Jonathan Calleri on loan from Juventus and Deportivo Maldonado respectively.

The latter of these signings played a big part in West Ham's first massive embarrassment at London Stadium, which came in a Europa League qualifier against Astra

Giurgiu. Having been knocked out by the Romanian outfit the season before, it seemed almost unfathomable that they could be humiliated by them again. Having drawn 1-1 away from home, they went and lost 1-0, with Calleri missing two gilt-edged chances to beat goalie Silvia Lung Jr. Former Paris Saint-Germain and West Bromwich Albion midfielder Filipe Teixeira was the only man who got the ball in the back of the net that night.

Then there was the whole Dimitri Payet debacle, which saw him leave London Stadium. The Frenchman had been one of the most prominent heroes in West Ham's final season at Upton Park, but he was to be the club's first big villain at the new home. Plenty of fans couldn't believe what he had done to the club that had helped him get into France's squad for the 2016 European Championships, due to how much he had elevated his reputation in east London. There was disgust about the way the former talisman had conducted himself, and disappointment that one of the club's greatest talents for years had been lost.

Despite the many frustrations that term, things didn't actually end too badly in terms of results as West Ham finished 11th in the table, and one big positive to be had was the emergence of Declan Rice. This came after he had won the Dylan Tombides Award in 2015/16, which had actually earned the then 17-year-old a place in the matchday programme for Upton Park's final game. It wasn't to be known when he came on for the end of the Hammers' final match of 2016/17 against Burnley, but this was someone who would stand out in the early years at London Stadium. There has been an immense feeling of pride shown towards the midfielder, who has dealt with adversity in his short career having been on the receiving end of a backlash after switching his national allegiance from Republic of Ireland to England. By the age of 21, he had already played over 100 games in claret and blue, as well as becoming an England regular, while he has often been linked with big-money moves away from London Stadium.

At the end of that campaign, there had also been a feeling among some that they were going to give the club the benefit of the doubt, considering the move to a new stadium. However, that same treatment wasn't afforded to the players, staff or board. Slaven Bilić was to find that out in November 2017 when he was sacked, with the Hammers in the relegation zone. A shocking performance in a 3-0 loss against Brighton & Hove Albion certainly didn't help his cause. An equally toothless display in a 4-1 defeat at the hands of Liverpool proved to be the final straw. The club's statement after the manager's departure read, 'The chairmen and board of West Ham United would like to place on record their thanks and gratitude to Slaven and his team for their services over the past two-and-a-half years, but believe a change is now necessary in order for the club to move forward positively and in line with their ambition.'

The board had also taken a dig at players they had signed, as David Sullivan told the *Guardian*, 'I'm very involved with physically bringing in the players,' before stating, 'I'm not involved in the strategy. The manager said he wanted [José] Fonte from Southampton and [Robert] Snodgrass from Hull. My kids begged me not to sign them.' It is quite sensational that the West Ham co-chairman was willing to openly say this when Fonte was still at London Stadium and Snodgrass was still technically a Hammers player, as he was halfway through a loan spell at Aston Villa when the article went out. 'Everyone tagging me in this like you're all surprised. Thanks for your support MR CHAIRMAN' was Snodgrass's response on Twitter. It is to the midfielder's credit that he still managed to come back from that loan and make a positive impact for West Ham, earning a lot of respect from Hammers fans.

Ambition was the key word when the board were pitching the move, but there were plenty of fans who felt it had disappeared once West Ham actually arrived at London Stadium. Board members blaming others didn't change that. Therefore, supporters will have picked that word out when reading the statement after Bilić's sacking. Hiring David Moyes, a man who had failed miserably at Manchester United and Real Sociedad before getting Sunderland relegated, didn't exactly feed the fans' appetite for excitement.

There were some good games during the Scotsman's first tenure at London Stadium, with the victory over Chelsea bringing joy, while a 3-0 win over Southampton was arguably one of West Ham's greatest performances at their new home. Marko Arnautović was key to both of those displays, bagging three of the four goals scored across the two games, and became a popular figure after Moyes had moved him from the wing into a central area. The Austrian provided plenty of other moments to remember, including the time he did the Irons sign away against his former club Stoke, as well as his cheeky skill and emphatic finish against Huddersfield Town.

However, things weren't always great under Moyes's leadership, and that came to the forefront during a 3-0 loss against Burnley in March 2018. Ashley Barnes scored the opening goal of the game, while Chris Wood got himself a brace after coming off the bench, crowning a win over a West Ham side that wasn't at its best. However, that is not what the day will be remembered for, as fans took a stand against the owners while the match was still going on. First of all, with the score still at 1-0, one supporter ran on to the pitch and was angrily pushed over by Mark Noble for doing so. Then another grabbed hold of the corner flag, ran to the centre spot and planted it into the ground – giving a nod to the protests against the Bond Scheme years before. Others ran on to the pitch, but the release of frustrations was also evident in the stands.

Fans turned to the section where the board was sitting and they didn't hold back. Banners were held aloft with messages such as 'some people create their own storms and then get upset when it rains'. Fans were chanting towards the directors' box where Sullivan was sitting, leading to him getting up and walking off. As a crowd gathered below, things such as 'you destroyed our fucking club' were venomously chanted. London Stadium had often been referred to as a bowl or spaceship – whatever people wanted to call the ground, it was filled with hatred and despair that day.

'Since we've moved to the stadium, every time we lose a game we get a lot of stick and the board get a lot of stick and I think you could tell today that the fans have had enough. It looked like that out there to us and they wanted to show their emotion,' Noble said to BBC Sport after the game. 'When you ain't winning, especially when fans probably come to games – not all of them, I must say – with the hump anyway, and when it goes wrong, West Ham fans know how to show their emotions.'

Thinking about Noble's admission, it is quite incredible that it came less than two years since the captain had been applauded for the gratitude he showed the owners during his speech. Moving to London Stadium had come about with moving to 'the next level' constantly being mentioned – if anything, it felt like the club had regressed.

Despite the feeling of impending doom during that game, the Hammers managed to stay up. Moyes wasn't kept on, however, with Manuel Pellegrini taking over and Mario

Husillos coming in as his director of football. Large amounts were spent upon the Chileans' arrivals, with Felipe Anderson, Andriy Yarmolenko and Issa Diop among those who joined, coming in from Lazio, Borussia Dortmund and Toulouse respectively.

Things hadn't gone to plan at the start of Pellegrini's reign, though, as the Hammers lost all four of their first league games, conceding ten goals and scoring just two. It was six days after the fourth of those matches that *Final Score* was released, starring Dave Bautista. It was an action film, mostly set at Upton Park, in which Bautista's character had to stop a Russian terrorist from killing thousands of fans as the Boleyn Ground hosted its final match – a semi-final against Russian side Dynamo FC in this case. In the film, there are motorcycles tearing through the concourse, shootings on the roof, Bautista flying into a scoreboard that still had 'Farewell Boleyn' written above it, and a massive explosion that takes out a large chunk of the West Stand. Having been away from West Ham's spiritual home for a year and a half by that point, there will have been plenty of West Ham supporters watching it and focusing on the surroundings as much as the action, as we saw the seats we would have sat in, the kiosks selling hotdogs and parts behind the scenes that fans wouldn't have been able to see before.

Back to the real world, and things looked fairly good in the league for the Hammers, who finished tenth that term. However, there was embarrassment in the FA Cup after a 4-2 defeat in January at the hands of AFC Wimbledon, who finished that season 20th in League One. Arnautović had refused to play in that match, trying to force through a move away, having become the star man. The forward's transfer eventually came to fruition in the summer of 2019 after further disruption had been caused. The Austrian's brother and agent, Danijel Arnautović, didn't help relations. 'He's not a cow or a horse which you bring to market,' he told Sky Sports News. 'He's a highly talented footballer who is simply being used by West Ham. He's just a number to them. To them he's just a commodity.'

The bluntness of West Ham's statement when Arnautović eventually left gives an indication of everyone's frustration towards him, as it read, 'West Ham United can confirm that Marko Arnautović has joined Chinese Super League champions Shanghai SIPG for an undisclosed fee. The 30-year-old Austrian departs after two seasons at London Stadium, during which he scored 22 goals in 65 appearances in claret and blue.'

As the 2019/20 campaign began, there was more hope that West Ham would take the leap forward that the London Stadium move had been designed to allow. More signings were made to help that process along, with Sébastien Haller, Pablo Fornals and Roberto Jiménez among those who came in, joining from Eintracht Frankfurt, Villarreal and Espanyol respectively. The latter of these names played a large part in de-railing West Ham's season after it had started promisingly, when he came in for the injured Łukasz Fabiański.

The Spaniard had put in a shocking performance during a 4-0 Carabao Cup loss against Oxford United before coming in to play Premier League matches. That trend continued as he was caught in no man's land against Newcastle United, before then letting a Jonjo Shelvey free kick go in from range. He had a calamitous moment with Fabián Balbuena to gift Burnley a goal, before punching a corner ball into his own net in the same game, and then let in two soft goals during a 3-2 loss against Tottenham.

The Spurs game had proven to be the final straw and in the next match, David Martin reminded everybody why it is that we all love West Ham so much. The son of Alvin Martin had originally come in as the third-choice stopper, signing on a free from Millwall but never expecting to play a game. Due to just how untrustworthy Roberto had been between the sticks, Martin was called upon at Chelsea with little expected of him from many. At 33 years old, Martin was making his debut for his boyhood club and it was clear to see this meant the absolute world to the goalkeeper. Every single thing he did that game got a cheer from the West Ham faithful, but when he made his triple stop, passers-by will have been forgiven for thinking the Hammers had just scored. Martin's performance was enough to keep a clean sheet, and Aaron Cresswell was able to score the goal that secured all three points at Stamford Bridge.

There was an outpouring of emotion from Martin at the final whistle as he fell to the floor in floods of tears. As he was picked up by his team-mates and given a hug by Rice, it offered a reminder that Martin was living the dream of every young kid who had turned up to watch West Ham back at Upton Park. He'd had to wait a long time, but the stopper had got himself in a position to wear the shirt and was the hero of the day once he got it on. Things got even more emotional when he went over to give his dad a hug in the stands.

This was exactly the lift Hammers fans had needed, and at most games that followed this one, the main chant coming from West Ham supporter sections was, 'We've got a chance, Martin's in goal, we've got a chance, Martin's in goal, Martin's in goal.' The good times didn't last for Pellegrini, though, as he was sacked just under a month after the victory at Stamford Bridge.

Carlo Ancelotti was among the names being linked with the West Ham job when speculation around Pellegrini's departure had begun. It was Moyes who came in again, however, which caused further frustration. Like his first time in the London Stadium hotseat, while there were some losses that were hard to take, West Ham also put in some brilliant displays, including beating Bournemouth 4-0, while there was a 3-2 win against Chelsea, a 4-0 victory over Norwich City and a 3-1 win against Watford after fans had been prevented from entering stadiums following the outbreak of coronavirus. The latter results had been helped by the January signings of Jarrod Bowen and Tomáš Souček, who joined from Hull City and Slavia Prague respectively and ensured that the Hammers stayed up.

The summer of 2020 was a tough one for everyone across the world due to coronavirus, and people were looking for things to make them feel better wherever possible. West Ham didn't provide too much respite for supporters at first, but instead handed them one more reason for uproar. That came due to the sale of Grady Diangana to West Brom. Following a season in which the youngster had impressed at The Hawthorns in the Championship, there was real excitement about seeing the Hammers academy product playing a role in the first team.

That wasn't to happen despite Moyes, Diangana himself, the West Ham fans and players all wanting him to stay. Even Noble spoke openly against the board's decision to sell, tweeting, 'As captain of this football club I'm gutted, angry and sad that Grady has left, great kid with a great future!!!!!' There were no gatherings to protest because of the national lockdown, but it was easy enough to see how furious so many had been left by what they posted online. Fans had grown so frustrated that #GSBOUT became the top Twitter trend in the UK almost immediately after Diangana's departure.

In the end, there was reason for joy in the summer, as Vladimír Coufal joined Souček in coming over from Slavia Prague. Saïd Benrahma and Craig Dawson also came in on loan from Brentford and Watford respectively. The first half of the season had its fair share of high points, including a 4-0 victory over Wolves, an incredible comeback to draw 3-3 against Spurs and a well-earned point against Manchester City, as well as wins over Everton and Leicester City. Results like this helped to earn Moyes greater popularity.

There was to be one more reminder of the lack of direction in some of the recruitment since the stadium move, though, as record signing Haller was sold to Ajax 18 months after joining, with the club making a considerable loss. While Benrahma's loan was turned into a permanent deal and Jesse Lingard was signed on loan, there were further frustrations that Haller was not directly replaced. It was also emotional to see Snodgrass following Diangana to West Brom due to how popular the Scotsman had become.

'I do think about the last game, especially with circumstances and how things have gone at this athletics stadium. I pine for Upton Park, but the move has been done now and there's nothing anyone can do about it,' says Jeff Geggus. Phil Parkes has echoed his thoughts, saying, 'I think it's the worst thing we've ever done. I think Sullivan and Gold have screwed everybody over to go to this new stadium which is totally useless for football. It's useless for the fans to watch it from. They could have still been at Upton Park, I don't like the new stadium at all so I don't go.'

Georgina Hunt has added that even one of the most cherished things about West Ham now feels different, 'I don't know if "Bubbles" is as special anymore in the new stadium. I still find it really unauthentic and I just feel like we're kind of placed in this sports stadium, rather than it being a home. So, that song that I heard on the last game is a song that made me feel quite sad because I knew I wouldn't hear it the same way.'

While Tony Cottee doesn't have the same disdain for London Stadium, he does still think of the Boleyn Ground. 'I understand all the reasons, all the economic and business reasons behind the move, but there's certainly a big part of me that really misses the old ground and the atmosphere and everything it stood for. All my goals and all my memories, everything for me, is at the Boleyn. It's not at the London Stadium. I know we're trying to create new memories in there and that will come over the next 100 years. I've got twin boys who are 22 and I say to them, "When you have your children, they won't know the Boleyn and they won't have experienced it." Upton Park will be a train station, it won't be a football ground like it was, which is sad, but that's what will happen as we go through our lives and everything, but you know the memories will never fade.'

One thing that some people suggest may have faded is the club's identity. 'You're not West Ham anymore' is a chant that has been sung by many away fans at London Stadium. Having been the gritty east London club at the Boleyn Ground, West Ham are now in this big stadium with an atmosphere that is far less hostile. Martin Godleman suggests that he doesn't see that chant as an insult, though, 'I like that song because that actually shows a respect. And then when you go online and you see all these Millwall fans saying it's terrible what's happened. You think, "You're a Millwall fan, why would you have sympathy for West Ham?" And there's strings of them, someone will say something, and then all these Millwall fans will come out of the dirt and say, "It's terrible, I loved Upton Park."'

Though Joe England adds, 'A lot of people have said since we moved from Upton Park most of it has died. When I talk to people I say you can't be like that, we've still got to get behind the team, West Ham is still alive, it's not dead, it's not Bury, we've still got a club.'

Following the final game at Upton Park back in 2016, there won't have been many doubts in fans' minds that the stadium would live long in the memory. While this book and other forms of media ensure the stadium's swansong is immortalised, its legacy would have stood strong for a generation without all of this. A 112-year history is impossible to erase, even if the place where that was made is knocked down and covered in flats. Maybe this has hung over the club more than expected as everyone tries to acclimatise to the new home.

Comparisons to the Boleyn or comments such as 'we didn't leave Upton Park for this' have often been heard, and I've thought those things too. One thing that I've said many times is that the Boleyn's swansong was the best night of my life. The only issue with this is that it's then almost impossible for anything we ever do to compare with this. As Daniel Hurley puts it, 'It feels like if we never win a cup, then we've got that. I can't even believe that winning a cup would be as good as that night.'

As fans, we struggle through the tough times full of rubbish results and poor performances in pursuit of the ecstasy attached to seeing the best game of our lifetimes. At points, I've struggled to deal with the fact that mine probably came when I was still just 20 years old. While people of different ages attended that game, over time that's something I and many others have had to accept, especially as the Boleyn Ground and its crowning glory fade further away into the past.

While there is still plenty of frustration towards the owners, Moyes and his team have shown the fanbase how good things can be on the pitch. In mid-February, the Hammers sit outside of the Champions League places on goal difference and comparisons have been made to the 2015/16 campaign. Members of the playing squad are completely idolised by supporters, while Moyes has plenty of West Ham fans happy to admit they were wrong in their judgements of the Scot when he was re-instated. For many, this will never make up for the Boleyn being gone, but it does offer an indication that the West Ham faithful can enjoy their football at London Stadium.

It is also important to note what has happened to the local area left behind by the move. Vivian Archer, the manager of Newham Bookshop, states, 'It was only on the home games on Saturday that we were packed and we miss that. It has an effect but we didn't rely on that, whereas other businesses around here did.' John Newman, who works in the same shop, adds, 'It's going to change now. House prices are going up around here, that will drive rents up, that will drive shop rents up, because people will think it's becoming more gentrified, more middle class: we can move a business in here now, people are shopping local, let's open a restaurant. The Boleyn Tavern is having a major refit, that will make a difference. The irony is West Ham played elsewhere before Upton Park and who remembers that? Things move on.'

There may not have been much of a move in terms of the distance between the two sites, but leaving Upton Park has definitely had its impact on the club's former home, while the matchday experience is almost unrecognisable. Some may even argue that what has changed the least is what we see on the pitch. It only goes to show that things have undoubtedly moved on already, but the Boleyn Ground, its 112 years of history and the greatest of swansongs will not be forgotten.

Acknowledgements

FIRST OF all, I would like to thank my family. To my mum, you've been even more excited about this book than me, and your sacrifices have played a massive part in me getting where I am now – for that I'm eternally grateful. My sister Marie, nephews Jake and Bobby, and niece Georgie, have also listened intently whenever I've spoken about what I'm doing and it's always nice to know that I'm making you proud. To my dad, thanks for all the years you took me to Upton Park, even on days when you probably didn't want to. Without you I wouldn't have been a West Ham supporter, let alone someone who attended the final game at the Boleyn Ground and is now writing this book about it.

I also want to thank all of my friends and colleagues who have taken an interest in my work. From the moment I announced that I was writing this book I've had nothing but positivity and that's massively appreciated. Whether it's been having a laugh about certain moments or sharing my updated word counts, I've loved sharing this experience with you all. A special shout goes to Josh Browne, Oli Dyer, Ollie Sirrell, Haydon Stevenson, Tom Symes-Brown, Dan Bennett, Aaron Richards and Robert Villiers for all of the encouragement.

A massive thank you goes to Paul and Jane Camillin at Pitch Publishing for deciding to take this book on. I also have a lot of appreciation for Duncan Olner, who designed the brilliant cover.

It's important for me to thank the people who were interviewed for the book. This simply would not be what it is now without each and every one of you and the time you gave me. I know how special the memories of that night are and for you all to share yours with me means the world. In alphabetical order, they are: Aaron Cresswell, Bobby Zamora, Brian Holmes, Dan Lawless, Daniel Hurley, Darren Randolph, David Blackmore, Freddie Bonfantini, Geoff Martin, George Parris, Georgina Hunt, Jacqueline Lange, James Datson, James Jones, Jeff Geggus, Joe England, John Newman, Joseph Fordham, Mark Gevaux, Martin Godleman, Matt Datson, Nigel Kahn, Phil Parkes, Rob Pritchard, Roberta Moore, Russ Budden, Suri Krishnamma, Tony Cottee, Tony Gale, Vivian Archer and Winston Reid. A special thank you goes to Tony Cottee for the heartfelt foreword he wrote – its sincerity blew me away.

I also want to give another mention to Rob Pritchard, who spoke to Aaron Cresswell and Darren Randolph on my behalf, as well as digging out some old features about the game. I truly appreciate your efforts. Further thanks go to Ben Campbell, who allowed this to go ahead. Another thank you goes to Patrik Bergabo from Sporting Kansas City, who allowed me to join a press conference to speak to Winston Reid.

There are many people who've written me off throughout my career, but there are also those who have shown so much belief in my abilities. Gary Firmager was the first man to put my name in print, as he gave me the chance to write for *Over Land and Sea*. Joseph Fordham reached out for me to write for *No Place Like Home* and has shown continued faith in me ever since. Omar Saleem allowed me to write for *These Football Times*, which played a large role in me developing my long-form writing skills. Chris Darwen helped me to secure my first job in the sport journalism industry, which came at Snack Media, something I'll always appreciate. Ever since I e-mailed Nick Judd about working for envee media, he has been nothing but supportive in his mentorship. There are so many others who have allowed me to contribute to their publication and given me the advice that has helped to shape me as a journalist and writer. This includes the lecturers at Bournemouth University and some teachers from The Harefield Academy. I'm truly grateful to have worked with so many great people.

Thank you to the players, staff and fellow fans who made the years at Upton Park so special for me. That was my favourite place in the whole world and while we can't go there anymore, the memories made at the Boleyn Ground will endure for a lifetime.

Finally, I want to thank you, the reader. Writing a book has been something I always dreamed that I would do. For you to buy and read this makes all of the work I've put in worthwhile. I hope you've enjoyed reading this book as much as I've enjoyed writing it.

Bibliography

Books

Hogg, T., *1895 – 2005 Who's Who of West Ham United* (London: Profile Sports Media, 2005)

Hurley, D., *The Greatest Escape* (London: Pitch Publishing, 2020)

West Ham United official programme vs Manchester United, 10 May 2016

Williams, B., *Home From Home* (London: Biteback Publishing, 2017)

Websites

theathletic.co.uk

twitter.com

www.11v11.com

www.bbc.co.uk/sport

www.dailymail.co.uk

www.express.co.uk

www.independent.co.uk

www.manchestereveningnews.co.uk

www.premierleague.com

www.skysports.com
www.telegraph.co.uk
www.theguardian.com
www.transfermarkt.co.uk
www.whoscored.com
www.whufc.com

YouTube channels
FIFATV
FourFourTwo
Manchester United
Sky Sports Football
Spencer FC
The Emirates FA Cup
West Ham Fan TV
West Ham United FC
West Ham United FC videos

Documentary
Iron Men